Liam J. Callaghan is a 21-year-old originally from London, now living in Shrewsbury where he studied at Shrewsbury School. "The Project" is Liam's first novel which he wrote during college, beginning his writing as a hobby that swiftly developed into a passion and determination to overcome his dyslexia and achieve the goal of becoming a published and professional Novelist.

Dedicated to Isabella, Kay, James & Judy.

L. J. CALLAGHAN

THE PROJECT

AUSTIN MACAULEY
PUBLISHERS LTD.

A CIP catalogue record for this title is available from the British Library.

ISBN 9781786125668 (Paperback)
ISBN 9781786125675 (Hardback)
ISBN 9781786125682 (E-Book)

www.austinmacauley.com

First Published (2017)
Austin Macauley Publishers Ltd.
25 Canada Square
Canary Wharf
London
E14 5LQ

'Pride, envy, avarice – these are the sparks have set on fire the hearts of all men.'

Dante Alighieri, Inferno

Chapter 1

Worlds apart

He had meant to shave, having considered it last night whilst lying awake in bed. Now it had come to it though, the thought never crossed his mind. Far too busy pondering the big day ahead. And this was a very big day, huge! He was nervous and had reason to be.

What had only yesterday morning been an acceptable and impressive landscape of stubble was now rough and untidy around the edges. Stubble aside, he was a very presentable individual. Six feet tall and lanky, he was what you would call 'easy on the eye'.

Meanwhile, on the other side of the Atlantic;

The man picked up a cut throat razor, shaving with a swift yet cautious motion, not a single drop of blood in sight. By his facial appearance alone it was clear to anyone this was a man of taste and style. Jet black hair parted to the side, effortlessly falling into place thanks to his skilled barber and his own care and attention. An image of Michael Corleone springs to mind.

London;

Reaching the bedroom of their cramped apartment, the dishevelled lanky form stumbled awkwardly towards a bulky and heavily worn dresser, rescued from a charity shop by the lady of the house. He grimaced as he yanked at a badly warped drawer, which finally gave way to reveal its disappointing contents; a boring array of men's briefs and socks.

A rather depressing pair of black trousers and whitish shirt lay on the beaten, war zone dresser. He shuffled into them aggressively, retrieving a plain Casio and Velcro wallet from the dresser before heading out of the room.

New York;

Perfectly manicured feet slid smoothly into a pair of strategically placed leather slippers before striding into the bedroom. Its vast expanse of walls sponge painted in a dark wash of purples, blues, greens and greys gave one the illusion of entering into a dreamland, a monstrous bed sitting centre-stage, luxurious Egyptian cotton cascading down to kiss the floor.

Double doors carved in polished cherry, dark lines like rivers of chocolate flowed, meandering naturally through the flawless piece of wood. The door swung open to reveal a walk-in wardrobe fit to accommodate the most fastidious of Beau Brummels.

Crystal white light bathed the room Scandinavian-style neither too bright nor too dim for sensitive, early morning eyes. An impressive array of tailored business-wear lined the outer walls, surrounding an island containing a collection of glistening jewels, a number of wristwatches stealing the show.

The fastidious male dressed with care, installing cufflinks with dexterous precision and skill. Sliding a rose gold Bulgari onto his wrist before scooping up an elegant pocket book as he left the room. Italian loafers echoed past opulent rooms towards the elevator.

He reached crisp morning air, the Rolls Royce attended by a man of military stature greeting his employer with a respectful,

"Morning, sir,"

No trace of acknowledgement from the boss. Not even a subtle nod.

London;

"Sam….don't forget your **papers**!" the feminine voice instructed. She would like to think he had remembered it but knew what a scatter brain he was when nervous. She could usually tell which emotion he was experiencing as, like a lot of men, he wore his heart on his sleeve without realising it.

Of course, he tried to protect her from his own worries and she'd always been touched by the fact that he didn't want her to worry about him.

"Shit, I really gotta go!" he announced, consulting his cheap wristwatch, checking it twice, as if he doubted its loyalty.

"Keys, keys, keys," Sam repeated, whispering the mantra to himself. As if repetition would reveal them.

Reaching on tip-toes, proffering a goodbye kiss,

"Love you." Spoken in the softest most supportive tone she could muster.

Sam smiled widely but said nothing. She could tell it was forced. Her kindness did not go unappreciated, but his mind remained focused upon the task ahead.

Grasping at an old leather shoulder bag, darting towards the front door as Seren called enthusiastically after him,

"Go get 'em!"

Unsure whether the words reached his ears just before the battered door slammed.

Chapter 2

Perspectives

Sam had always had a confidence problem. Seren had known this before she'd ever met him. As a fresh young spirit she had worked nights behind a bar in her local pub. Her father had set it up without her consultation but she hadn't really minded. At the time she was attending college and the extra cash had covered her wild teenage lifestyle.

Always the party girl, confident, energetic, outgoing and rather gorgeous. Naturally, the boys flocked to her. Only the equally popular and outgoing 'lads' (as they were known) of course. Sam was not amongst them. He'd always been more the music, books and studying type. When presented with the simple choice of football or staying in with Stephen King, it was always a foregone conclusion.

She had never been a believer in fate, often pondering on the small, random acts and circumstances of life which in time can manifest into such a big part of your life. Meeting Sam, had seemed a small, random incident at the time.

The memory was so vivid, she could even recall the weather, a typical English winter evening, damp and cold. After all, it was one of the most important moments in her life and its memory was kept fresh by regular perusal.

The pub was always full of the local rabble, college boys flashing Daddy's credit card to impress the girls. These 'lads' as Seren referred to them were always gathered around the bar, practicing their cheesy chat up lines and pitching their wares to the delightful new barmaid. At first it had been a bit of a laugh. But after a few weeks the whole act had become tiresome and stale. They just didn't appeal to her. Sure, they were always stylishly dressed and well presented, but they were also bullish and loud.

Sam, however, was well hidden, sat at the back of the room, book in hand, next to a small window, which he had opened partially and was leaned towards in order to breathe in the fresh air. Trying to relieve the assault on his senses of the thick stench of cigarettes which was leaving him dizzy.

He began to wonder what he was doing there. He thought he would give it a go. 'Who knows maybe you'll enjoy it' he'd thought. He'd thought wrong, very wrong. It was not somewhere he enjoyed at all. He stuck out like a sore thumb, a lonely figure in amongst a deafening concerto of conversations.

'Maybe if you didn't come alone you'd appear less of a tool?' he told himself. But friends were not really something he had naturally acquired. It didn't bother him and he'd always imagined that was the reason for the strange little conversations he often had with himself. Like there were two people inside him. The most predominant of which was his shy, polite and cautious self. The self he was mostly made up of and considered his true personality. However, there was another part to him, a confident and straight shooting part which was in the main held captive. It could never escape any further than the occasional conversational battles offered up internally. Sometimes he wished he could release the beast within... but he didn't have the key. And so this brave creature was trapped in the back of his mind by his nervous self, rarely given the chance to air its views.

His father had always provided everything he'd needed in terms of friendly conversations and the life lessons a young man must learn to survive. Maybe that was why he'd never developed any strong friendships. Superfluous to requirements. 'Don't worry yourself, people are mostly miserable morons anyway!' he thought, consoling himself.

In a moment of calm when everyone was served and drinking away, peeping through the endless sea of conversation directed her way, she saw him. A young man in a bright green V-neck sweater. 'Gosh, that looks like something his nan knitted him.' She giggled then felt a stab of guilt. He was slouched overlooking rather pathetic, clearly cocooned in some deep and meaningful train of thought.

It was a mere instance, just a moment before the crowd reconfigured and he was gone but that was all she needed. This bright spark somehow knew that here was someone worth getting to know. The fact that he stuck out from amongst the crowd, his negative to her positive, 'He's cute.' It was subtle but definitely there and something she'd not experienced before. Seren was genuinely intrigued by this stranger.

'You're an idiot, you look like an idiot. You're like a fish trying to walk. It's a pointless endeavour. Just go home!' Sam gave himself a rather forceful admonition. Convincing himself to leave as a feeling of embarrassment built within him like a nearing hurricane. So small on the horizon but building in menace until the feeling consumed him.

Sam placed hands on knees, instructing himself to stand up and walk to the door. He looked up and there, like a beacon of hope through a sea of nothingness was a very pretty young barmaid. Not just any pretty barmaid but the loveliest, most captivating young lady he had ever laid his teenage eyes upon. He was instantly smitten, the very sight of her causing his stomach to seize up. His throat was dry and his heart pulsated like a rabbit's.

Sam tried desperately to compose himself with a deep breath but before he could finish their eyes met. *'Is she actually looking at me?'* He very much doubted it, passing it off as a glancing look, but her eyes hovered over him. *'Jesus, she's looking at me, she is, she is'* the air caught in his lungs. He knew she was looking, but part of him didn't believe the cheeky smile he received as he gazed back blankly. He had another few words with himself,

'Oh God she's smiling, what does that mean? Is she mocking me? No, I don't think so. Don't be a prat, compose yourself and smile back!' Sam's thoughts were scattered as

14

the classic side effects of instant attraction kicked in. Logic was out the window and all that was left was a warm fuzzy feeling, mixed in with a generous helping of nausea.

He made an effort to compose himself once more, caught up in this surreal game he'd never played before. No idea he was playing with a pro. He shuffled, sitting up straight before smiling back at her. It was a respectable enough smile but he couldn't see it to check, '*You look like a serial killer, you're grinning. Stop grinning!*' But before he did, he received a playful wink.

His head exploded with euphoria, quickly followed by disbelief as doubt crept in and he had another quick internal chat, '*She must like serial killers…*' quickly replaced with a happier argument, '*She likes you, idiot! Do something… Like what? Anything!*'

Seren's cheeky wink came as a surprise even to her. She hadn't thought to wink, it just sort of happened and she was a little taken aback by it. 'Well, I've winked at boys before and no doubt I'll do it again… not boy's you've never even met. You don't even know him!' she reprimanded herself.

Emerging from the initial spark of attraction came another feeling that was new to her. 'Am I nervous? I am!' It look her a moment to place this alien feeling, but she'd read just about enough love stories to know it by definition. Her immediate fondness for this boy was subtle, but it was definitely present.

'Why are you nervous, this is silly,' Seren had a go at convincing herself it was absurd to feel so strongly about a complete stranger. But no matter how absurd a thing is, but feelings know no logic. That's not how they work, they don't abide by the rules.

The two had now been locked in a mutually exclusive connection for around five seconds, which wrapped in the definition of space time itself isn't a particularly long interval. However, when associated with gazing into someone's eyes, it certainly felt significant to both parties. As quickly as it began though, that moment was over as the sea of people once again swayed and the connection was lost.

Unfortunately, the confident party was the one stuck behind a bar, guarded by large football players. Internal dialogue screamed out, *'Go... Go on you prat!'* But was sidelined by nerves,*' Go and what? Ask her out? How about going and ordering a drink. That's what you do in a pub! I dunno. I don't really drink. Fuck the drink! That's not the objective you prat, just go talk to her! GO! She winked at me though so won't she come here? No, no, no – you're the man. YOU approach her, that's the gentlemanly move.'*

Sam concluded it was right for him to approach her. That was the polite thing to do. He took a moment to calm himself and run through his strategy. He felt like a firefighter waiting for a brief moment before manning up and entering the inferno, an intense moment which appeared both beautiful *and* dangerous all at once.

For the second time the curtain closed in on the view Seren was enjoying. Forcing her eyes back to the dull but inevitable scrum, their brash mannerisms making it blatantly obvious how much they thought of themselves.

Seren was reminded of the lyrics to a Shania Twain song she was fond of. 'That don't impress me much!' She fought hard against an inappropriate and sudden urge to laugh. Managing to confine it to a brief yet wide smile, averting her gaze just in case someone dared to presume she were smiling at them. 'As of course these overconfident, arrogant pricks would.'

Seren found herself judging them in a way she never had before. Yes, occasionally she had considered them tools whose heads were planted firmly between their rear cheeks... But never had she passed such damning judgment, this was completely out of character. She turned her attention back to the mysterious stranger.

Walking up to that bar and asking this gorgeous girl for a drink wasn't much of a strategy, but it was something. It would do. *'It doesn't matter, you just have to talk to her, you have to! Don't let this moment pass!'* With these final words of encouragement he sprung into life and up out of the chair.

'It's that boy – the stranger,' she thought. Somehow he'd sparked negative feelings towards the locals. Why? 'Because he's different and different is sexy' she concluded. Of course it was! Every day she was faced with these presumptuous bozos who demanded her time and attention and she was obligated to provide it to a degree.

'But you don't know this mystery man, he might be the same?' She pushed this silly thought aside, somehow she knew he wasn't. No, this boy was different, special even. And her curiosity was piqued. The newbie intrigued her.

Standing up and away from innermost thoughts Sam suddenly realised the obstacle before him. The mass of men he must get through was a task in itself. He dove in, squishing and squeezing and twisting his way through the smallest of gaps.

Seren had formed her strategy, she would approach him. She suspected he was not a particularly confident fellow from his slouching posture. His body appeared to want to curl up into a ball and hide. And of course there was his general 'nerdy look' which she knew she shouldn't judge, but generally it was safe to say such fellows struggle when conversing with the opposite sex. Especially when there was attraction and Seren felt confident that there was.

'I'll ask Jane if I can clock off early!' She decided, Jane being the landlady and therefore, her boss. A lovely, slightly stocky woman who'd taken a particular shining to Seren. 'She just likes you because you bring in a load of smitten boys who drink and drink to try and impress you' her cynical side had whispered. She now knew better.

After asking Jane most persuasively, Seren collected her reward, "Go on then," Jane indulged her favourite.

After a tiresome ten seconds the bar was in sight, but only the bar. No gorgeous girl. The inner dialogue scolded,

'Agghh, you blew it! Waited too long you idiot!' For once he agreed with himself, he was indeed a Royal prat. *'And so we come to our prestigious prat of the year… No, hell, make it the decade, which goes to Samuel Lowell for letting the most gorgeous girl he'd ever set eyes upon escape.'*

Sam looked up and down the bar frantically searching. Leaning forwards over the counter to check both ends thoroughly. But it was no use. She had gone.

'Prat, prat, prat,' Sam repeated to himself inwardly as he sauntered back towards the exit, feet heavy with disappointment. It was so clear now, what he should have done. Now the lion had slunk off to lick his wounds he was left feeling flat and convinced he'd never see her again.

'Of course you will, you know where she works!' optimism piped up. Meanwhile, his favourite mantra continued to demoralise in the background, 'Prat... prat... prat'. He left that pub a different man. One with a gorgeous girl on his mind. Completely oblivious at that point to the life they would share in the future. The small, random acts and circumstances of life pulling the strings of his own.

Five minutes, that's all it took for Seren to get ready. A swift transformation from the characterless black uniform and neatly tied back hair into the party-going punk girl she truly was. Her thick blonde hair flowed down her delicate spine, unbrushed yet naturally alluring. White ripped jeans were accompanied by a tight tank top. Both effectively showed off her petite slim body. Physically she could have passed for the most graceful of ballerinas.

She'd only been five minutes, 'Only five minutes' she thought as she came from one of the upstairs rooms. Seren bounded down the stairs. Confident he'd still be there, what was five minutes after all?

About to turn the corner back to the bar she stopped in her tracks. 'It'll take you months to get through there!' she thought, opting for an alternative exit. Far more efficient to sneak out the back door. She turned and fled towards the rarely used back way (Which she had employed on many other occasions). Grasping her thick coat from the hanger as she passed, shutting the door with such force she heard it slam loudly behind her, the sound resonating throughout the carpark.

She found herself quickening into a jog as the thought of fleeing filled her with a sudden excitement. There weren't many 'James Bond' moments in a country girl's life. Just a little imaginary enhancement required and we had an escape scene on our hands!

Seren darted and sprung with all her speed round the side of the building, not a moment to lose. She made sure to duck dramatically past the small but low windows, taking no chances. If the rabble spotted her it was game over! Someone was bound to make a move. Now for the tricky part, entering and leaving the premises unseen then escaping with the target undetected before retreating to an undisclosed location for coffee and a chat. The scene was closing in fast as she headed for the front door.

Bursting through it, the heroine immediately recalled she was not in a film and that back in reality her behaviour was 'weird'. Luckily, the mass of over-exuberant conversations drowned out the sound of her enthusiastic entrance with ease.

Loitering momentarily just inside the doorway, attention turned back to the reason for her erratic behaviour. 'The mysterious stranger! He's gone…' Disappointment hit home with the brief sharpness of a cold gust of wind.

'He's just nipped to the toilet, silly' optimism spoke. But this was unlikely. No, he was gone.

Recalling the tale as she often had, Seren realised that in fact, 'technically' speaking, this wasn't the story of their meeting. It was more a preview. But every time she reminisced it wasn't long before her mind retreated back to her own favourite version of the couple's first meeting. Like a vinyl record stubbornly repeating itself over and over.

Though they had not even talked, the subtleties of body language had spoken for them. The smiles, the body language and, of course, the cheeky wink all spoke as plainly as words. Seren's memories were not distorted, just not bound to the 'technicalities' of life. They were romantic recollections.

Their first 'technical' meeting had in fact taken place a few weeks later. When Seren happened to mention her mystery man to her girlfriend Beth, who then told her boyfriend John (Who by some miracle was actually paying attention) which provided him and some mates with a good old laugh 'oh girls 'eh!' they'd say whilst chuckling away. But one of the mates just so happened to know that memorable and rare character from his dorm. And so bipity bopity boo the Chinese whispers moved back up the ladder and two weeks later the two had officially met and instantly hit it off.

Chapter 3

Underground

Sam had always hated this place. It was not that he minded being closed in, even the most cramped elevators didn't bother him. No, it was the feeling of the place, the vibe it radiated. Leaving the bright shimmering city above, the interminable walk down the grey concrete steps descending into a realm of grim obscurity. Sam had always imagined that it was the closest thing to visiting hell this world had to offer.

The never-ending footsteps of countless people echoed dull commutes. The screeching and screaming of trains' occasionally interrupting the dull tone with a deafening violence. And of course, there was the smell. The sickening cocktail of damp and piss, with the aroma of the odd hobo thrown in for good measure. Even that wasn't the end of a commuter's misery, with the constant threat of delays, line closures and the odd 'jumper' disrupting daily services. The only thing to do was to switch off and go on auto-pilot.

He would always leave the underground a little deflated, with the feeling another little piece of his soul was gone. As if the place itself were a living, breathing entity, recycling the negative feelings of its thousands of daily commuters.

Sam paced briskly up and down the platform of his local railway station, following the yellow warning lines as he waited anxiously for his train. '*Stop worrying, you'll be fine! Everything always seems more daunting than it is*' Sam's voice of reason spoke up, trying desperately to convince his nerves to leave him alone. But they didn't, they restlessly pestered him. He knew he'd feel better once he arrived. It was the waiting, the suspense that played with his nerves.

It was a mere fifteen-minute walk to the station from home. Assuming an energetic pace which Sam traced the depressingly familiar journey. He was not one to hang about and enjoy the views. But that was likely because there weren't any. If there had been then he may have slackened his pace, who knows. He wasn't short of appreciation for fine architecture. It's just it never seemed to be in his vicinity. Except on the rare occasion they'd managed to save a bit of money to travel into the heart of the city. A rare treat on special dates.

The cul-de-sac where the two love birds lived was itself run down. Appearing sadly unloved from the outside, the once white painted windows and door were now blistered and cracked like a 15th Century oil painting. Green moss began to breed between the bricks, residents unable to keep up with the constant maintenance of the tall narrow buildings. Once respectable houses, they had now been converted into small flats.

It never seemed to bother Seren that this was their home. She never gave off that impression anyhow. She'd always been much too busy focused on the interior which they done out cheaply but well. She'd definitely managed to make it cosy and homely. Still, Sam was most definitely not proud of it, or even contented with it. He wanted more, dreaming of a life in the inner city which he was headed for today.

Westminster. That was his destination. W1, and though only half an hour away by train it felt worlds' apart. A world Sam longed in his bones to be a part of.

Sam's relentless pacing ceased, as the pitch black tunnel before him caught his eye. He gazed blankly into its nothingness, strange fascination meant he was unable to take his eyes off it. The longer he looked the more his blank mind began to fill with terrifying thoughts at the notion, 'anything could be down there'. The unknown always breeds fear. Sam realised this, accepting that it was just a tunnel. A man made structure underground through which electrified tin cans pass. Yet still his adult mind was spooked by childlike imagination, '*could be anything down there you know! Don't be stupid it's just a tunnel.*' His logic dismissed the child within. Although the thought did at least alleviate his skittishness, allowing him respite.

His gaze remained uninterrupted and finally a pair of bright lights appeared from a sightless corner. They drew closer and closer until the steel snake glided out from its hidey-hole and slowed, accompanied by its screaming soundtrack.

Sam's attention turned to the swift migration of humans that had assembled around him. A herd of cattle all moving together towards the gate, waiting for it to open. '*Well, that's a pleasant analogy!*' his inner voice spoke up sarcastically. '*Yeah, well... it's true,*' came the swift reply. And it was true. They were like cattle. The alter ego had the last word,

'*Except cows gather only to be assaulted by a milking machine... you're heading for the city of London, definitely the more thrilling of the two!*'

This notion lifted his spirits and Sam's attention turned back to the journey ahead. These thoughts filling him with an equal measure of nerves and anticipation.

As the train slowed to a creeping halt the strange and unavoidable game of 'Let's guess where the doors are going to stop' began. You couldn't help it. Sam believed it was a culmination of two factors; Number one, and most obvious, was the optimistic search for a seat. It seemed rarity always bred value; the train seat being a very illusive commodity indeed. Secondly, was the more obscure and natural streak of competitiveness built into us. It was stupid and infinitely childish, yet somehow beating the crowd, or if you were really skilled being the first aboard, left you with a mild sense of smugness and empowerment.

Sam joined in. He embraced his competitive streak with enthusiasm. Heck any joy, no matter how small, retrieved from such a mundane part of daily life should be squeezed dry. Besides, he knew the key to this game was to lock onto one specific door as early as possible, and track it. Using his vast experience to determine where it would land. He stalked it like a tiger does his prey. Slowly shuffling to the left, his gauge constantly adjusting.

'And BOOM! Nailed it!' he congratulated himself as amongst four or five 'pros', Sam came out on top, the door coming to rest right before him.

However, before total victory would be his he'd have to weather the awkward social niceties, waiting for the departing passengers to exit the steel beast. Making sure to stand back a polite amount, but not so polite one of the vultures around him could steal his rightfully imminent victory.

The doors sluggishly parted. Immediately a rush of people burst out onto the already crammed platform. Sam's space was dwindling into one the human body was not designed for. He wriggled and squirmed like a worm through dense mud. He was in, and in pole position.

'*Yay.*' His inner voice was accompanied by a small smile, quickly disintegrating, eyes narrowing. '*A seat... eyes on the prize, you prat!*' He sprung into overloaded action. Eyes scanning whilst his head pivoted and leaned for angles around the few standing bodies. God knows why you'd stand if there was a seat, but he knew people did. Perhaps they didn't trust who or what had been on the seat.

'There... there in the corner!' His eyes clamped down on one at the front of the carriage. Likely overlooked, it being the furthest from any doors and a pain to get to, just outside the driver's cabin.

Sam didn't care. If he'd just been travelling a short two or three stops he wouldn't have bothered, but for half an hour's journey he would claim that seat. He weaved skilfully in and out of the standing bodies all holding onto the overhead handles beginning to gently sway with the train's motions. All so zoned out to the world, Sam's overactive imagination had an interesting thought '*they look like swine, hanging from meat hooks, lifeless in the moment.*'

Sam allowed his knees to buckle and came down hard upon the plastic seat. He felt it bend a little under the sudden shock of his weight. As if he'd caught it napping, but it quickly awoke, reclaiming its moulded shape.

It was now that his nerves really got his attention. Since leaving the apartment, the sickly feeling had faded into the background, his mind blissfully distracted by other things. Directing himself to the station, constantly checking his timings, getting the right platform had all kept the nerves in check.

But now all that was left to do was sit and relax… sit and wait. Wait for one of the most important days of your life, a real game changer. No, he would not be relaxing on this journey.

Sam's attention refocused on distracting himself. Looking left, almost leaning on him, was the doorway to the driver's little cabin. Leaning forwards, he could spot him through the glass window. A small bald fellow wearing a visibility jacket. To Sam's right, a large stocky bloke sat. So large in fact his left shoulder invaded Sam's side, causing him to muse, '*Bet he plays rugby… If he doesn't he should. Reckon he'd make the England team on size alone.*'

Sam's attention shifted to the window opposite, where the lights flickered off and on as they passed in and out of the brief tunnels. He imagined it was like standing outside in the dark looking into a room where the lights flicked off and on again and the rooms were different every time, like the train was a gateway to places which, in a way, it was.

Sam's interesting thoughts were rudely interrupted by the ruby player bloke who had opened a newspaper to a ridiculous width across Sam's line of vision. As if he were being rude on purpose. '*Well… if not, it's certainly un-fucking-intentionally rude!*' Sam's temper spiked but swiftly simmered back down, quickly realising that this was just people being people.

However, it was called back immediately when this oaf's colossal right leg came up, over, and down onto his left. Sam watched in horror as he witnessed a pea sized chunk of wet mud dislodge from the oaf's industrial boot and land on Sam's freshly washed, blackish trousers.

'*WHAT THE FUCK! God damn... what an inconsiderate shit!'* Sam screamed inside, briefly fantasising about 'twatting' him, his head so hot with rage it felt as if smoke was steaming from his ears. He wanted to get up, shout and curse, making sure he got his perfectly justifiable and reasonable point across. Which would be something along the lines of, '*DON'T BE SUCH A COCK!'*

But the opportune moment passed, rage diffused and Sam said nothing. Normal service resumed as his body unclenched and settled back into the plastic mould.

If there was one thing, besides money, Sam wished for more of, it was confidence. Something he'd lacked as a boy and just never really had the chance to grow into. It wasn't that he suffered from a lack of it or anything. There was usually little anxiety or self-doubt within him. He had the utmost sympathy for those who did live with such strong self-doubt, often empathising about how dreadful it would be, unable to leave your home without feeling secure, as so many do.

Sam imagined his confidence was at about an average level for a lower class man, which was ok, he supposed. But it was times like this, when he knew deep down he should stand up for himself and be heard, that the wish reared its head. '*This isn't Disney... Prat!'* Sam distracted himself from pointless, wishful thinking.

His body leaned abruptly left, then right, then back again with the stuttering motion of the train as it jerked to a halt, approaching the station. Like all commuters, Sam could always tell the not so subtle differences between an experienced and in-experienced driver. This driver obviously being the latter! So much so in fact the train itself seemed nervous to arrive at its destination…much like Sam. Stuttering and jolting along, the train eventually came to an abrupt halt upon the platform.

'*Must be this guy's first day on the job*' he thought, the scathing comment causing Sam to frown at himself for a moment for being so harsh, *'I suppose we all have to have a first day.'* But he didn't take it back. This was the most jolty, stuttery train he'd ever been on. Sam knew immediately where they were. This journey wasn't new to him, just a rarity. Still, bursting to make sure he checked the illuminated platform sign and found himself crouching down to bring the full text into view, "Euston" it read in bold black lettering.

It reminded Sam of The British Library, which he knew was a mere five-minute walk from Euston. He only knew this because Seren had mentioned on several occasions it could make a pleasant afternoon out. So the fact was imprinted somewhere in the back of his mind as important but it was of no importance today. Today Sam had bigger fish to fry. If the Library had been a succulent salmon, he was attempting to harpoon a gigantic whale.

The doors opened and the familiar chaos resumed, people off and on… always off and on in a bustling hurry. *'You're not the only one with a place to be you know.'*

Amongst the seven or eight people – Sam couldn't be sure exactly how many came aboard, there was such a random clashing of bodies – entering the beast was a withered old lady. She looked so small and weak, Sam imagined a gush of wind would be all it took to topple her over. Initially, a modicum of pity grasped at Sam which was swiftly pursued by admiration as the phrase 'Good on her! Still using the tube' quickly followed.

Sam was unaware of his pleasant smile generated by his inner conversation whilst continuing to gaze at her with respect. And as she made her way gingerly towards him, walking stick in hand providing much needed support and balance, their eyes met and she immediately reciprocated. With a much wider smile of her own that amplified the deep wrinkles etched into her face; demonstrating wisdom to Sam as she ground to a halt two meters from him.

His admiration and respect for this plucky pensioner had briefly brushed his manners aside. *'Your seat… give her your seat!'* his gentlemanly manners programmed into him by a loving father having been roused. And he sprung from the warm plastic mould towards the lady but she had turned away obviously not wishing to fish for a donor.

"Excuse me… excuse me…" Sam altered his tone several times before finally grabbing her attention,

She turned suddenly with a sprightliness Sam was not expecting. It threw him a bit but she just smiled back, her eyes glinting, apparently much pleased by the possibility of even a simple conversation.

"Hello… I was wondering, if you'd like a seat?" Sam found his tongue. The question accompanied by a polite gesture back towards the plastic chair.

Her smile widened again, until it seemed to cross from cheek to cheek. "That's very kind of you. Thank you." Her voice was liquid silk and didn't seem to match her appearance at all. Sam had imagined a rough, even crackly tone forged by years of wear and tear. This lady continued to amaze! She moved cautiously towards the seat.

"What a gent." She extended a compliment, which Sam somehow knew was genuine and not the sarcasm more often aimed at fellow human beings.

Slowly she edged down before her legs finally gave way to a short drop and sudden stop. Sam shuffled back to where she'd stood, grasping tightly to the overhead bar. *'You mocked them… but now Mr Lowell, you have become one of the swine,'* Sam smiled briefly at his own little irony.

"Going into the city?" Sam surprised himself as the random question blurted out in the direction of the pensioner. The fact was he'd do almost anything right now to distract himself. Anything to keep his mind busy and off the thought of where he was heading as the dreaded nerves had crept back causing this little outburst. But it wasn't just the randomness, it was a stupid question, *'Yes… of course she's going into the city, that's where this train goes… Prat!'*

This combination of randomness and stupidity didn't seem to faze this old lady though, not one bit. Sam imagined this was because she'd lived long enough to see everything there was to see. Once you've seen it all, there's no surprises left… which he supposed could be seen as good or bad, depending on whether your glass was half full or half empty. Sam had mostly focused on his being half or even three quarters full.

After a brief pause for thought she replied, "Yes! I'm meeting a few friends for tea at Claridge's." Sam was once more surprised by the lady. This time by the casual mention of one of the most luxurious hotels in London.

Sam had been so absorbed with admiration and respect he'd failed to notice her attire, until now. She wore a long elegant cream skirt which swayed elegantly with the train's motion. Above was a black polo top beneath a fitted jacket, matching the skirt in colour and design.

Sam honestly believed The Queen of England herself would have been happy wearing that outfit. A feminine Rolex peaked out from the sleeve and a string of generous-sized pearls around her neck finished the ensemble.

It all made sense now... He knew there was something about her, an air of sophistication which he hadn't quite captured from her elegant voice and charming smile alone. Sam was immediately drawn in to her and now he knew why. It had always been the same, he'd always been beguiled by 'posh' people. Their elegance and charm had always fascinated Sam, but what Sam really admired more than anything was their large helping of self-confidence. He imagined it was all down to a good upbringing, expensive education and all that.

Sam supposed that when this lady said, "tea at Claridge's" that meant the works, tea, sandwiches, scones and cakes!

Yes, it was all clear... setting aside the fact she was taking the tube...Sam puzzled, '*Why the hell is she doing that?*'

The pause following her answer had by now drawn out to at least twenty seconds. Sam's deep thoughts broke as his rudeness dawned, "Oh, sounds lovely... I've never been." He'd finally found some words but they came out distant and insincere. '*She must think you don't care!*' Sam witnessed her smile fade, having mistaken his hesitation for boredom.

He really hadn't meant to sound disinterested, realising only too late as the perky passenger turned her attention towards the window opposite her. Sam thought about rejuvenating the conversation but stopped himself, his inner voice concluding it was best to leave her in peace.

Before the opportunity to relax and the nerves returned Sam turned his attention to the well-used shoulder bag he'd almost forgotten. It had been a gift on his 18th birthday from his father and he'd treasured it greatly ever since. It hardly left his side. A durable and quality possession made of proper Italian leather. The sort that just gets better with age, like a fine wine.

Unfolding the flap, he retrieved two lonely pieces of paper; the top page was titled 'Interview with Miss Andrews.' Underneath was a professionally polite, yet brief letter of confirmation which he'd read at least five times. Each time he perused it the words filled him with a subtle optimism. Shuffling the pages, glancing at the second page which was crammed with scratchy notes that only the author could be expected to comprehend. This was Sam's comprehensive list of potential interview questions.

He centered his thoughts back to the dreaded interview. Going through the notes reminded him of how well he'd prepared for this opportunity, this golden opportunity he longed for. This was it! His big chance to unlock the key to the door and enter the business club where wealth and power thrived. His dream was alive and kicking.

Chapter 4

The meeting

Exiting the train, Sam stepped amongst the masses and adeptly navigated his way towards the way out, whilst willing himself not to allow the negativity of the place to infiltrate. But any such feelings were quickly stamped out as he came up the steps and into the vast Victoria Station. The cold draft and thick stench was replaced by a warm ray of daylight streaming into the architectural masterpiece from the glass windows above. Fresh, scentless air passed into his lungs. The building itself was like a gigantic, grand greenhouse made up of painted steel. The cream pillars strengthening the bare skeleton above.

Sam saw it as a place whose mood depended upon the whims of the weather. A grey, clouded day would dampen the mood in the space, still making it marginally more pleasant than the underground... the yardstick against which Sam measured all misery.

However, this was not one of those days. Today the sun beamed down radiantly, bathing the space in amber and, like a mood altering drug, it soothed Sam's frayed nerves. It was as if nature itself was backing him. Just the boost of optimism he needed. An extra spring of energy was injected into his pace and Sam was almost bounding towards his meeting.

It was a short walk to the address that Sam had scribbled on a sticky notepad earlier that day. Retrieving it three or four times along the way, just to triple and quadruple check he'd remembered it right. The time flew by as Sam's neck got the workout of its life, rotating and rolling around as he moved from landmark to landmark. Big Ben, Westminster Abbey and the Palace of Westminster – they were all in sight, at least for the duration of this mini hike.

It was the scale of the place that always got Sam, the grandeur of it all. The place made him feel proud to be a Londoner. To call Westminster your home… to walk to work every day with such a stunning view was surely worth the extravagant price these buildings commanded? If you had it, of course.

Before he knew it Sam had reached his final destination. This was it, W1J 7QY. The phrase 'End of the line, sport' waltzed into Sam's consciousness with sudden randomness and in an American accent. Then all thoughts were blown out of the water as X marked the spot. He had finally made it and he was on time.

A building rose impressively in front of him, its design modern and minimalistic. The frontage was set in a seamless collaboration of what appeared to be black granite and glass. Though its design was clean cut and professional, its size and boldness gave it a grand status all of its own. It had a new-age grandness that could not be compared with Cathedrals or ballrooms. No, this was unique. Sam was no expert on the mechanics of architecture, but even he knew this place was something special.

Cautiously, Sam approached. The building gave off such an aura of luxury he felt humbled just standing in its presence. *'Come on, it's only a building… This isn't your first time,'* he admonished, in an attempt to shake off his nerves.

Coming closer he spotted two men dressed in deep purple tails and top hat. They stood like posh guards either side of the revolving doors, a glass jeweled centerpiece. Sam's eyes were drawn upwardly to two words "The Keaton," each letter an individual masterpiece of golden art, their hidden back-lighting created a luminescent glow. *'Such extravagance... What's the inside going to be like?'* Sam's inner child got the better of him.

He wasn't ashamed to admit he was a little intimidated by it all. His heart was pounding; he could feel sweat beginning to bead on his forehead.

One of the men tipped their hat to him, followed up by a,

"Good morning, sir."

Sam replied with an awkward smile. He felt a bit of a goon who had no idea what was happening. Overwhelmed, he had wandered out of his comfort zone. Unsure of the protocol dictated by this alien situation he found himself in. He hadn't been to 'posh' school. Sam was pretty sure he'd never had a hat tipped to him in his life!

'Stop getting hysterical, calm yourself down you prat! They're just people... It's just a hotel, you've been to one before.' The voice of reason calmed him as he realised his hysteria was getting out of hand. He had another word with himself; *'Turns out nerves plus an alien situation equals panic... Who knew?'*

He made his way through doors that responded to his presence automatically. *'But of course... Rich people don't open doors themselves'* He enjoyed a private joke. As soon as he was inside Sam felt out of place, now doubting that he deserved to be anywhere near such a building. The lobby itself seemed larger than the building he lived in. From the high ceiling two crystal chandeliers sparkled in the daylight as they reached out towards the black marble floor. So pristinely well-polished, Sam stared at his reflection.

He moved ever more cautiously towards the front desk, situated at the far right of the space. Made more self-conscious by the deep echoing of his best shoes upon the hard surface. Sam adjusted his steps to perform a softer reverberation.

He negotiated an interesting table which stood boldly in the centre of the room. Its edges and legs curved and moulded; a sculpture of natural art made of some dark wood Sam was not familiar with. He left a generous and respectful gap between them, not daring to hazard a guess at its value, inexplicably worrying that he may cause damage by his proximity to such a priceless item.

Nearing the front desk, Sam ran through his opening statement in his head, determined not to fluff social convention of conversing with the hotel staff. Though, before he could make the substantial trek across the room Sam was approached by a man whose purple livery matched the guards outside. He spoke without hesitation.

"Good morning, sir. My name is Tomas, welcome to The Keaton. How may I assist you?" Sam was addressed with a level of concentration and respect he had never received from a stranger before. His eyes were locked onto Sam's awaiting his response. It slightly resembled that gaze your mother gave you when you told her what you learned at school today…undivided attention.

"Morning…," Sam spoke hesitantly, disconcerted by the sudden and bold diction of this Tomas. He glanced down at the piece of paper he'd remembered he still clung to. It was almost completely scrunched up, caught in the grip of his tightened fingers. Panicking slightly at the silence, which began to draw out between them, he rushed to un-crinkle the paper to reveal his scribblings. Searching for the name he knew he'd written down underneath the address… It began with an A, *'Miss… Andrew?'* he trawled his memory banks but still wasn't sure, and reluctance to embarrass himself if at all possible made him mute. Tomas stood by patiently. Hands clasped smartly behind his back. The paper now smoothed out somewhat, a name came into view and the torturous silence was punctured,

"I'm looking for a Mrs Andrews… I have a meeting with her," Sam finally continued with an inward sigh of relief.

Earlier this very morning Sam had considered himself to have an 'average' helping of confidence. Now he wasn't so sure. He was beginning to feel as though he were teetering dangerously close to acute anxiety. The pounding heart, profuse sweating and shaking hands all screamed, *'BAIL! We don't belong here.'*

But that was ridiculous and his logic knew it. This was a golden opportunity and he wasn't about to allow some nervous manifestation to ruin his chances.

'Suck it up!' He internalised the three words as forcefully as he could in an attempt to frighten off his nerves... Of course, it didn't work. But he was adamant he was not leaving. He recalled one of his father's many, many motivational phrases, 'You never know where an opportunity might lead, Sammy. Jump in with both feet... No matter how deep the water.' The wise words marched through Sam's mind, like the motivational push of military drums. Even when he was nowhere to be seen, his father stood behind... pushing him on.

Tomas smiled in acknowledgment of Sam's statement, pausing to ensure Sam had finished speaking,

"May I take your name?" came the polite request.

"It's Sam... Lowell," he replied, fishing for his own last name as nerves clouded his thoughts.

"Very good, sir, please follow me," Tomas turned and walked across the vast lobby, past the reception, and through towards the back of the hotel. Tomas would glance occasionally back at Sam, just to make sure he was still there. *'He's checking to make sure you're not stealing anything... NO! He's just being polite,'* Sam's two characters played out one of their brief sparring duels. As usual, optimism gaining the upper hand.

They were now in a large open office space. Hidden at the back of the building a good distance away from the posh clientele. *'Couldn't have the worker drones fraternising with the customers could we?'* Sam held back a sudden urge to laugh. The urge swiftly dissolved as he remembered he himself was a humble drone and the comment seemed far less amusing.

Thomas finally came to an abrupt standstill in front of a door, the title "Manager's Office" was stamped across it in a somewhat conservative font.

"I'll just check if she's ready to see you."

"Sure." Sam shrugged his shoulders casually. His attention still focused on the font, wistfully imagining the words related to him. What a confidence booster that would be!

Tomas knocked three times with his knuckles... A sharp, yet pleasant tone sounded. Clearly well practiced, Sam wondered if there was a 'door knocking' course was required for such a position. *'Maybe even a certificate?'* Sam forced back another sneaky laugh. His sarcastic side always galvanised into action when he was nervous. Laughter was a good defense mechanism.

Sam's thoughts briefly turned to the master of sarcasm himself, Chandler Bing... Good old 'Friends', one of his favourite shows. He was so fond of Chandler, possibly because he reminded him of himself, Sam often thought that might be where the sudden sarcasm came from as if he were playing that very character himself in those nervous moments.

There was a pause as Tomas listened intently for a response. It was not a particularly long pause, but felt like an age.

"Enter," a feminine voice reached faintly through the door. Tomas opened it a foot wide and poked his head through the gap.

"Mr Lowell to see you, Mrs Andrews." Under normal circumstances he wouldn't have been able to decipher the words. But this was no such situation. Sam's focus on the other side of that door was now fixated on the enticing possibilities that lay inside.

"Yes, show him in please, Tomas." He craned his neck, blatantly eaves-dropping but didn't care for any opinions on this side of the door.

"Please" Tomas pivoted back to face Sam, pushing the door wide before stepping to one side. His arm stretched out into the room, gesturing for Sam to enter.

"Thank you," Sam acknowledged with a small nod, finally able to nail a reply. He walked through the open doorway. The woman's faint voice now made sense as he witnessed the deep room. She sat typing at frantic speed at a glass desk. Walking over to her was the longest few seconds of Sam's entire life... His heart beat explosively. He surreptitiously wiped his palms on his trousers in anticipation of the approaching handshake which no doubt would naturally follow.

"Mr Lowell." She beamed at him with an impressive, white smile and bright, intelligent eyes. Shooting energetically from her chair, she seemed genuinely pleased to see him and if this was a managerial act, which Sam suspected it was, it was a bloody good one.

She moved briskly round the desk. Hand out confidently early, directing the expected brief but forceful handshake, the bolt of strength in her arm surprised Sam as he adjusted his own to match.

"I'm Samantha Andrews, manager of The Keaton London," she stated with a confident pride.

"Really great to meet you," Sam chimed back. So caught up in her welcoming face he'd forgotten to introduce himself, although the efficient Mr Tomas had given his name...A clear indication of interview nerves, she looked past it politely. Sam couldn't really be blamed; Mrs Andrews was rather striking.

Sam guessed she was around forty, but still got it in abundance, *'Mrs...'* Sam mused, appreciatively, *'Lucky husband.'* This was natural of course. All men do it, they see a pretty woman, they appreciate her. Can't be helped. Millions of years of evolution has hard-wired an automatic response. Doesn't mean anything, Sam could never cheat on Seren. Not because he couldn't do the deed without enjoying it... the body is only a series of chemical reactions, after all. No, it was because his protective feelings for her were too strong, he could never hurt her like that. No decent gentleman could. And this was what Sam always aspired to be.

"Please, have a seat." Mrs Andrews guided Sam to the nearest of two leather chairs with a feminine gesture.

"So, from our conversation over the phone I'm presuming you have a firm understanding of the role?" Samantha inquired in a tone that conveyed seriousness as she moved back to her side of the desk, eyes fixed on Sam. He could tell already she would be analysing every answer he gave. Whilst this was unnerving, it also helped him focus on his words.

"Yes… I believe so," Sam replied with a moment's hesitation that he immediately came to regret. It had no doubt set off an alarm bell in the interviewer's head, her diagnosis of him probably shifting from nervous to extremely nervous. '*Yes. You should have just said YES, YES I understand! YES, I'm up for it! YES, I'm confident! Prat!*'

This sudden upward trajectory of self-awareness caused Sam to remember his shoulder bag which sat untidily upon his lap. His pounding nerves amplified the severity of the situation. '*THE BAG, THE BAG… get rid of THE BAG.*' He shuffled it hectically to the floor but this only made things worse, with Mrs Andrews no doubt thinking, 'this man is nervous as hell. He's not up to this. He doesn't belong here.'

Sam's imagination ran wild, well and truly on the loose, out of control and running free. '*Oh God she knows you're nervous, she can see it… Well you've made it obvious enough! Oh God, she's already regretting meeting me and it's not been five minutes!*'

Sam wanted desperately to disappear into the cold floor, out of sight. But before his vivid imagination took over completely it was reigned in as Mrs Andrews spoke, "From your CV I noticed business… well, isn't exactly your field. I'm curious as to why you're pursuing such a drastic change?" Samantha gazed, wide eyed over his CV once more. Clearly impressed by what was set out before her.

Sam knew that the contents of that piece of paper was the only reason for the continuation of this interview. The only reason she'd given him the time of day was probably down to her baffled curiosity. He didn't apply for the job expecting to hear back… Frankly it had started out as more of a joke to lighten the dull, depressing act of applying for work online. To enhance the mood, Sam found himself applying for all sorts of high ranking positions, so out of his depth they were completely beyond his horizon. Sam had taken his father's advice to its sarcastic limit, also applying for a CEO position which had provided him with a good chuckle.

Amongst the endless list of mundane positions was one in particular that stood out to Sam. It was part time which was exactly what he was after, but that wasn't the attraction. Sam thought the job title, "Business Assistant" a little vague. Still, the key word was business and this word alone had enticed him.

Whilst other teenagers looked up to mainstream celebrities such as Kanye West, Johnny Depp or Justin Timberlake, Sam's admiration centered on businessmen like Richard Branson, Steve Jobs and Mark Zuckerberg.

He had always found such people fascinating and worthy of notice. The strict code they lived by. The promise that through hard work and commitment you can do something that matters. That makes a difference. A positive contribution to this world. Such people deserved the respect they received because they'd earned it. Sam dreamed of becoming such a man. A man of respect and passion. A man with confidence, who knew what he wanted and went right after it.

"Part time Business Assistant required for immediate start and for the foreseeable future whilst current job holder is on sabbatical," the description read. Sam skimmed through the rest which detailed the job in tedious depth, having already decided he would apply. He might as well. He was a bright man and quick to pick things up. Sam didn't pay much attention to the description itself, it just didn't seem important.

Hey presto, a week later Sam received a short concise letter from 'The Keaton Hotel, London.' His father was right, as they often are.

Though he'd made it to the interview itself, Sam knew reliance on first impressions alone, well, to put it bluntly, would have left him royally fucked. This rush of newfound knowledge filled Sam with a devil may care attitude. After all, his first impression couldn't possibly get any worse. Shy of assaulting his potential employer, the bottom of the pit had already been reached. Nowhere to go but up. *'So come on you prat, just go for it! No holds barred!'* Sam unleashed his true self upon the woman's question. Deciding to not just answer it, but attack with furious truth.

"My father, he always wanted me to follow in his footsteps. He's a great man and I've always looked up to him as my hero. Ever since I can remember, all I wanted was to make him proud. He deserves that after everything he's done for me. So I worked. I worked hard towards the goals he set for me...' The passionate rant paused abruptly. Sam recalling the sickening fact his father remained oblivious to the drastic change in his career trajectory.

"Recently I've come to realise that... my father's dreams for me and my own may not coincide."

In all honesty Sam was not sure on that last part... the nagging question constantly present, 'Are your fathers dreams yours?' He didn't know. Truly, he'd always enjoyed the path his father had chosen for him, he loved it in fact. He was an empathic person, he loved helping others... But if he didn't at least try, attempt to explore other options he would never know if something better may have been possible. That nagging doubt would remain there for the rest of his life.

"I guess I'm just exploring other options," Sam finished off. Taking in a long breath, he felt exhausted. All his energy having been channeled into the mini rant.

Sam realised his words, "I'm just exploring other options," must have come across as very weak. *'I'm passionate about business!'* or, *'I won't let you down!'* would have been better options, he thought... *'At least it was the truth, better than blowing smoke up her fine ass.'* Something Sam imagined happened on a daily basis.

Samantha closed the papers. Clasped hands together on the desk, her penetrating gaze turned its full force back upon him. There was a pause during which Sam could see the deep thought reflected in her eyes. As if what he'd said had spoken to her in a profound way. Making her rethink the judgement she'd all but passed on him. It was a positive gaze. Maybe it had been his shocking honesty?

"Working at The Keaton requires a very specific level of professionalism!" Mrs Andrews stated with serious conviction, 'The statement seemed somewhat random on initial response, but Sam intuitively read her words for what they really were. Not a statement, but a question, a chance to convince her... What she was really saying was, 'Are you sure you're up to this?'

Sam's nerves had almost completely evaporated and for the first time since entering this prestigious domain his mind was completely clear.

"Mrs Andrews, I believe I would be good at this job... this would be a huge opportunity for me an..." Sam was interrupted by the dull ringing of a telephone.

Mrs Andrews turned her attention to the number on the display, her eyes widening in surprise. It was clear this was unexpected.

"Excuse me, I have to take this." She snatched at the phone with immediate urgency, seemingly fearful it might ring out again.

"Carter... good morning," she answered in a deferential and cautious tone.

Suddenly it seemed the tables had turned and now it was Mrs Andrews, the high flying business woman who was under some pressure. Sam relaxed back in his chair, enjoying the break in the tense atmosphere, which had built up to a crescendo.

"Now? His next visit isn't scheduled till next month," she queried with obvious concern. Whoever was coming had the power to scare the crap out of her.

"No of course... it's not a problem, I'll have a room made ready immediately," Mrs Andrews finished before putting down the phone. She let out a sigh, conveying to Sam the unspoken word, thought, *'Shit...'*

Her deep reverie was interrupted and she was back in the room. Returning her attention to Sam she spoke somewhat abruptly, "Please excuse me, Mr Lowell, I'll be back shortly," then stood up. No time for an explanation and not a moment to lose. Sam was intrigued, was it a celebrity? Some diva who was expected next week but had decided to arrive early.

Mrs Andrews moved swiftly across the room and out the door, before Sam could so much as turn in his seat to watch her go. About to retreat into his imagination, Sam was dragged back. His ears pricked up as the peaceful lobby suddenly erupted in sound, footsteps and voices filled the air. Sam wondered what the hell was going on and found it a physical challenge to remain seated. Mrs Andrews had closed the door and there were no windows. The sound of panic was all he had to go on. 'Bet it's an A-lister... David Beckham, or maybe even royalty!'

Before Sam's imagination could embellish the door opened and Mrs Andrews re-entered, "Sorry about that," her apology was sincere and she seemed back to her confident, professional self. Relaxed by whatever she'd been out to do.

'Sounded like she started a fight!'

"Not a problem, something the matter?" Sam enquired out loud.

"No, no... the CEO is coming in any minute and... well we weren't expecting him," she tried to sound blasé and unfazed... But it was clear to Sam from her erratic behaviour and the frantic manner in which she was tidying her desk before him, she was no such thing.

The desk itself wasn't even untidy and yet it seemed imperative she clean. The stationery was brushed into one of the desk drawers with one swoop of her arm and the papers stacked as neatly as possible without the use of a ruler. Sam was stunned as she even took the trouble to remove and relegate a photo of three young children, presumably hers, to a drawer.

'What kind of satanic person was this man?' Sam presumed it was a man as his overactive imagination sprung

back into life with questions bulging at the seams. *'Is this the owner of the hotel? Will I get to meet him? What will he be like?'*

"He runs a tight ship," Sam stated as he continued to watch Mrs Andrews' erratic acts. It was somehow wrong to meet a confident businesswoman and then five minutes later see her reduced to a scared little girl. Acting like she'd broken Daddy's favourite gadget, waiting nervously for the consequences.

She paused for a moment, passing one final scan over the desk.

"Mr Keaton is a very... unique individual... indescribable really. He's a brilliant businessman, a genius really."

Sam's curiosity spiked at the prospect of meeting a man that Mrs Andrews, a successful businesswoman in her own right, rated so highly as she continued her praise of this apparent bastion, 'A genius no less... How many people do you know that get called that?' The answer was none. Whoever this man was, he was the real deal. A true entrepreneur. Belonging to the same group of people Sam had grown up admiring. Alongside his father. An excitement built deep within him. *'Don't blow it Sam... Try and act professional,'* Sam's body didn't want to play that game, it had other ideas. He hadn't felt this giddy since going to see the latest Star Wars film.

The Rolls Royce came to a gracefully gradual halt outside the hotel's rotating doors, a doorman already at the rear door of the car before it had come to a complete stand still. Immediately recognising the importance of its contents, he opened the door before standing back, respectfully.

The occupant exited the car, doing up one of his jacket buttons as he walked briskly towards the entrance, driver walking closely behind at his left shoulder. The remaining doorman held his form perfectly, looking straight ahead, lacking the courage to look the intimidating man in the eye as he passed. Italian shoes resonated throughout the peaceful space. An aptly matching soundtrack for his bold and confident pace. The timid staff silently went about looking busy.

There was a muffled buzz from Mrs Andrews's telephone.

"Yes," she answered, firmly pressing a button as she spoke before releasing it again. It reminded Sam of walkie talkies, *'Whatever happened to them?'*

"Mr Keaton has arrived, Ms Andrews," the speaker fizzed. The announcement snapped Sam violently from his thoughts.

"Thank you, Bethany,"

The office fell silent as they both waited in equal anticipation. Neither able to speak as formulated a plan of speech. Mrs Andrews to her manager, Sam to an unknown hero.

During the ten seconds' silence the two exchanged nothing more than a smile as their eyes randomly crossed the room, the insulated void sustaining the suspense. The ordinarily undetectable metallic twisting of the doorknob sounded out clearly, slicing through the vacuum like a knife.

Sam was suddenly filled with panic as decisions flooded his mind, *'Do I turn? Do I stand? Do I stay facing Mrs Andrews?'* Once again Sam found himself painted into an alien situation... Out of his social depths. What's the protocol? The uncomfortable notion allowed his nerves to gain a foothold once more.

Before he could dwell further, and just in time as his nerves were about to implode, Mrs Andrews leapt to her feet, un-crinkling her skirt with her palms. Sam immediately followed suit, minus the skirt part of course! He concluded his best bet was to mirror her as best he could.

Sam heard the door fly open with a swift swoosh of air. His mind now wrestling with the question, 'Should I turn?' He didn't. He could distinctly hear the footsteps of two men enter the room. But one set stopped at the far end of the room, whilst the others thundered deeply towards him. Closer and closer. The suspense was killing him. He wanted to turn, but his joints were frozen in place.

"Mr Keaton, sir, what an unexpected pleasure. We weren't expecting you." Mrs Andrews tone balanced gracefully between excited sincerity and professionalism.

Sam watched her, stunned. A flash of eye contact screamed at the immobilised Sam, 'Turn around!' the statue turned around feeling like he was back at school again, waiting for the teacher's permission. Sam had already made a decision to learn from this PhD. of business from whom he aimed to absorb every ounce of information he could. But now he was about to upgrade and meet the Professor. Sam's body slowly pivoted to face this bastion of the business world.

"Thought I'd grace you with my presence before I leave for New York," Mr Keaton casually orated his opening line. The man's words hinted a typically English sarcasm… Yet his deep, monotone speech and poker face conveyed firm professionalism. It was the most inscrutable face Sam had ever seen. Eyes and brows remained dead whilst mouth released cool, eloquent words.

Keaton was flawlessly presented in a black suit of the highest quality and fitting. Dark eyes corresponding with thick black hair, combed back with meticulous precision. Standing over 6" tall with a posture almost robotic in its perfection. He was what Sam would have described as an 'intimidating figure.'

But it wasn't just the way he'd presented himself which left Sam in complete awe. The man's presence had a profound effect on the atmosphere in the room, regality radiated from him. Complete and utter confidence, which struck you hard. Like the building, the man left Sam wondering if he belonged in such company. It was what he imagined standing before The Queen would feel like. Excitement and awe mixed in with nervous fear at the power standing before him. Sam would give anything to have such self-worth. He was mesmerised.

Mrs Andrews reported back, "Well it's great to have you back, sir. I have managed to secure the Presidential suite for you… Hope you'll be comfortable." She negotiated the tightrope of social interaction with perfect execution. Once again there was no notable reaction from her superior. But Sam imagined that was about the best you got and that the wry expression was usually only ever discarded with negative intent… '*He does NOT look like the kinda guy you wanna piss off.*'

Sam's admiration for Mrs Andrews continued to escalate. It was clear she knew exactly the right words to say to such a difficult man. There was no hint of a pause nor any hesitation. This seemed incredible, as Sam realised her dialogue would have been measured and re-calibrated prior to delivery, yet it all seemed immediate and instinctive. This was the admirable skill of being able to hold your own when faced off with the most intelligent and intimidating of people. A skill that would have been earned through valuable experience.

A moment of silence then Keaton's inscrutable charcoal gaze changed direction, shifting position towards Sam. Sam felt the full force of those black eyes' piercing scrutiny and felt utterly exposed. Naked. The radar locked onto his very soul, scanning him like a book, feeling him out.

Sam twitched uncomfortably, he desperately searched for words. Anything to break the spell, but he couldn't think past the intense probe.

Mrs Andrews' impeccable manners abruptly rebooted and Sam was saved, "This is Mr Lowell. He's here about a position at the hotel," Keaton's eyes tore her down. The subtle, yet clear clenching of his brow and jaw conveyed disappointment. As though she'd distracted a deep train of thought which he had considered extremely rude.

To Sam's horror, the silence resumed. And there was no chance even Saint Andrews would interject a second time. The assessor continued with his calculations. The man saw everything; cheap suit, dull shoes, functional cheap wristwatch. All of which spoke to him with detailed complexity. The movement of Sam's weight from one foot to the next and his inability to find a resting place for his hands screamed 'gauche'. This scrutineer was exceptionally good at reading people. He could pick up the physical manifestations of emotion that we all give off in sweet ignorance. Like a wolf, he possessed the ability to sniff out weaknesses… It appeared that Keaton had nothing to gain by ripping him apart, only interested in commerce. He lived it. Breathed it like air. No, this was something else altogether. The entrepreneur was intrigued.

"Mr Lowell… Alexander Keaton," it had felt like an age, but finally someone spoke and it was, of course, Keaton. Sam now knew without a doubt this predator was the orchestrator of every province he entered. A large, right hand approached Sam who felt honored by the simple gesture. Sam instinctively felt the man's interest in him but was baffled as to why and convinced this would be a rare thing.

Taking a wild guess, he imagined it was because in Keaton's world, of high end business and professionalism, people like Sam weren't on his radar.

Whatever it was, the two shared a long, forceful handshake with Sam matching Keaton's strength.

Sam responded with a genuine honesty, "A privilege to meet you, sir."

Keaton's next enquiry demanded the conversation pick up pace, "Tell me, Mr Lowell, what makes you believe you'd be a valuable asset to my hotel?"

Sam could feel the weight of responsibility resting on his reply, its dead weight pressing its physical presence upon him. A brief second's hesitation then, recently learned tactics were applied as the quick study willed back his 'devil may care attitude' which had worked so effectively on Mrs Andrews.

And so, for the second time that morning Sam let himself go, "I know I may not appear on the surface to be someone who would fit in here… But appearances can be deceptive and I have been brought up to believe that anything can be achieved through hard work and determination, two traits which I possess. Traits which in my opinion, sir, are extremely valuable assets."

An agonising pause of silence drew out, Keaton's deadpan visage remaining loyal. Sam had no idea if what he'd said conveyed intelligence… or stupidity. As a sickening doubt began to creep into his mind, Sam perceived the smallest, briefest of smiles. It was a Mona Lisa smile, in fact, it was so subtle Sam wasn't sure it could even be classed as a smile. So brief and unexpected, he doubted his own eyes.

But this was blown out of the water by what Keaton uttered next, "Well then… how about a meeting, this evening. Eight O'clock?"

Sam had to stop himself from physically stepping back in amazement. If he'd chosen a list of 'most unlikely questions' to be asked next, that would have been right at the top.

He was just about able to fashion a polite response, fearing his silence would be construed as rudeness; "Yes of course."

"Until eight then," Keaton's tone gave the distinct impression it was time for Sam to leave. It was time for him to catch up on private business matters with his Manager.

Sam smiled weakly. Trying his best to condense his ecstasy. Before turning towards the door, Sam gave a faint nod that mirrored the bow of respect one would address to a respected superior. He was mesmerised.

Sam turned, walking briskly, but not too briskly towards the door. It was the first time he'd noticed, or even considered the other man who'd entered the room with Keaton. A middle aged fellow with greying hair, which accompanied by his muscular physique suggested a dangerous past. He looked like ex-military, which Sam thought made sense… Keaton's body guard, slash man servant.

The figure remained riveted to his post as Sam made his way past and out of the doorway. All the while unaware Keaton had turned back to observe him, as a scientist would a rare species, with professional curiosity. As though Sam were some new breed he had not encountered before.

Sam had to use all of his self-control to contain his overflowing excitement until he was out of the building. His mind was buzzing with new found optimism and hope for his future. His vivid imagination couldn't help but run wild once more at the endless possible outcomes of a private meeting with this new acquaintance.

Sam had been completely oblivious to Keaton's existence an hour ago. But, he knew enough about The Keaton Hotel chain to know he was a very, very powerful man.

Finally, he was outside in the cold city air. Sam could let his self-control go, giving way to his emotions which resurfaced, resulting in a beaming smile and perplexed laugh. He needed to release the adrenaline that coursed through his veins. In his overwhelming state of euphoria, he felt the sudden urge to blurt out his joy.

Given the chance to step back from this moment and view himself dispassionately, Sam would realise his response was a tad dramatic, but he was presently unable to see past his own vivid imagination.

It was the surreal nature of it all. Like winning the Lottery or rising to fame it was completely unexpected, and therefore not something your emotions are prepared for. There was no measurable comparison, no rational gauge for such a situation. Tonight, Sam would have a meeting with his new hero, in which anything was possible. And that was that.

With an explosive cocktail of hormones and imagination still prowling, Sam's attention turned to the human need to tell someone, anyone his news. The first name that popped into his head was of course, Seren. He needed to talk to her, now! This couldn't wait. He couldn't wait. The whole thing just sounded so unreal in his own mind, no matter how many times he repeated it. Sam needed to hear Seren's voice, to hear her accept it.

Seren had always played the role of 'the sensible one' in their relationship. After all, someone had to be, and she was always better at it. Seren was naturally grounded and realistic

49

about everything. Always able to take a step back and really look at a situation with judgment... Whereas Sam's wild imagination always left him reaching for the stars, usually with unrealistic ambition. This child-like attitude was one of his most charming features, and had caused Seren to fall hopelessly in love with him.

This natural contrast between them worked well, all relationships require balance... Often why you find opposites attract. And right now, Sam needed Seren to rebalance the equation. She was the anchor that kept his wild imagination grounded to Earth, stopping it from floating off into the void. And right now he was dangerously close to doing just that.

Sam fumbled erratically about his many pockets. Checking his inside, outside jacket and finally pulling an old Nokia from his trouser pocket. He had to concentrate hard on the small digits, to counter his shaking fingers as he dialed. The phone rang twice.

"King's College Hospital... reception," a bubbly enthusiastic voice chimed down the line.

"Anna its Sam! Is Seren about? Need to talk to her," he enquired politely. Once again having to reign in his joy. It would have been inappropriate to direct it towards the Hospital secretary, their relationship never having moved beyond the occasional phone conversation necessary to catch Seren at work.

She'd never have her phone on her at the hospital... Took her job very seriously and hospital staff weren't supposed to have mobiles on them. The signals can interfere with the delicate and in some cases, life dependent equipment.

"Oh Sam, it's you!" Anna rejoiced at the familiar voice. She'd grown fond of the short conversations the two of them had whilst waiting for Seren. Mundane as they were, they provided a nice little break from her repetitive job.

Anna chuckled, "Seren told me all about the interview; we all had our fingers crossed down here, all rooting for you!" Her speech was rushed and playful, as if short on time.

He murmured appreciation of Anna's support, imagining her to be the gossipy type.

He came back, "That's actually what I need to talk to her about. You see…" Sam stopped himself, before he spilled all the juicy details that he was desperate to share. He wanted to say it, to hear it, out loud… But what he wanted was overshadowed by what was best in the circumstances. He needed to tell Seren, first. She should be the first to know.

Sam resumed, having altered his statement, "There's been an interesting development. I can't say any more. Couldn't wait till I got home, I just need to talk to her, now!" Sam barked, doing his best to convey urgency, which he could only hope wasn't mistaken for arrogance, immediately regretting the omission of a simple, 'please' on the end of his request.

Sam's concern was swiftly assuaged by the return of her consistently, bubbly voice, "Hang on a minute, lovely, I'll see if I can find her."

"Thank you!" Sam blurted quickly to make sure he caught her before she left the line silent.

There was nothing for a minute for two. Sam's ears clung to the strange static as he patiently waited for the pager to find its target… Completely zoned out to the background noise of the city surrounding him. None of that mattered right now. He was suspended in this moment of waiting… waiting… waiting to hear the familiar voice. A voice he knew would dispense joy and logic with a balanced dosage.

The drawn out silence wasn't unusual under these circumstances. Sam amused himself with a ridiculous comedy sketch starring Anna as she ran around the gigantic maze of corridors in the hospital, calling out "Seren… Seren!" Sam had only been there once, to meet Seren. He didn't like it at all. Reminded him of a well-lit dungeon. He came back to reality, reigning in his overactive imagination, visualising her tactically calling sections of the building where Seren may be working that particular day. Roots were constantly re-shuffled, taking into consideration staffing fluctuations. No matter how skilled Anna's tactics were, it always took time to find any member of staff amongst the hundreds.

A familiar voice spoke with anticipation, "Hi, darling, how did it go then? Anna said it seemed like good news."

A cynical wave washed over Sam and he immediately pushed it down, replying, "Really well… In fact, really, really well! Surreal," Sam gave a light chuckle. His words were so stuttered and scrambled.

"What do you mean, surreal?" Seren inquired quickly, her interest stirred. She'd only seen him this giddy once before.

Sam took a deep breath, steadying himself enough to explain in clear English, "Well, I was having my interview with the manager, which was heading towards a crash landing, when the owner of the company happened to walk in! And… I have a meeting with him tonight at eight!" Sam's speech rising to a crescendo.

Alarm bells screamed but Seren paid them little attention, unwilling to burst his bubble just yet. Enough positive energy was mustered, allowing her to cloud her concern, whilst also conveying interest in his situation, "What… that's fantastic, I mean what's the meeting about?"

"I have no idea," Sam began with humble sincerity, "I don't think he's the sort of man to explain his methods… but I don't think he's doing it just for a chat, this can only be a good thing!" Sam clung desperately onto the vision of the half full glass.

Seren's concern increased as she now had the feeling that this stranger he'd only just met already had Sam in his power. Seren was disconcerted.

But she couldn't say what she needed to over the phone, it would have to wait. For now, it was back to the acting game, "Yeah… I mean that sounds great."

Sam knew that for some reason Seren was suspicious. He knew the news had struck some negative emotion. Over the phone, with only her voice to go on he couldn't quite put his finger on it, but he did know one thing, it wasn't positive.

There was a short pause, as Sam formulated a response. He wasn't about to start the conversation they needed to have over the phone either. But before his well thought words could escape, Seren came back, "Hun, you'll have to tell me all about it later, I really have to get back. We're under-staffed again!"

Sam suspected this was a line, still it was probably best to terminate this conversation now, and so he accepted it, "Okay I'll see you later."

Having killed the conversation, Seren swiftly returned to her work. Submersing herself and ensuring she was too busy to think.

Sam was a little surprised by Seren's reaction. Of course, he'd expected her to impart calming, grounding logic. He knew exactly why her mood wasn't a positive one. It was with good reason, Sam knew that. However, he'd just not anticipated that the balance would come crashing down so decisively on the negative side. Sam was aware she hadn't meant to be unkind or unsupportive. Still, Sam's hyperactive energy faded as the adrenaline drained away, imagination retreating, logic taking its place.

Now in the eye of the storm, Sam found a moment's peace. Zoning out of downtown London, an idea surfaced, 'Fate.' It was something he'd never seriously considered before, but he did now… Coincidence was a reality of life, but could it really stretch this far?

A man, who ever since his teenage years had worshiped the entrepreneurs of the world, longing to meet one of them, to be able to call one of them his mentor, finally had a chance, an opportunity to do so… by means of a delicate series of events; just happening to decide on exploring his options, just happening to stumble upon the hotel job online amongst the infinite options, just happening to run into an entrepreneur… Could they really all just be random events? Coincidences? Or was it something more. Sam opted for something more.

Chapter 5

Aspirations

Sam had retreated to a cafe, just a half mile down the road from the hotel. Afraid to wander too far, in case some unlikely disaster prevented his return to the hotel by eight. This was of course ridiculous, but Sam was taking no chances. This meeting could turn out to be one of the most important moments of his life.

Sam's mind returned once more to the small, random acts of circumstance, which he now believed absolutely to be nothing less than the aforementioned 'fate.' At eight o'clock Sam would be at that hotel, no matter what.

As the first cup of coffee touched his lips Sam's thoughts turned back to the last time he had been so full of hope. As a child, of course. Looking back now as a grown man with a grown man's problems such times seemed so far away. So distant, they felt more like dreams than memories. A life, which now seemed so wonderful and carefree, but at the time was just plain old life. Childhood never feels special in the moment. Oscar Wilde was right, youth is sometimes wasted on the young. It's not until you look back through the eyes of an adult you realise how precious those days were.

Sam recalled a scene from childhood when he had been around thirteen. Sam had never been good with numbers – dates or ages. The memory's beginning, was in fact a rather sad one. As a nerd through and through Sam had always been a target for bullies, school being their stomping ground. There were many such tyrants throughout the overcrowded public school Sam attended. Many of whom he'd encountered at some point during his years. However, there was one in particular, a brash and thuggish individual using his superior size and strength to act out his authority. He was in the year above and so would have had no affiliation whatsoever with the little nerd… If not for the school bus, that is. That battered white minibus Sam had come to dread.

For months, twice a day, every morning and evening Sam was placed helplessly within the tyrant's grasp. It had begun, as it always does, with a little light ribbing and the occasional dead arm which then escalated. Like a crack junkie's lust for more, the abuse was driven further and further by the need to inflict pain.

The silence and lies he fed his parents finally caved in. Sam could take no more and he unloaded his mind onto his ever comforting father; his bully, the bus, everything. His father had given him a sound piece of advice, "people sometimes hurt others when they are in pain themselves."

This wasn't the moment of hope and wonder Sam recalled. No, as good as his father's advice was, it hadn't really helped the situation at the time. This was the mere prologue, the introduction. It was what his father did next that made the memory so special.

The following morning Sam was awakened by a gentle jolting motion. He opened his eyes to see his father sat beside him. Perched on the edge of the bed wearing a wide smile and performing the gentle motion with his two large hands, which carefully pressed Sam's delicate shoulders repetitively, "Sammy, Sam! Come on… Got a surprise for you," he insisted in an excitable, yet soft tone.

Sam, like most teenagers, was not a morning person. And his father had to persist for a while before he managed to drag his son from his near comatose state. Out the bedroom, down the stairs and into the living room where Sam's drowsy body was completely and suddenly shocked into wakefulness. To his delightful surprise, before his eyes, stood a bright red shining new bicycle.

"It's all yours! You like it?" His father broke the stunned silence as he gazed upon his much loved son... Eyes widened and mouth dropped towards the floor.

"Wow... It, it's awesome! Dad can I take it out, Dad can I!"

That was it, that weekend was the best of his childhood; the two of them had shared their love of cycling. But it wasn't just the bike itself and the endless laughs the two shared because of it that made the memory so special. It was also the sense of freedom it bought Sam. That was the true sense of hope and wonder. That red bicycle let Sam's mind run wild with adventure.

Looking back through the more developed mind of a young man, Sam came to the realisation that after that treasured weekend with his father, he'd never seen the bully ever again. Sam had been able to ride the two miles to school, which he did every day. No more dreaded white minibus. No more bruises, mental or otherwise. That red bike was not only an adventure... It was an escape to salvation. In this moment of sudden enlightenment, Sam had realised the man his father was.

Sam's attention now turned to that very same character. If there was one thing which he dreaded more than anxiety, it was disappointing his father, the one who'd given so much to him. Sam wanted his father to be proud of his line of work... but he also wanted to follow his heart, which right now was gunning for the eight o'clock meeting.

This was the greatest dilemma he'd ever faced, *'What dilemma? Keaton hasn't even offered you anything yet. Let's be realistic, currently there is no dilemma. Just a chance, a chance for something of which we have no clue. So just calm down... After the meeting, then comes the dilemma. If any,'* Sam had a few words with himself. The notion calmed him. After all, currently, there was nothing on the table. No cards, not a single one.

Sam had been in the coffee shop over three hours by now. Caressing a third cup of coffee, he sat gazing out of the window across the street, his eyes were drawn to a beautiful

Aston Martin which had stopped at a set of lights. He admired the boldness of it, the loud statement it made as it drove away with a deep and thunderous growl. In that moment Sam's dreams became amplified; he wanted to be confident, he wanted to be rich, to have freedom and power. Sam wanted to be an entrepreneur. He'd never before linked himself to that particular word but now he wanted to become a well-respected businessman, a man of sophistication and taste, a gentleman.

Sam's attention was now constantly switching between his Casio wristwatch and the clock on the wall above the door, constantly pitting the two devices against each other, as if one of the timekeepers may attempt to fool him.

The seconds rolled on at a glacial pace, until finally at twenty-five to eight he could no longer hold out, decisively stepping out for the hotel and chance.

Chapter 6

The Position

Sam arrived back at the hotel at quarter to eight. A full fifteen minutes was early by anyone's reckoning and far exceeded a safe buffer... five minutes would have sufficed, ten at the most. But it didn't matter, could have been an hour early for all he cared, just as long as he wasn't late. Sam didn't pretend to know this Mr Keaton from their brief meet. And yet, he would have put a substantial amount of his pitiful savings down on the man not accepting tardiness. Such men would quite rightly consider it rude and unprofessional.

No, fifteen minutes early was good. It gave him time to relax (as best he could) before the meeting, to go in cool and composed with collected thoughts. What you didn't want was to burst into Keaton's company sweating and panting with scattered thoughts because, well, that was surely as bad as being late.

Sam knew from extensive reading that entrepreneurs like Keaton could be extremely difficult to work for because they like things done in a certain way, being very particular about things such as punctuality. And if you can't keep up then you're out. But if you can keep up, the rewards could be plenty.

'Stop it! You're getting too ahead of yourself again... He might just need a new doorman, reign in that imagination! It's on the loose again,' Sam forced himself back to reality and reason. But he couldn't reign it all the way in, it was too strong. Especially now his logic was beginning to agree with

his fantasies. The thought that Sam could not, no matter how he tried, get out of his consciousness was, 'Why would the owner of the company want a meeting with me?' It was a tantalising question. The CEO of a multinational business did not take time out of his hectic schedule to deal with minor tasks… Such as hiring a minion, or even a business assistant to the London manager. No, Sam knew that in business, time is money! And Keaton didn't seem the type to waste it. Such a busy man would only personally hire those who would be closely associated with him. Sam's impatient mind postulated an abundance of answerless questions. The tantalising answer to all of them would be known soon enough.

He was back in the great lobby. Sam's self-consciousness was subdued having been here before, but still somewhat present. His body articulated, *'You don't belong here… GET OUT!'* churning the contents of his stomach. But the nerves were soon dampened at the reassuring sight of Tomas approaching, wearing a beaming smile of recognition,

"Good evening, Mr Lowell. Good to see you again, how may I assist you?"

Sam couldn't help but be impressed. This young man had remembered his name, considering the number of guests he must address daily this was admirable. Must be at least twenty? Thirty? And yet from amongst the, no doubt, wildly more impressive people that came through this hotel, Tomas had remembered their brief encounter. To the rich guests accustomed to it, it likely was nothing much to write home about, but for Sam the gesture had substance, lifting his confidence. It was a nice feeling to be remembered even by a stranger. It made him feel respected, valued, important. Of course his cynical side might say, 'Ah, he's just doing his job,' but that wasn't really the point. It didn't matter if the young man had been trained to do it. How it made you feel in the moment, that's what mattered, that's one of the many qualities people who paid the exorbitant prices were paying for, the service.

"I have a meeting with Mr Keaton, at eight." Sam felt there was no need to delve into deeper explanation, no doubt Tomas knew who Mr Keaton was… His name was above the door.

That was the real tragedy of nerves; they warp your personality, or at least that's how it appears. Like throwing a damp, dull veil over a unique sculpture of art. Their individuality hidden out of sight under a shaking, sweating mess, tragically locked inside an impenetrable wall of anxiety they can't break free from. Trapped in their own personal cage.

Tomas paused for a short moment, considering his response carefully, "I see. Would you care to wait in the gentleman's lounge, sir?"

"Sure." Sam said in a casual, friendly way. Almost as if he were beginning to view this young man as a friend. He supposed that was the idea really. You want your guests to be as comfortable as possible. When are you ever more comfortable than when you're with a friend?

"Please follow me, it's this way." Tomas gestured casually before leading Sam across the space and through leather bound double doors. They reminded Sam of the famous leather door of M's office in the James Bond movies. He'd never come across one in real life and was strangely fascinated by it.

Beyond the doorway the atmosphere had changed dramatically. The friendly yet corporate lobby, with its practical, bright white lighting and grand space was all worlds away now. Replaced by a much smaller, intimate room, stretching out lengthways, it was no more than ten meters wide, with a comparatively low ceiling. A small bar where no doubt a variety of alcohol and cigars were at one's disposal. The dimmed, yellow lighting and roaring open fire in the centre of the room made for a cosy atmosphere. The space was deserted but for two elderly men, sat in the far corner quietly discussing private affairs. Large leather armchairs were dotted around delicate coffee tables. This was indeed aptly named as 'the gentleman's lounge.' It's exactly what Sam would have imagined. He felt much more at home here and even hoped Keaton would come to him, although he doubted it.

"I will inform Mr Carter of your arrival, sir," Tomas explained plainly, waiting an extra moment to convey yet another warm smile before walking away. Leaving Sam in a man's dream-world of fire, leather and alcohol, concluding '*Yes, I could happily spend time here.*'

Sam deliberated, 'Who is Mr Carter?' But he immediately lost interest as it didn't really matter. He was likely just one of Keaton's many employees. Sam imagined if he were ever lucky enough to work for the man he'd be meeting too many to keep track of and would in fact be one of them.

Making his way to the closest armchair he sank gratefully into it. Placing his hands on the worn armrests and crossing his legs, like he thought a gentleman might do, he couldn't help allowing his imagination to run riot once more. He imagined himself as a high flying globetrotting businessman of vast importance, relaxing after a long day of meetings with important people about important things. Sam closed his eyes to enhance his other senses having a go at some mindfulness; he listened to the crackling of the fire, the light chinking of crystal glasses – the two old men toasting to something, the feel of smooth leather as he ran his fingers along it, the light concoction of jasmine, whisky and leather which filled the air… The smell of luxury. Sam was now in a state of total relaxation. Though he fought it, he could feel himself drifting away into a drowsy dreamland.

"Mr Lowell," Sam's drifting mind snapped abruptly back to attention at the strong gruff voice which came from behind the chair.

Sam stood up and turned to face its owner a moment of panic passing through him as he feared he had indeed drifted off into a deep sleep and missed his meeting. This quickly passed as before him stood the man who earlier that day had entered Mrs Andrews office with Mr Keaton. This must be

Keaton's right hand man, which placed him right where Sam wanted to be, inside Keaton's inner circle.

"My name is Carter; I'm Mr Keaton's personal assistant." The man spoke with a military bluntness that matched his muscular, hard exterior. Sam knew when Carter said 'personal assistant,' he meant; body guard and personal assistant.

"I thought you were," was all Sam could think of to reply, feeling like an idiot as soon as the words left his mouth. His nerves having got the better of him, it was the best he could do under the pressure of intimidation. Not only did this ex-soldier bear down on him at well over six feet tall, he presented the recipient of his emotionless gaze with penetrating precision, giving the impression of a man who'd seen things, horrific things, witnessed war firsthand. Sam was sure Carter meant no offence making the decision to give this soldier a large helping of respect.

"Mr Keaton will see you in his room. If you'd like to follow me," Carter explained with blunt efficiency, not a man for wasting words. This didn't bother Sam in the slightest for he knew he was entering a world of action, not words. A world where money thrived and time wasn't wasted, being the most valuable commodity.

Carter led Sam from the comfort of the gentleman's lounge and into a corridor where one of many elevator doors stood open. As they reached the doorway Carter stepped to one side, inviting Sam to enter the small space first. It was then that Sam's nerves began to pop as reality loomed. Soon he would have his chance to impress a man who could give him everything he'd ever dreamed of at a mere snap of his fingers.

Sam walked into the space which had now become intimidating in itself, all attention focused on Carter as he pressed the button labelled 'twelve' which lit up white. Sam watched the numbers above the door as they moved up at an agonisingly slow pace. He focused as hard as he could on them, counting along in his head loudly, hoping it would pull his mind from the nerves which now took up residence in his churning stomach. He could sense the sweat coming, stress hormones working overtime. Sam tried to will it away but the outcome was inevitable, his body won the battle.

Sam didn't want to do it, but he had no choice. His body was screaming out for him to break the torturous silence. *'SAY SOMETHING! ANYTHING!'* Yes, anything, anything at all, just say something to stem the tide of nerves which multiplied like locusts.

Finally, Sam gave in and interrupted the silence, "Don't suppose you have any idea why Mr Keaton wants to see me?" It was a relevant enough question. Still Sam felt awkward asking it. It seemed child-like, immature. Memory took him back to school years when boys would ask other boys to ask girls if they liked them. Once again, Sam had made himself feel like a moron... Still anything was better than the physical manifestation of nerves which were somewhat dispersed.

"I wouldn't know, sir. Mr Keaton doesn't divulge such information."

Sam was growing rather fond of Carter's speech, it was short, concise and to the point. No dicking about just simple clarity.

"I see," Sam replied with vague disappointment having allowed himself the luxury of hope for a glimmer of information. The silence didn't last for much longer, the elevator 'pinged'. They had reached their destination. A well-spoken automated voice announced their arrival, an image of Joanna Lumley vaulted into his mind.

The doors parted and Sam's eyes goggled at the luxurious scene set before him. Black marble slabs reached out across the floor, matching the dark ceiling, diminutive inset LED's twinkling in a night sky. Concealed lighting gradually turned from royal purple to sapphire blue, illuminating the textured slate wall to Sam's right. The ever changing colours created a dramatic mood in the dark spartan space.

Two low, elegant sofas in ocean blue suede sat opposite each other, centre-stage. Penned in-between them, a glass bowl perched, opaque spheres of gold, white and black suspended on a glossy black table.

Sam's eyes were drawn back to the mood changing wall where at the back, in the corner, three rectangular glass sculptures rose majestically out of the ground and almost found the night sky. Swirling green's and blue's danced through the glass, illuminated by concealed lighting which percolating from the ground up.

At the back of the room, staring straight back at Sam a seamless glass panel revealed a spectacular view of the London cityscape, the evening lights of the city adding to the drama of the scene. Sam struggled to contain raw admiration as he gazed upon the view set before him, imagining himself sat there all night. Just looking out and waiting for the sunrise.

Sam had imagined many, many times what it would be like to be rich, to afford all the many privileges this world has to offer. Imagining something and seeing it with your waking eyes was something else again. But now Sam was there. The reality of wealth stood before him and captivated his senses. He was instantly hooked. Hooked on the mood, the elegance, the grandeur and the quality of it all. It was like stepping into a different world of possibilities you didn't know existed. You never know what you're missing until you see it and now Sam had. He knew, there was no going back. The way he lived would never be enough for him now, he'd always want more.

"Right this way," Carter cut into Sam's thoughts with pressing urgency and he dutifully followed out of the room, down a long corridor towards the other side of the suite, managing to sneak a peek into some of the rooms en route, including the magnificent kitchen/diner.

'THIS PLACE IS HUGE!' Sam imagined this suite was more like an apartment which made up the whole twelfth floor.

They stopped outside a closed door at the end of the corridor. Carter knocked three times.

"Yes," the acerbic voice resonated from behind the door. His tone was so distinctive in its deep voiceover smoothness that Sam was sure he would recognise it at any point in the future.

Carter opened the door aggressively before stepping back, gesturing for Sam to go inside and into the dragon's lair.

Sam paused, suspended in a moment of self-doubt. Unsure if he should wait for Carter to announce him? But the man just stood, a statue with no indication of doing anything. With a deep breath, Sam walked forwards and into the room.

The space was bathed in darkness, but for a solitary desk lamp, its lighthouse beam cutting defiantly across the ocean of darkness. Beyond the light sat a creature yet more sinister; one who appeared to be at perfect ease in his natural habitat, he owned it. Sam was drawn towards it like a moth to the flame.

Keaton was just a silhouette, his chair turned facing the window away from Sam. The ever busy entrepreneur taking a rare moment's peace to gaze out on the stunning view he owned.

Sam continued to approach with caution. He didn't want to startle Keaton, or disturb some deep thought he may be tracing.

The door slammed firmly shut behind him and Sam propelled himself forward. As he reached the desk, Mr Keaton rose slowly from his seat, fastening one of his jacket buttons before turning casually, left hand resting on the back of his chair. There it was again, that soul piercing stare. There was a small hiatus as he looked Sam over once more, still studying, taking down mental notes derived from Sam's subtleties.

"Have a seat," Keaton said, his deep monotone more like an instruction than a request... No doubt used to people obeying his every command. He gestured momentarily to one of the two suede chairs opposite him. Sam sat quickly, glad to relieve his tense leg muscles which had seized up. With perfectly measured skill Keaton pushed his chair around with his palm and sat, facing Sam. As he placed his left hand on the desk, Sam's eyes were drawn to an elegant gold timepiece. The room was as silent as it was dark, the only sound was Keaton's thumb slowly tapping the desk and the eerily muted night sounds of the city outside.

There was not a chance in hell Sam was going to break the silence first. He had nowhere near the confidence required to pluck a topic out of the air and force it upon Keaton. He doubted many people did. Sam was back at school again and in the presence of the professor. Speak only when spoken to.

After a good ten seconds of intense eyeballing Keaton finally spoke, "Why are you here?" The question was blunt and sharp, but there was a hint of intrigue in his eyes which momentarily broke through the inscrutable countenance.

Sam took a moment, constructing his answer with care, preferring to endure a brief silence than release an unjustified answer.

"I'm here because… I want more out of life." The answer seemed short and oversimplified. It wasn't much of a detailed explanation. However, it was everything this quick study imagined Keaton wanted; short sincerity that got right to the point. And from Keaton's immediate reply, which delved deeper, he knew he'd done well, "More what, exactly." The thumb stopped tapping, as though Sam had reached the next level of his intrigue, scaling Kilimanjaro for the summit of interest reached only by the rare few.

"Truthfully, sir; more freedom, more confidence… more money." The last two words sent an ugly wave of shallowness over him, but at least it was the truth. In fact, truth be told, it's something most of us want. And the final word seemed to dispatch a shock of pleasure into Keaton as he shuffled momentarily in his seat, raising his right hand to his lips which he softly pressed with his knuckles.

Sam could imagine the complex cogs in Keaton's mind working away, but what they were thinking was well guarded by the prize worthy poker face.

His right arm shifted back down to his lap before he replied, "Are you unemployed, Sam?" The question was casually delivered but he'd used Sam's name… His first name no less. This was a new personal touch, which Sam considered positive. Keaton's intrigue slowly cranking up the gears with Sam sweating and striving to achieve it.

"No, I'm working in retail part time at the moment… down in Surrey," Sam explained quickly. Choosing not to disclose his other venture, he correctly sensed that although it was impressive, it was not something that would fit in well with Keaton's ethos.

"You don't enjoy retail?" Keaton asked immediately. Sam was aware the man knew the answer to that question from what he'd just said. Entrepreneurs were notoriously good at reading people and their deepest desire, the secret door to compliance. Find out what you want, then offer it to you, buying devotion. Some say there is no man more trustworthy than a bribable one. No, he asked that plain, boring question because he wanted to see if Sam could twist the conversation back to Keaton's interest. Which he did, "No, sir. It's always been the world of corporate business that's excited me." His passion emotively conveyed.

Keaton paused with the posture of a statue. Then leaned forwards, out towards Sam. His hands clasped together on the desk. It felt as if this was it… The million-pound question was coming, the big one. Keaton just said one word

"Why?"

It was such a simple little word, but Sam felt the overbearing menace that three letter word had in this moment. It could make or break him.

He retreated into deep thought, before answering,

"It's a natural longing that's built up inside me. The desire to be part of this world of more. I feel like it's what I'm meant to do. This is where I belong, sir. I feel it in my very bones and I'll do anything and everything to be part of it."

On finishing his speech Sam felt shocked at himself. His initial passion had rapidly strengthened and deepened into this dark and cold longing. In that moment there was nothing but fierce passion and he honestly convinced himself he would do anything for success. He hadn't meant to go so far, it just sort of happened naturally and just as doubt began to infiltrate, it was stamped out by the same brief smile he had witnessed Keaton deliver earlier that day. Clearly his dark passion had spoken to the businessman.

Without warning Keaton suddenly got to his feet and turned back to face the stunning cityscape, Sam felt summarily dismissed. The movement left him momentarily confused as to what was happening. Sam was convinced he'd said the right thing but now he wasn't so sure. Had he read the man wrong? Was getting up and facing away a sign of boredom? Disappointment? Or was it positivity? Or dare he think it, trust? Whatever it was Sam knew one thing… The man had made a decision, one way or the other.

Sam was about to find out. He could feel it. It was make or break time. The tension was palpable; his heart racing to keep up with his breathing. Keaton turned 180 degrees and looked right into the interviewee's soul, casually serving up the question, "What would you say, if I were to offer you a position. Working for me personally?"

A bolt of adrenaline exploded, igniting his entire body into electrified life. He felt, in that moment, a man who could accomplish anything. Run a marathon? No problem. Scale The Eiger? Bring it on! It was as if the whole world had disappeared and all that was left was Sam and his Idol. The hormones subsided and reality resumed.

Sam focused on mirroring Keaton's composure in the face of this unexpected statement, but the idea had hit him like a train… Too many emotions to control. He was immobile.

"You're interested, I presume?" Keaton pushed for a response, knowing full well what the answer was by Sam's apparent inability to construct a simple sentence.

"Absolutely," Sam was eventually able to find a solitary word from amongst the turmoil within.

"I've been searching for a worthy business assistant, you'd be shadowing me during all business affairs," Keaton expanded as if it were necessary to further entice Sam. As if he needed to! But the man seemed to be enjoying the effect the news had. Such power over another person's emotions seemed to excite him, although naturally, he would be careful not to show it. To gather even a glimpse into Keaton's true self would take considerable skill; reading between the lines and beyond them. You would have to be bloody good at it.

"It sounds like a great opportunity, Mr Keaton. One I certainly couldn't pass up." The words just tumbled out of Sam naturally. He'd totally surrendered, raw enthusiasm drowning out the small logical part of his mind which screamed, 'What about Seren!'

"I have to return to New York tonight on business. I'm back here on Friday, my secretary will contact you with the details,' Keaton explained with vague detailing. But it didn't matter, he could have said anything at this point, Sam's consciousness only picked up the words in a quiet undertone… Far too busy still mulling over Keaton's offer which repeated again and again, a reverberating echo in a grand salon.

Even if he had been paying full attention, and managed to muster the most logical, level headed state of being, was he going to say *'Sorry, that's no good for me. I'd like to forego this once in a lifetime opportunity please'?* I don't think so.

Sam's wild imagination was now out of sight, way out of the solar system, beyond the galaxy, landing somewhere in the outer reaches of other-worldly dimensions. It was violently snapped back to reality as the door opened and the now familiar gruff voice announcing, "The plane has arrived, sir," Definitely back down to earth, now!

Keaton briefly consulted his wristwatch before deducing time was indeed up.

"Until Friday then," Keaton's voice quickened ever so slightly. He'd been cruising in third gear and had now shifted abruptly up into fourth. Still not at full speed but certainly acknowledging the urgency of his next appointment... Whatever that may be.

Whilst Sam was reluctant to leave his hero's presence, politeness kicked in and told him it was time to leave.

"Thank, very much, Mr Keaton. I won't let you down," Sam squeezed out one final moment to say what he felt needed to be said. Keaton said nothing. The inscrutable Sphinx standing fast. He simply gestured back towards Carter, who led Sam back to the elevator.

Sam entered alone, puzzling over the many buttons for a moment as he struggled to comprehend, eventually finding "L." He pressed it firmly, waiting for the doors to close before letting out a long sigh containing too many emotions to express.

"Did that just happen?" Sam asked himself out loud, running hands through his hair as he began to laugh uncontrollably, joy and disbelief blended together.

Chapter 7

Disparity

Sam was nearly home now. Sauntering down the dark, lonely streets of his town. By now his racing mind had settled down somewhat, rationalisation having crept back in. He thought of Seren and wondered what she might say… He'd agreed to this job without discussing it with his partner. *'That wasn't very clever was it?'* she'd certainly be upset, they were supposed to be a team after all.

And then another thought crossed his mind, 'For all you know the job could be based in New York!' With this realisation came a much more practical one. Sam only knew two things about the job; one, he'd be Keaton's 'business assistant,' two, he'd be shadowing his boss during all business affairs. Both were very vague and didn't give much away.

But Sam felt pretty safe presuming he'd be travelling a lot. Lots of time away from Seren. He didn't like the thought of leaving Seren alone in a neighborhood he considered rough. The idea worried at his conscience for a brief moment, before swiftly swinging back to the upsides.

Yes, Mr Keaton had been vague and yes, Sam should have discussed it all with Seren before agreeing. But there was no point obsessing about it now. The fact was this was the opportunity of his lifetime and precisely what he wanted had presented itself before him and he'd be an idiot to pass it up. *'It's fate… this is supposed to happen to me. Dive in at the deep end!'* he reminded himself, his surety erasing any doubts.

Sam was surprised he wasn't running home, sprinting to tell Seren the news. He didn't care she'd try to drop the anchor. That didn't matter he just needed to share this with her, the one person he wanted to share everything with.

But there was something which stopped him from doing this immediately – the perfection of this moment. Sam's sauntering pace had bumped a 15-minute journey up to twenty. Between the station and home Sam was completely alone and in his current state of mind he felt as if the city were his.

It was not the first time he'd made his way home alone in the dark, of course not. The lonely view, the quiet, everything was the same as always… everything but Sam. He felt reborn, had been handed a fresh start where anything and everything was possible. It was that rare feeling of newfound freedom you discover when you first journey out into the world. A young eagle spreading his wings wide for the first time and soaring into the sky of hopes and dreams. *'You never made the leap… After school, you just went back to school.'* Sam's ghosts returned, prodding him with *'what if's?'* and *'you could have's!'*

Meanwhile, he was busy worrying about his current problems. Predominant of which was always money – specifically, lack of it. Surely the most worried about reality in the cosmos, the pecuniary numbers ruling our lives with ruthless mathematics. And Seren and Sam were located securely in the lower class bracket, a world where worries about money are always there, because *it* isn't. As soon as *it* came in *it* was gone again. The Usain Bolt of the fiscal world.

But that was washed away now, all of it. He was set to take the leap once more and this time he wouldn't fail. Fate had given him another chance and for the first time Sam made his way home with his hopes and dreams intact. So he sauntered – *All* the way home.

Just before turning the corner of his street Sam's eyes were drawn to the liquor store opposite him. 'Never had there been a greater excuse to drink,' He thought and changed course decisively. It was a small corner shop and so wasn't exactly stocked up on Dom Perignon. Sam just grabbed their most expensive bottle of champagne, which was a non-vintage Moet... twenty quid, a lot of money, *'Well... A lot of money to you now,'* ever the optimist.

Sam knew he wouldn't be able to help his new found hopes and dreams infecting his daily life. His imagination had been rebooted and was now omnipresent in the background. As he paid for the champagne, he couldn't help consider a future where he would look back on such extravagance and laugh.

Sam leaped up the stairs, taking three even four at a time as he made his way impatiently to the second floor. He reached the door, stopping momentarily as he contemplated his big reveal, deciding to wrestle the bottle into his shoulder bag that still dangled, ever faithful.

Seren emerged from the kitchen, feet dragging, exhausted from a long day of walking and standing. Her body was eager to finish the tea and crash, but the unmistakable creak of the old rusted lock meant Sam was home. This comforting sound energised her.

The door flung open violently, almost coming off its rusted hinges, Sam's effervescence providing a newfound strength. Sam stepped through the doorway, not giving one thought to closing it behind him, his attention fixated on his beloved standing in the kitchen doorway across the narrow hall. There was a tense silence as neither spoke, Seren because she was exhausted and Sam for an entirely different reason. He looked Seren up and down, his eyes filled with sudden animalistic hunger. She was still wearing her nurses' uniform which clung to her petite figure, curving out at the hips and chest.

'Later Sam, LATER!' He snapped himself out of it, realising there were more pressing matters at hand. He walked briskly to her, caressing her cheeks in his hands before stealing a long passionate kiss as his consolation prize.

"It went well, then?" Seren threw him a cute laugh as their lips parted. She gave a high pitched yelp of surprise as Sam grabbed her by the waist, lifting her light body effortlessly into the air whilst walking into the kitchen.

Sam couldn't keep his hands off her, they longed to run up and down her smooth skin.

'Control yourself. YOUR NEWS! Headlines first, sports later.'

"We. Are. Celebrating!" Sam rejoiced, almost breaking into song. He swung the shoulder bag skilfully round to his front before placing it gently on the kitchen table and pulling out the champagne, waving it like a trophy before Seren's eyes.

"Sam! How much was that!" Shocked at the extravagance, she tried not to smile, but failed miserably. She snatched the bottle from him. Her eye's glaring disapproval whilst exposed pearly white teeth betrayed her own curiosity.

Sam shuffled over to the counter where he leant causally before dropping the bomb, "Oh, I think we can afford it, seeing as Mr Keaton offered me a job as his personal assistant!" He couldn't resist a smug smirk which stole across his face.

However, this quickly disappeared as he witnessed Seren's immediate reaction to the news. The pearls vanished as her smile retracted faster than a recoiling cobra. The infectious and sudden joy she had contracted off him was replaced with a look of disappointment as her mind caught up with the news.

She dropped the bottle dramatically upon the table. "What?" That one simple word conveying a myriad of questions she needed answering; what are you talking about? What happened? What the fuck's going on?

Sam didn't know what to say. He was as stunned at her reaction as she was at his news. He suspected, no, he knew from her tone on the phone earlier she had doubts at the least, but he wasn't expecting such persistent resistance. It threw him. But he needed to speak, to say something. The tigress glared, awaiting an explanation.

Deciding it was best just to explain what had happened, Sam began, "Keaton invited me for a chat, asked me a bunch of questions and then he offered me the job... completely out of the blue." He let a smile slip out as he recalled the bizarreness of it all. However, this was speedily rubbed out as Seren's expression didn't falter.

But what had happened in the meeting didn't matter to Seren who then asked the question she needed to ask. A question she already knew the answer to, "I don't understand... his PA... I mean that's a full time job, right?"

"Yes of course! He asked me to be his personal business assistant. Mr Keaton himself, can you believe it?!" Sam got carried away, he couldn't help it. Explaining what had happened just brought the memory back to him, excitement its natural accompaniment.

However, Seren was one hell of an anchor and dragged him swiftly back down to Earth with one simple question.

"What about your studies?" She inquired in the most serious tone she could muster.

There was a long silence, the topic Sam had so skilfully avoided for the last two hours stood like a brick wall before him... blocking his hopes and dreams. At least, that's how he saw it now. Something that had started out as a beautiful thing, a noble cause to please his father, which his mind had now twisted and morphed into something evil, something that stood between him and his precious fate.

Sam's mood was shocked into change and he spoke with a slow calmness, "Nothing is certain yet... Okay. I haven't signed anything. His secretary is going to send over the details, I'll look over the contract, and we will make a decision... together?" He was convincing, but he knew the words to be hollow. He was taking that job, he was sure of that now. There was no way this opportunity was slipping through his fingers; he was poised on the edge of that diving board.

Seren was taken in by Sam's words and her concerns subsided. She genuinely believed he might not take the job.

"It's just that you're nearly there sweetheart, I… I don't want us to throw away everything we've been working so hard for – you're so close." Seren began to tremble as she got to the root of her fear. She was about to cry but Sam saw it coming and rushed to wrap her tightly in his arms, galvanised into his role as her protector. The tears receded and she hugged him back. Her nails digging into Sam's back but he didn't care.

There was only one thing which equaled Sam's lifelong dream of becoming a successful businessman with confidence and respect, and that was Seren's happiness. In fact, though initially the job offer had sparked his own selfish fantasies he knew deep down he would be taking this job for Seren too. He wanted her to be happy and secure, always. To expunge the worry about bills or being robbed in the night. He wanted to provide his woman with everything she deserved and to look after her in every sense.

Sam spoke softly, "I don't want you to worry about anything, you hear. Whatever we do, we do it together, always."

Sam wasn't going to mention 'the job' anymore this evening. It was clear how the topic upset her. Right now what she needed from him was comfort, and by God he was going to provide it. There was nothing… Absolutely nothing he hated more than seeing his sweet angel suffer.

And so he would carry her to the sofa and let her sleep whilst he finished the dinner. Then they would retire to bed early and sleep the night away. For tomorrow was a fresh page.

Chapter 8

Wisdom

The following day was a living nightmare for Seren. Never in her life had she done so much worrying in one day.

Last night Sam almost had her convinced, she had hoped, believed even that he was only considering taking this new position. But having removed the rose tinted specs and reviewing the evening with clarity, she realised the truth. He was resolved. Anyone could have seen it. Sam would become Mr Keaton's personal business assistant... *'Whatever the hell that means? His bitch, basically.'*

Seren wasn't one to get angry without good reason but she felt she had it now. For three years they had struggled... Three years of shit jobs and shit pay, fighting together and for what? So Sam could throw it all away because of a childhood fantasy. She sounded like a bitch when you explained it like that. The girlfriend who kept her boyfriend on a tight leash and wouldn't let him follow his dreams. She didn't want to be that girlfriend of course she didn't, she wanted Sam to follow his dreams. That wasn't what had pissed her off, it was the fact they were supposed to be a team working together towards a goal they both planed for, and now he'd just decided all on his own that there was a new plan. Seren felt betrayed, that her opinion was redundant. She knew this was a tad dramatic and that Sam's intensions were good but she couldn't help the way she felt. The bottom line was that Sam had made a decision which would soon affect both their lives in a dramatic way without so much as passing it by her first.

So, she was royally pissed off, but that was nothing compared to what really frightened her. The real reason that every fiber of her being screamed out, 'DON'T LET HIM DO IT' Seren's uncharacteristic anger towards Sam was just a shield… A shield she used to hide her true fear. Something she would never tell Sam… She couldn't talk about it. A painful memory from her past was dislodged and resurrected from its cold grave, 'Sam, will become your father' it spoke. She didn't want to revisit that emotional minefield and adroitly pushed it away.

Seren trudged through the long day. Not about to let her personal problems get in the way of her duty of care for those in need. In many ways her job had been her salvation. It was tough and every day just seemed to get busier and busier but she loved it. Helping people was very important to her. She'd always maintained the belief that there was karmic justice in the world and no matter how exhausted she was at the end of the day, she knew she'd had a positive impact on someone's life. That she'd made a difference and that was her personal reward.

It was 7:15 and Seren was set to clock off at 7.00pm… But she didn't want to go home. She didn't want to face Sam, along with the new reality he had forged for them. Seren wanted to work and work and work until her problems just drifted away. Of course they never would, but it was a nice thought.

Having wrestled back and forth with the idea of returning home, Seren decided she would make one more stop first.

She walked briskly down the white tube lit walkway, turning left then right then right again down and endless maze of corridors, negotiated automatically and entirely without conscious thought.

She reached the ward labelled "Elderly Services Department," and entered one of the many rooms. It was relatively small, for a hospital anyway. Five beds on each side of the room symmetrically arranged, all occupied with frail women.

Seren could understand why hospitals left many people uneasy. To be blunt and truthful they were full of sickness and death and Seren saw plenty of it. But she chose to focus her attention on the living and the elderly in particular, who always had a story or two up their sleeves. However, this evening it wasn't a story she was in need of, it was advice. And Seren knew one particular old lady who fit the job description nicely.

She didn't want to talk about her problems, she just wanted to bury them. But avoiding Sam and her home forever wasn't practical. Wants and needs are seldom the same thing and Seren needed to talk through this, but not with Sam. She was too angry with him. No, she needed someone standing outside the storm, someone level headed and with the wisdom developed over a long life. Thankfully, Seren had many such people at her immediate disposal.

Seren made her way to the back of the room, to the bed in the far left corner where the wisest old woman she knew rested. The two had met by chance, as most do, when Seren was rostered in to settle some new guests in, Nina Astley being amongst them. She had stood out immediately to Seren with her 'devil may care' attitude. This lady didn't care what anyone thought of her and always spoke her mind and Seren respected her greatly for it. She was the sort of person you could sit and talk with for hours and never revisit the same subject once. And Seren habitually returned to read stories and chat.

"Hi, Nina, how are we today?"

She announced herself whilst pulling across the blue curtain to give them some privacy. Seren had completely ignored the fact Nina's eyelids were shut tight. Knowing full well these old gals tended to drift in and out of light sleep constantly, even during the day in fact. After all, there wasn't a lot else to do in a hospital. So you couldn't be too shy about waking them up. Sure enough, intelligent blue eyes opened and she was fully alert, mind still as sharp as ever.

"Well, I'm still sitting here in this old decrepit meat sack so… pretty shitty, girl."

Nina spoke in a dull, honest tone. Yet her words were so comical it seemed to be a joke.

"Nina! You shouldn't use words like that."

Seren's ready smile attempted an escape as she gently admonished whilst knowing full well it would only encourage this irreverent patient but she couldn't help it. There was just something inherently hilarious about a ninety-year-old woman cursing.

"Why not? Has free speech been abolished?"

Nina snapped back with her sassy spunk that had drawn Seren to her. Eyes widened and arms gestured wildly, proffering yet more comic genius.

"Yes, and I know you're not a lady but some of these other poor women are… Probably never heard words like that in their lives, bless them."

A motherly sympathy washed over Seren as she looked over the other beds with warmth. A mood which was swiftly demolished by Nina's reply,

"Ah, Bless them me arsehole, they can't even hear me!"

"Will you keep your voice down."

Seren couldn't help but allow a small giggle to escape but Nina was gradually becoming louder and louder as her overflowing passion escaped. The professional returned and immediately smothering her mirth, mimed disapproval with a gentle frown.

Nina went blank for a moment, crossing her arms in silent protest before a sudden confusion grabbed her. The carved wrinkles deepening further as her ever expressive face scrunched up tight,

"What are you still doing here anyway, coming to disturb me peace?"

Seren knew Nina well enough by now to know behind her brash exterior lurked an extremely caring person. And that when she said 'what are you still doing here' what she really meant was 'go home.' It was always crystal clear when the exasperation was real, her violent body language would make the bed rock. Seren had only witnessed this once, when one of the less experienced nurses dropped hot chocolate in her lap. Boy, did that girl get a talking to. It had been one of the most brutal yet strangely, comical displays of anger Seren had ever seen.

"Unfortunately for you, I have another hour left and a new book!"

Seren sang as she pulled a small novel from one of her practically large, Mary Poppins pockets.

She just wanted to spill all of her problems, tip them out on the table so that Nina could help sort them. But she couldn't just come out with it. She feared if she delved right into it she wouldn't be able to stop, she'd ramble on and on all night about her and Sam and their plans and now Sam's new plan. No, if she was going to talk about it; it had to happen naturally, flowing within the set boundaries of the conversation.

Luckily, Nina's wit and intelligence immediately detected something was wrong,

"You may be able to bamboozle these other old wind bags, but you can't fool me girly. I may be blind but I hear the clock chimes just fine! Get home to your husband."

Nina was adept at hiding her disability. She had an amazing talent for finding you in the room just by your voice and steps. Her heightened sense of hearing compensated and it was quite disconcerting when she appeared to be looking you directly in the eye.

Nina had employed a clever little tactic for timekeeping. With her she had bought a small alarm clock, nothing fancy but on the hour every hour it gently chimed the numbers and Nina knew Seren's shift ended at 7.00pm on the dot and the seventh chime had already sounded.

Consciously Seren hadn't suspected she would be found out so soon, but maybe on some subconscious level she had known or at least hoped.

Seren replied,

"And skip Stephen King's nail-biting 'Misery', I don't think so…"

She still couldn't do it – couldn't come out with the reason she didn't want to go home, lacking the courage to delve into her feelings.

Still, she'd made it perfectly clear from her poorly faked cheer there was something she needed to say and Nina didn't waste any time,

"What's wrong girl? Why so reluctant to go home?"

Nina's sassy tone had vanished, replaced by soft enquiry, asking the question Seren needed to answer.

Seren placed the book back in her pocket. Pretence vanished as she pulled up a chair beside Nina, sitting silently for a moment as she calculated how much to reveal.

She began,

"Sam's taking a new job, nothing's official yet but… I know he's made up his mind, before he even spoke to me, the decision already made… He's giving up his studies,"

Seren spoke of Sam's studies as if it were a lost lover. To her the feeling of betrayal was equal to that of a cheating beloved. Working so hard for so long towards a common goal which she had now found out they didn't share after all. Suddenly the dream they had shared evaporated into nothingness, as if it never were.

Nina's mind rankled with snide comments directed at Sam for the pain he, knowingly or not, had caused her favourite. But such judgements didn't have a place in this conversation, they wouldn't help Seren and so batting them down she simply asked,

"What's the job?"

A seemingly harmless enough question which Nina immediately regretted asking as Seren's eyes watered and her lip trembled. Nina had unwillingly cut right through to the wound.

"He's going to become a businessman." She spat the last word out bitterly.

This answer was meaningless to Nina, it would have been meaningless to anyone. Unless you knew about Seren's father, that is. Which Nina didn't. In fact not even Sam knew much about the man other than the fact he had been a successful businessman back in his day. Nina was about to learn more about Seren's mysterious Dad than had ever been shared previously.

Nina lay there in silence. What could she say? She had no clue what the problem was beyond Sam's seemingly undemocratic decision. And she wasn't about to go fishing for the answer. No, wisdom had taught her to be patient over the years and she was not about to rush headlong into such a delicate subject. Intelligently, she sat in silence, until her friend was ready to share the main course in her own time.

Following this brief period of tranquillity, Seren gathered all her courage... Preparing to journey back to her past,

"My father..."

She began sheepishly, clearing the lump in her throat,

"He was a businessman. He worked for some tech company, I don't know who they were or what they did. I didn't honestly care I was only a child... But I cared about him. From as long as I can remember up to when I was eight he was everything to me,"

Seren's smile stole through her tears as her best memories came flooding back to her,

"We used to spend so much time together, laughing and playing. I was his little princess and he was my hero."

Seren suddenly stopped, wiping the streams of tears away with a shaking palm. Nina could see she didn't want to go any further. The poor girl just wanted to end the story there, at the good times. But Nina knew she needed to go on and provided the gentle push of support she required,

"Something happened?"

Seren nodded slowly,

"He umm... got promoted, to managing director... And everything changed. Him and my mother they were so happy, so overjoyed they were moving up in the world, joining the middle classes,"

Seren gave a dark chuckle born of irony,

"We had more money, a bigger house, more stuff... But he was coming home less and less, every month he was travelling more and more as his workload got bigger and my time with him reduced… His enthusiasm for life just seemed to slowly drain away as if the job was destroying his soul. I tried to ignore it, remain optimistic, kept telling myself it would pass, it would pass and I'd have my father all to myself again, things would go back to the way they were… But they didn't. And it was on my sixteenth birthday that I finally realised I'd really lost him… He missed it, away on some trip to America and I knew then that he'd become someone I didn't know anymore. My hero, my father who used to put family first had slowly morphed day by day into someone driven by money and power… That job stole my father away from me."

There was a tense silence as Nina took it all in, connecting all the dots before she spoke,

"Sam isn't your father."

"I know,"

The statement was flatly acknowledged. 'Knowing the two most important men of her life were wildly different and that just because Sam was venturing into the harsh world of business, like her father, didn't necessarily equate to the same result… But it was a harsh world. One Seren knew the realities of. It didn't matter what the business was in the end; it was all just a matter of numbers on a spreadsheet and the numbers had to add up no matter what the costs.

Yes, on the outside looking in it was a bright world bathed in money and success. But the grass always looks greener and in the shadows lurked risk, stress and hard, hard work with the power to drain your soul down to the last dregs.

It was a world built for a certain type of man. Money obsessed, hyper active, testosterone pumping, self-righteous bastards who were born to chase money. Those rich adolescents who had gathered at the bar all those years ago; they had become such beings.

Sam wasn't one of them, that's why out of all the men she could have chosen she chose him. Not because he was confident or manly but because he was sweet and an innocent. And so finally the real fear which haunted Seren was exposed,

'That job will turn Sam into your father. It will turn him into one of the lads!'

She'd lost a father she couldn't lose Sam too!

Nina summoned all of her experience and prepared to do the impossible, to convince Seren that everything would be alright, even though wisdom had taught her it possibly wouldn't, she wanted to give her friend hope. She decided to tell a story of her own,

"You know, trust is the most important part of any relationship, sometimes you've just got to take a leap of faith and trust your man... Now George, my husband, he liked to think of himself as an inventor, God rest his naive soul..."

"I didn't know you were married?"

Seren exclaimed, her own troubles briefly breached by sudden curiosity,

"I'm not one to be blabbing about my whole life story you know! And don't be interrupting me!"

Nina's sassy temper returned momentarily before Seren's sweet face forced her attention back to business,

"Anyway, as I was saying, George was my husband for over forty years, a good man, but he was always obsessing about money, always trying to come up with some get rich quick scheme... Almost burned down the garden shed once with one of his stupid inventions,"

Both women shared a brief laugh at poor unfortunate George's expense,

"But eventually, in his own time he came to realise there is more to life. But he has to discover it for himself... Your Sam is a good man, like my George. You have to let him follow his dream or he will resent you. Then, in time, he will realise some dreams should continue to be just that – dreams."

Nina smiled widely and kindly reached out a trembling old hand towards Seren, who grasped it tightly.

Seren was consoled. Nina had done exactly what she needed her to do, exactly what Seren knew she would,

85

provide the insight of experience and reassure her that everything would be alright in the end. She swallowed the soothing balm whilst accepting the possibility that Sam could still end up becoming her father. Not even Nina's wise anecdote could conquer that fear. No, some wounds never heal and the consequences of them stick with us forever, carved into our very souls. Wise souls accept this and view their experiences as opportunities, rather than problems.

But there was comfort to be found from Nina's own personal experience. It was an illogical comfort of course. What happened to George had no real relevance to Sam and yet it still conjured a newfound hope and optimism within Seren... why?

It was because Seren honestly believed Sam was the best of men and if George could escape being seduced and consumed by the idea of money and success, then so could Sam. What Nina's story had made Seren realise was that she already had faith in her man... she'd just forgotten it, swept up in this sudden storm of panic which had dug up some old wounds from the past. But Nina was right, Sam wasn't her father. Not yet.

Seren smiled widely, her beautiful glowing self had returned and she reached back into her pocket, retrieving the book,

"One chapter... Then home,"

Seren promised and began to read.

Chapter 9

Quitting

Whilst Seren spent her day in a living nightmare of *'what if's'* about the near future, Sam was living his own nightmare which played over and over... The reality of his retail job. Well, he always said it was retail but that was only because he never wanted to utter the words, 'I work in a supermarket.' In fact, technically he couldn't even say that. Lose the word 'super' and then you had a more realistic definition, which was apt really as it certainly wasn't a 'super' job.

The store was a strange paradox. Inside it was your local convenience store stocking everything from bandages to booze. Then, outside the front door was a small market stall, which three days a week Sam had to get in early to bring out. Trailing in and out with boxes of fruit and veg. The only reason Sam's position had been part time, the only reason the store was open three days a week was because that was all it could afford. Sam didn't know the finances of the place, he didn't care in the slightest but he knew even Lord Sugar couldn't stop this tragedy from haemorrhaging cash.

During the vast spans of time between the rarity of a paying customer Sam chose to stand outside. Even in the mid-winter freeze it was the lesser of two evils, at least outside there was some form of view and fresh air. But this did mean facing off the bitterness of the street, not just the weather, which was brutal this time of year making the raw fruit and veg like handling cubes of ice, but the people too.

Especially the local adolescents who would stare and snicker with judgmental glances as they passed by, living their young care free lives. Sam for a moment wishing he was them. Of course, Sam could never be sure it was in fact judgment and laughter at his expense, but that's how it felt.

Occasionally he'd drum up the courage to try and force something nutritious upon the miserable locals, who would flash him that sharp glare door to door salesman get, which basically said, 'Fuck off!' These irritable Londoner's, who for some reason weren't at work themselves on a week day were like aimless zombies, occupying their time by passing through this tragic little street.

And it was tragic, the kind where the betting shop had the highest number of visitors during the day and the pub at night. Not only that but to top it off they were the most attractive buildings on the street, standing three stories side by side with a featured brick roof. The betting shop, the pub, a chippy and the market Sam worked at were the only four buildings of twelve which weren't boarded up. The small street had been left behind by a modernising city which had drained the very life and soul out of it, leaving it weak and helpless.

The place where Sam worked was the most tragic looking building of the bunch, setting aside the mass of deserted ones of course, penned in tightly between the chippy and a public toilet. It stood a pathetic one story high with a flat roof. It looked like a council building which had been sliced down to the base.

Sam's hatred for the job wasn't because he believed he deserved more than those around him… It was because he wanted more, for himself but more importantly for Seren. There was a drive and determination deep within him which longed to be released. The restless lion which for years had been kept securely caged by his lack of confidence wanted to go out into the world and make something more of himself. But now this shiny new opportunity Keaton offered him had woken the beast which smelt blood. Its time had finally come. Sam now possessed the key to unlock the cage where the lion dwelled. A confident, raging beast that wanted to take on the world.

Every day Sam was filled with the same sickening feeling of self judgment, *'So, this is what your life's become?'* `In that briefest of moments the fact that this job was only part time and temporary until his studies were completed didn't compute. He was there now and that is all that mattered. All that ever really matters is the reality of the moment you're in, you can't escape the surroundings constantly perceived by your senses.

The essence of this dull street of concrete and dilapidated buildings had slowly infiltrated and poisoned Sam's mind, warping the reality of a mostly blameless local community into something to be despised. Not even his vivid imagination could escape his self-made prison. Its perceived feral negativity was too ferocious and Sam's overactive imagination was under constant attack, his thoughts plagued with the paranoid judgement he perceived. His intelligent mind fantasising because it wasn't occupied with anything else. A bored mind is indeed a dangerous one.

'But now I can escape…' This cheerful thought suddenly burst forth, a ray of light penetrating the drab darkness, as Sam wrestled a large cabbage into a small bag for an elderly woman, who waited somewhat impatiently. It had clicked into his mind like a moment of pure clarity. He had been given the opportunity he so desperately needed. The chance to break out of this bubble and make his way to the guided promised land of the business world.

Sam had planned to wait until his new job contract was signed and stamped for the sweet satisfaction of quitting the market stall slash corner shop. But in this moment it just made too much sense to go ahead and leave. *'Why wait?'* Day by day he could feel this occupation sapping his very soul. Every day he left another little piece of his enthusiasm for life behind. Like the store itself were some evil demon which fed on the lost dreams of its workforce. *'Well, it's not going to take my dreams away from me.'* The lion would wait no longer, it was about to break free. *'This little old lady will be the last customer I ever serve.'*

Sam marched with a forceful purpose into the building to the back of the store where the owner's office lay. His task consumed him with such ferocity and blind will he forgot the simple curtesy of knocking. Bursting through the doorway to see the familiar sight of his greatly overweight boss, leaning back with his feet on the desk watching Top Gear reruns on Dave.

The sight of his lazy boss, who every day came in no earlier than eleven and spent all day in his sweaty chair watching TV whilst Sam ran the shop, sickened him. Sam's strong will and sudden righteousness was blended with a toxic cocktail of rage… *'All the long days of doing everything from serving customers to cleaning the bathroom whilst this lard arse sits all day long, putrefying in his own filth without lifting a finger.'*

Sam's body surged with adrenaline and before any objection could be made to his rude entrance Sam snapped, "Now listen here, you fat fuck," the man's jaw dropped and his eyes widened. He'd never so much as heard a complaint from the good natured Sam, never mind cursing. But that Sam was gone, he wasn't going to be pushed around anymore.

Sam paused for a brief moment, he was about to have a nice long rant about how this man before him didn't deserve to be called a businessman. He wasn't a businessman at all – he hadn't earned that title, but on reflection, *'he in't worth the ten seconds.'* All Sam wanted to do was to go home to Seren and so he simply said calmly, "I quit." And walked out of the door heading for the bright new future that awaited him.

'No more waking up dreading the day ahead, no more riding the sweaty and depressing tube twice a day, no more wishing my days away, no more wasting my life trapped in a place forgotten by time.' Sam mentally prepared himself for something more.

90

Chapter 10

A call from New York

Sam arrived home at around six. The hour long train journey had mellowed his racing mind which had so hastily quit his job. As trigger-happy as that decision had been he still didn't regret doing it. He was wrapped up in a warm sense of newfound freedom, released from the shackles of that depressing occupation.

Sam had imagined being that eagle with a second chance to leap from the nest and soar into the sky, but now he felt he was there, standing with his wings outstretched and ready to jump.

Friday could not come soon enough. Sam would sign the paperwork and he and Seren would begin their new life of plenty together. *'Providing she agrees, that is!'* The thought popped into his mind and was quickly brushed aside.

He made his way to the kitchen, dropping his trusty shoulder bag on the hallway floor where it slumped pathetically. On the counter stood a lonely bottle of wine the couple had opened the previous weekend. That was their weekend treat, no romantic dinner out, no cinema and popcorn; just a cheap bottle of red and Freeview telly. But all that was soon to change and Sam decided to 'cheers' the two glasses worth left in the bottle in celebration of this notion.

Retrieving a large wine glass from the top cupboard he sauntered into the lounge where he slumped into his desk chair, filled the glass and turned to the ancient desktop computer he'd bought second hand. It stared blankly back at him.

Sam had already finished his first glass by the time the computer fired up into snail paced action. He wanted to find out some more information about this mysterious hero of his. Apart from the obvious fact Keaton owned the hotel which had his name above the door, Sam knew nothing about the man. He'd presumed he was just your typical entrepreneur having worked his way up to the top via hard work and perseverance.

But this was the first time Sam had had the opportunity to stop and gratify his curiosity in depth. As he prepared to type into the search bar Sam realised he couldn't remember the man's first name. So completely awestruck during their meeting, such details hadn't properly registered.

He typed, "Keaton Hotel owner" into the search bar and waited, tapping his fingers impatiently upon the desk as the prehistoric machine communicated with the shitty cheap broadband. Eventually the screen lit up with information about the mysterious man, delivering him in three-dimensional life.

Sam clicked the link labelled Alexander Keaton... Alexander, that was his name. Not that it really mattered as Sam couldn't imagine ever gathering the courage to call him by his first name. That seemed somehow inappropriate, impertinent even. The man radiated such harsh professionalism it seemed strange to Sam he even had a first name. It should just be Mr Keaton... Mr... that should be his first name and to Sam it would remain so.

Sam clicked on the first link of the search page which was of course good old Wikipedia. As the page loaded Sam wondered what it would be like to see yourself online. He'd searched his name before, like most people, but after a good ten minutes of researching for links to himself he'd found nothing more than a single picture derived from his Facebook page, and even that was on the fourth page of images. Sam thought he may as well have not existed according to the internet.

But what would it be like to have tens, even hundreds of web links and images all devoted to you, as Keaton clearly did. What would it be like to read about yourself online and find out things you'd forgotten or never even knew about yourself. Countless journalists trying to psychoanalyse you via their eloquent words... Surreal, was the only description Sam could think of. He imagined it would act as the perfect cure for his lack of confidence. A magazine article from Forbes or People should stock you up with enough confidence for a lifetime. It meant you mattered, that you'd made it. Yes, that's where Sam longed to be, on the cover of Forbes looking as professional and regal as Keaton himself.

As Sam's thoughts returned to Keaton he imagined the man wasn't likely the sort to have Googled himself. Even if he'd wanted to he was likely far too busy to carve out such idle time. Then it clicked in Sam's mind, that was it wasn't it? The people that sit around idly Googling themselves weren't the ones who appeared on the screen. It was the people out there, too busy working and making a name for themselves who made it big. Sam wanted to be one of those people and suddenly felt bad for sitting back and relaxing with half a bottle of red. *'So lazy, this isn't how you make money,'* Sam inwardly chided but then told himself it was okay, he consoled himself with the blissful thought that soon he'd be working directly for a man who'd made it in the real and the digital world as best a man can. And he'd get his chance to prove himself to the world, working day and night to make it happen.

The selected page sprung into lacklustre life and on the right of the screen was a portrait of the man, looking regal as ever in a black suit on a whitewash background. The lighting was so perfect the man almost looked approachable... even though his signature expressionless face had given nothing away. This was clearly the work of a great photographer. Sam imagined the poor artist battling with the editing for hours before he could print a photo which didn't portray the man as a successful serial killer... Though, Sam had heard somewhere that many entrepreneurs have psychopathic traits; ambition, confidence and charm all ticked the requisite boxes.

Sam began to read the wiki article,

"Alexander Richard Keaton is a thirty-four-year-old businessman from New York. He is best known as the founder and CEO of the Keaton Hotel chain which he started in early 2009. Since then the company has skyrocketed and has become one of the most prestigious names in the hotel business with locations now spanning across North America and Europe. Alexander Keaton is considered one of the most private and successful entrepreneurs of his generation with an estimated net worth of over two billion dollars."

Sam downed the generous gulp of wine remaining and fell back in his seat. He was in shock and couldn't quite believe what he'd just read. He had imagined the man was highly successful but as always seeing and believing didn't justify an equal response.

Sam had known for sure the man was rich. Any moron could have calculated that just by studying the man's outward appearance. Subconsciously, Sam had speculated around ten to twenty million as a likely ballpark, taking into consideration he knew the company was multinational. But there was a substantial difference between twenty million and two billion… '1,980,000,000 numbers to be precise' Sam's inner nerdiness getting the better of him and calculating instinctively. Alongside that, his idea of 'multinational' had been around two maybe three countries… wrong again!

Sam's eyes widened further and further at the prestigious list of cities; "New York, San Francisco, Los Angeles, Atlanta, London and Paris." Sam deliberated, if he could only visit those six golden cities in his entire life he'd be happy. Collectively, they had everything he could want.

The more Sam read the higher his respect for the entrepreneur soared. In seven years he had made himself a multi-billionaire and all before he was forty… There was no other word to describe him, the man was a genius and Sam would soak up every little detail of information he could.

Sam was glad to have been ignorant of the man's true status when they met as his nerves may not have survived the encounter. Everything about Keaton just seemed too good to be true. This sparked another internal debate, *'Everybody knows Wikipedia is not always to be relied upon, stupid! But why would someone lie about it?'* Sam even respected the fact he was named as a private individual rather than a corporate entity. There was nothing about his parents or past; he'd managed to keep it all respectfully and tastefully hidden, *'What class!'* He was not a boaster or even a talker, he was a doer and that, in Sam's opinion, was the best way to be. Let the work do the talking. *'Actions always speak louder than words.'*

Sam's image of Alexander Keaton materialised as a man who was everything he aspired to be – one of respect, confidence, integrity and of course, money. Sam now had a new dream. For Keaton to take him under his wing as a mentor. *'Hah, as if that's likely to happen!'*

Sam's attention was forced from the article as his pocket began to vibrate. He reached for his Nokia; the number was unknown.

"Hello?" he mumbled with conspicuous disinterest, his attention had turned straight back from screen to screen, it being a fairly safe assumption this was a sales call… once again he'd greatly miscalculated (which was completely out of character, he was a whizz kid at maths, after all.)

"Good evening, Mr Lowell, my name is Lynn Fox. I'm Mr Keaton's secretary calling from New York," the voice of a young woman explained in a charming American twang.

Sam's senses shifted towards the words which arrived in his ear as sweet, airborne honey. Before he could so much as acknowledge the woman she continued abruptly, as if racing the clock before moving onto her next mission.

"I'm calling to inform you that Mr Keaton has booked your meeting for tomorrow; one o'clock at The Dorchester restaurant," she stated with seemingly rehearsed precision.

Sam scrambled around the desk for a pen as he panicked to get down the two details. The fact that he knew exactly where The Dorchester was clouded by a rush of excitement.

"Thank… you very… much," he stuttered, his focus distracted by the desperate urge to find a pen. Worrying he'd suddenly become incapable of remembering two words and he didn't have this number or Keaton's so he'd be stuffed if he did. There was no pen! So he turned to the keyboard and wrote it in the search bar instead, "Dorchester hotel one o'clock." Now he could relax.

"That's not a problem, sir. Enjoy the rest of your evening," she replied and the line died before Sam could so much as think 'goodbye'.

In a social circumstance he'd have considered such abruptness rude, however, in this instance he accepted a foregone conclusion, that *'a woman in such a position would be run off her feet and therefore, had no spare time for niceties.'* Sam imagined many things had to be sacrificed in the name of efficiency but he didn't dwell on it, convinced no personal slight being intended. Shortly after this, another thought popped into his head, *'Short trip to New York, or maybe it had been postponed?'* He quickly dismissed the latter as preposterous.

Sam spent the next half an hour or so migrating his way from room to room with the objection of finding something to occupy this small gap of nothingness. He tried reading a book, watching TV and even took a shot at a nap but it was no use. He was completely restless and in the end resorted to pacing up and down, up and down the small apartment, occasionally stopping to gaze out of the window or at one of the many family pictures scattered about the place. Waiting for Seren to return home.

Finally, Sam's ears pricked up at the welcome sound of a key squeaking through the rusty lock. He leapt up energetically from the sofa where he'd been constructing random thought patterns for the last ten minutes. Bounding excitably to the door he pulled it open and out of Seren's exhausted lose grip. Longing to explode into conversations before the door swung open and Sam remembered the silent ritual of Seren's return from work.

Neither of them said anything just exchanged a warm smile that was enough to say they were glad to see each other. The two were a mirrored contrast. The long journey home from the hospital had allowed Seren's body time to relax and once it did the fatigue set in. Being a nurse was like running a marathon, being constantly on the go using massive amounts of physical and emotional energy.

Seren dragged her feet through the doorway before Sam slammed the door shut. He stretched his arm out across her back to her left shoulder and gently pulled her slender body towards his. Kissing her temple with comforting affection at which she briefly smiled.

Seren wanted to talk about the job, she wanted to tell Sam all about Nina and even her father. She wanted to tell him that she trusted him and wanted him to follow his dreams but to be cautious and take note and warning from what happened to her father. That the grass isn't always greener! And she didn't want him making any more rash decisions without consulting her. Seren had come to realise now that it wasn't Sam quitting his studies she really objected too, though she was disappointed by it, no, it was the fact he'd made such a big decision so rashly and without her. 'We are supposed to be a team Samuel! Don't ever do that to me again!' she had planned to say in a serious but loving tone.

But her scrambled thoughts refused to line up and she was too spent to delve into such complexities. The little focus that remained was honed in on Sam's warm body and the sofa which lay a tantalising ten feet away.

Sam using the reach of his left arm to grab her bag and drop it beside his own. The slumping shoulder bag lonely no longer, resting with an old friend on the aged splintered floorboards.

They moved as one single creature towards the sofa that Seren longed for. Sam knew this scene; it was a well-rehearsed one that didn't alter much during the week; Seren

97

came home looking like a zombie, Sam helped her to the sofa where she'd take a well-earned power nap sprawled across his lap.

Though Sam's reasoning for Seren's exhaustion was a bit tragic (she always claimed to love her job but Sam – even more so and somewhat conveniently now – believed she only did it because they needed the money and the truth was it was killing her inside just as much as his job was) he had come to enjoy this part of the day.

Seren would curl up on his lap like the cutest big cat he'd ever seen and just sleep. He'd run his hands through her golden hair, moving down her warm body. Enjoying the soft hums of pleasure she gave before she eventually stopped and he'd know she had drifted away. Sam would study her with a pure fascination born of love. It was the only time she looked truly at peace, her worries had vanished and the sight filled Sam with such warmth, for nothing was more enjoyable than seeing his girl at peace. He wanted her to be this way all the time but swiftly returned to reality with a few more pearls of advice, *'Don't be such a goon, everyone has worries at some point or another. It's a natural part of life.'*

When Seren awoke from her nap, they took up their usual positions upon the sofa, Sam squeezed bolt upright in the corner with Seren sprawled across it and she now managed to fight the urge to drift off for a moment – to tell Sam she supported him. She clung to that brief moment of consciousness and uttered the words,

"Take the job."

It was not the in depth lecture she'd planned on delivering but in her delirious state of exhaustion that was all she could muster.

It was exactly what Sam wanted to hear, and it fed his mind with the happy notion that she had come around and now saw this job as something that would be good for the whole team. Sam imagined that in her drowsy state Seren had unguardedly voiced what he'd suspected all along. That she hated her job, that she was tired of it and had just been sporting a brave face because they needed the money.

Sam's thoughts turned to Seren and his favourite musical artist, Peter Gabriel. He was their all-time favourite without a doubt, simply because his masterpiece, "In your eyes" always made them think of each other, it was their song. However, it was not this romantic love tune Sam's mind was drawn to but another of his famous hits "Sledgehammer." A song which he felt perfectly surmised his current situation, which was odd because the lyrics themselves were actually about sex. Yet, right now Sam had re-appropriated them to a completely different purpose.

Sam was oblivious to the original meaning... The first and second line he now took literally. He wanted to be and to provide Seren with everything she needed.

The third and fourth line he now saw as a calling card to stand up and be a man. Sam wanted to be Seren's sledgehammer, her protection, an iron strength that could protect her from the world the way a man should protect his woman. He wanted to be her weapon against all enemies. A force that could break down any walls.

'I'm going to take that job and I'm going to work and work and work to make sure she has everything she needs and is always protected.' Sam enunciated his newfound determination for duty, stating emphatically out loud,

"After tomorrow, we'll never have to worry about money again. You'll quit that awful job and I'll spend the rest of my life making sure you're happy... I promise."

He crouched forwards and kissed Seren's soft cheek before relaxing back filled with a sense of righteous responsibility. He had always felt protective of Seren and it was this that fed the raging lion which had now been released. He had never been a macho man, never been possessive about anything. But Seren had changed all that. She was everything to him and he couldn't believe she had stuck with him for so long. He was under no illusions that she could do much better and that he was punching well above his own weight. She could have any man she wanted, the kind Sam knew she deserved. A confident and respected gent, one with money who could afford her all the luxuries she deserved. A man like those who had hung around the bar where Sam first saw her, those confident and stylish young men who approached a girl they liked with no fear.

Seren never complained about the life they had together, but Sam had always assumed she was just too lovely to say what she really felt. The thought that lived in the back of Sam's self-conscious mind, *'she deserves better'* were a constant companion, habitually comparing himself against those he judged to be 'better men.' But now, finally Sam had the chance to become the man she deserved. And he WOULD do it no matter what the cost. He believed wholeheartedly his most important job was to provide for the woman he loved… in every sense of the word.

Chapter 11

The Dorchester

It was Friday morning, the big day, and Sam was up and raring to go, breakfasted, washed, suited and booted by 6.00 AM. The meeting itself wasn't until the afternoon but Sam was as giddy as a child on Christmas morning, except his present wasn't arriving until 1.00PM. But oh! What a present it would be.

It had been the slowest night of his life. Restless spells of tossing and turning under the humid sheets were set between stretches of time, which seemed to defy the very laws of physics as he gazed blankly up at the ceiling. The first few hours of insomnia had been a blast as Sam's mind swam with optimistic enthusiasm for the day to come.

However, once two or three glacial hours had passed by, his thoughts had become stale as they ran over and over like a broken tape with nothing else to play. And so Sam's mind couldn't help but delve past the boredom to deeper feelings.

Sam knew he was diving into the deep end of the pool but what he hadn't stopped to consider in the rush to get there was that he had no idea how to swim. Yes, he was a quick study and a very competent mathematician and that is the basis upon which all business is built really, numbers.

But now as he was trapped in between these stretching hours, Sam realised that in fact the business world was about a hell of a lot more than mere mathematics. The numbers, they lurked in the shadows where Sam was comfortable but to be successful in this game you needed to have the confidence to step out into the spotlight where the world could see you. Sam started to think about how he would feel, seeing himself plastered all over the internet and came to the disappointing conclusion, *'uncomfortable and sick!'*

But there were other things too. Sam recalled a brief book on business management he'd skimmed through once upon a time. During this deep night of nothingness, he rediscovered some of the key points. People skills, that was definitely one; you needed to have the confidence to articulate yourself and inspire others to see your ambition. 'Be bold and brave' was one of the subtitles, to have the confidence to make executive decisions under time pressure.

As the hours dragged along and Sam rediscovered more and more of the book's advice from the scattered information of the past he came to a profound realisation which churned his stomach. One word seemed to be repeated with consistent regularity; confidence. It was the one thing he needed but didn't have, it was the key to his success, he knew it. He made a decision to focus on the positive, *'Well, I will have an excellent mentor who will no doubt give me great advice. I am sure confidence will come given time.'*

All Sam could do as he lay alone in the darkness was hope with all his heart that the genius Keaton could somehow gift this illusive commodity unto him, by teaching him the ways of a businessman. He continued to fantasise, *'Maybe some of the billionaire's qualities will simply rub off on me.'* before concluding that it didn't matter how it happened as long as it did.

Sam was under no illusions about Keaton's ability to assess people. He'd felt the man looking past his skin and reading him like a three-hundred-page human novel filled with all the juicy details. Yes, he believed Keaton knew who he was and had faith that alongside all else the man had achieved, surely installing a little confidence in Sam wasn't much of a stretch.

At least that was the theory. That's what Sam had to believe because he was diving head first without a safety tether not into a pool but an ocean. One filled with sharks and currently he didn't even know how to swim and if he couldn't learn fast he'd either drown... or be ripped apart by the sharks.

This less upbeat thought consumed Sam for another eternity before finally his mind was spent and he slept. For an hour until 6.00AM which was not nearly enough to wash away his tortured ruminations. As soon as he awoke they returned. His mind which had been so enveloped in questions of optimism for his new position had now turned to the issues it presented for him. The points from that 'fucking book!' – as he now referred to – it poisoning his mind with all the things it claimed a businessman needed and Sam didn't have. Each point bringing forward the same word again and again; confidence, confidence, confidence. It teased and bullied him like a spiteful child.

Seren's eyes flickered open cautiously, stinging in the bright sunlight streaming in through the bedroom window. Her internal clock had woken her which was fortunate considering she'd not set her alarm the night before.

The gentle chiming would usually activate at a gruelling five thirty, factoring in time to gradually become fully consciousness before heading out the door by six thirty in a relaxed state of calm. Failing the alarm, Sam was usually there to lend a hand. However, today he was not and she felt a pang of regret. Was this going to be their life from now on?

The couple were like a well-oiled piece of machinery, but today its well-rehearsed rhythm had been broken by an irregularity, causing the delicate system to spin out of control as the parts weren't talking to each other.

Lazily taking in the time – 6.15AM- she was shocked into action as the realisation she was late brutally struck her consciousness, galvanising her into immediate frenzied action. She'd be missing her train if she didn't get it together pronto!

"Shit, shit, shit" Seren repeated with sharp feeling as she ran about the apartment collecting clothes, keys, bag there was no time for makeup or even a wash, 'What about a shower! There's no time I can have one there.' Meanwhile Sam was glued to the computer screen using Google maps to calculate train, bus, taxi and walking times to the Dorchester. His mind racing with mathematical figures trying to calculate which of the possibilities was most reliable. Absorbed in his own private world, he had forgotten to give her a prod and bring a comforting cup of tea per the usual routine. The mechanism was out of sorts.

It was not only Seren who was suffering from the malfunction. Though Sam would never ask for it what he really needed right now was a plethora of comforting words of motivation. This would normally be readily provided, but on this occasion, she, like him, was far too involved in the busy day ahead to recall today was Sam's big meeting. All those things she'd wanted to say about Nina and her father and how she stood by Sam were gone. Relegated to the back of her mind by her abhorrence of tardiness. After all, peoples' lives were literally at stake and she never forgot it. What she did was extremely important to her and so Sam would get no alleviation from that quarter this morning.

Sam had not even seen Seren until she came into the hallway ready to leave. He hadn't moved from the computer screen, he couldn't as his mind was still racing with complex calculations, engrossed in travel schedules and any possible delays he would need to factor in.

His eyes turned from the screen as Seren yanked up a pair of leather boots, snatched at her thick coat and opened the door without so much as a glance towards Sam. He watched in hope she would turn to him. Just a flicker of acknowledgment from those beautiful pools of blue would be enough. Those windows to the soul which still inspired him to become a better version of himself.

But he was left disappointed as she walked through the door and all Sam got was her voice shouting back irrationally,

"Bye Hun!" Her words barley escaping the closing door.

Sam turned back to the screen and the decision of the century,

'Christ just pick one! Take the train?'

'What if it's late? It could be late!'

'Okay... get a taxi.'

'What about the traffic? It'll be rush hour.'

'Well walk then! Just leave a good three hours early and take a leisurely stroll.'

'Then I'd have to leave at ten... Plus I'm useless with maps and I don't have fancy 3G, what if I get lost?'

'Oh for fucks sake, just man up and make a decision!'

'Okay... Taxi, yes I'll take a cab, but leave early. An hour, give it at least an hour to get there for the traffic.'

'Yes, great idea.'

After a painstaking argument with his alter ego Sam had finally concluded with the decision to take a taxi to The Dorchester.

Sam spent the rest of the morning trying to distract his mind from his own haunting thoughts with a good book. He knew there was no point in trying to prepare for a meeting with Keaton... The two times he'd met the man he'd been left completely surprised and flabbergasted. The man was more effective than a snort of cocaine... Not that Sam would know, he simply presumed and if cocaine did induce more adrenaline he doubted he could survive it.

Unfortunately, not even the ace of suspense himself Mr Stephen King could sway his stubborn mind.

'Confidence, confidence, confidence that's what you need...,' the inner dialogue now weighed in with its own personal opinion, *'You need to find some Sam, need to find your confidence and fast or you'll drown in the violent sea of business. You'll never get another chance like this again! You'll sink to the bottom and you'll never rise again, you'll never be seen again.'* Sam added a theatric scene at this point for good measure, featuring his inner voice receiving an Oscar. It had as usual gotten a tad dramatic.

Sam would get through two pages max before his eyes turned to the clock. The morning was almost as long as the night and when finally it was time to leave he felt a surge of relief, action affording him some solace.

He'd spent about ten minutes meandering around the apartment time wasting before he left; into the bathroom where he checked his teeth and hair, making sure the last two hours of sitting around hadn't left him unpresentable. Then into the kitchen where he made the last of around eight cups of tea, watching the kettle as it built up to the boil.

Sauntering with the warm cup in hand back to the pokey lounge where once again he turned to the photographs dotted about the space. And then eventually making it back round to the hall where he tied his shoes at a slow methodical pace. He found such simple everyday jobs somehow satisfying. The confident efficiency with which he tied those laces made him feel good about himself. Even if it was just a small confidence boost it still helped. Last but certainly not least Sam scooped up his trusty old shoulder bag and slid the novel he still held inside. He figured he could sit and read for however long he had before his meeting at one. He would certainly get there early and wanted to do so. At least then he could relax about the journey and worry about the meeting itself instead. *'Oh, the joys of anxiety!'*

As usual, there was nothing of real need inside the bag, but having it was a comfort. It's always nice to have something familiar when you're visiting a new and in this case, no doubt, intimidating place.

Sam knew The Dorchester was one of the top hotels, certainly rivalling Keaton's place and so Sam anticipated similar grandeur and luxury that would no doubt leave him feeling out of place and exposed.

Sam walked the couple of miles from home into the heart of his town and its main road where he knew a taxi would be much easier to come by. He was stood by the road a mere two minutes before he was able to flag one down. He got in and spoke as the cab rattled on its way, no doubt it had done well over a hundred thousand miles,

"The Dorchester please mate, how long to get there, d'you reckon?"

As soon as Sam entered a cab he'd inexplicably begin conversing with the man as if they were best friends, using

106

words like mate and bro. It was bizarre but automatic and Sam surmised it was likely due to the cabbie's friendly, conversational nature. There was always a relaxed atmosphere in a London taxi. Something Sam could really appreciate on this journey and he'd take any conversational distraction right now. Of course Sam couldn't help but inquire as to how long the journey would be. Even with all his in depth calculation Sam still harped on the ridiculous notion he might be late.

The cabbie gave a confident nod in acknowledgement of the destination before replying,

"Probably about twenny mins or so mate."

He spoke with a deep voice which conveyed the cockney accent stereotypically associated with London cab drivers. To be fair most of the cabbies Sam had encountered in his years in the city did seem to fit the bill. He had always liked it. There was definitely something pal like about it and Sam felt reassured, safe in the knowledge the London cabbie would get him there on time. Having completed 'The Knowledge', they knew the city like the back of their hands.

Only a few moments of awkward silence passed before the man initiated a nice simple conversation,

"You got a meetin' there or somin', or they just really strict about checking in times?"

Sam gave a short chuckle before replying through a wide smile,

"Got a meeting, about a new job,"

Sam's voice became excitable as his new favourite topic came up, he didn't bother to explain what it was, he knew the cabby's questions would lead them there,

"Done well to find something in this economy! What's the job?"

The cabbie's tone was filled with genuine interest but the way he spoke could just have easily been construed as intrusive. But Sam was too focused in on the man's interest to notice any negative notions, gladly explaining,

"You hear of Keaton hotels?"

Sam asked, knowing full well the answer,

"Yeah, course."

"Well er, seems I'm going to be Mr Keaton's business assistant,"

Sam tried his best to walk the fine line between sounding pleased and smug, believing he pulled it off nicely and the cabby's enthusiastic response seemed to render Sam's a bit low,

"Wow, that's awesome mate! Good for you, sounds like a hell of an opportunity."

The man was right of course, it was a great opportunity and this thought lead Sam back to his nerves momentarily until the cabbie piped up again,

"Must have been a lot a people applying for that job! You must have a brilliant CV."

Sam didn't reply and the rest of the journey was travelled in complete silence. Sam had retreated deep into a consideration this stranger had just shone a light upon. He'd been so involved, so caught up contemplating his dream, Sam hadn't stopped to think about how unrealistic it all was. He hadn't so much as studied business at college, come to think of it Mr Keaton hadn't even seen his CV!

Whilst Sam knew the man was clearly the sort who judged people upon meeting them and not on a piece of paper, he was frankly astounded at this realisation. Sam hadn't given so much as a reference. It was possible Mrs Andrews had sent his CV to Mr Keaton after their initial meeting but by that time the billionaire had already committed to a meeting and Sam had realised then such a man did not have time to waste for anything that fell short of absolute consequence.

Sam felt a substantial lift in his self-belief as he arrived at a profound realisation, *'Mr Keaton, the billionaire entrepreneur has chosen you!'* Out of all the countless professional businessmen with years of experience, who'd give a kidney for such a role, Sam got the job. Not because of experience or a fancy university education but because of himself. The only explanation for Keaton's decision was that he believed in Sam as a person and that was a great feeling.

After all, *'If a man like Keaton has faith in me then there's no reason for me to doubt myself.'*

Of course, this newfound enlightenment wasn't going to magic his anxiety and self-consciousness away, but it was a start. The image of a lion breaking out of his cage now popped up 'Monty-Python' style. It made him smile.

Sam turned to the window and the city streets racing by, beaming smile dawning as they entered Mayfair which was a place that Sam thought perfectly represented the opportunities this job offered up to him. They passed line after line of grand old buildings housing boutique hotels and shops.

Sam's attention was snared as the cabbie took one of their famous traffic beating shortcuts through a residential area off the beaten track. A row of perfectly symmetrical white residences that were pristinely maintained passed before his eyes causing them to pop. Sam counted five stories high at least!

He felt a long way from home but his positive mind couldn't help but wonder if maybe someday soon he could afford such a place. Logically, he was likely stepping over the line a tad. After all, he was becoming a business assistant to the CEO, not the CEO himself.

Still, Sam pondered the endless possibilities of the future, could he ever be comfortable in such a home. Or would it just leave him out of place, like The Keaton had. It depended he supposed if the beast could completely escape, it all depended on whether he would eventually become the man he dreamed he could be.

The Dorchester was on the far side of Mayfair, overlooking Hyde Park, of course. All the very best hotels have a view to boast about.

The taxi approached a large round island which lay before the hotel,

'Makes it easier to manoeuvre all those priceless cars,' Sam thought rationally before his cynical side escaped,

'Yeah, well they wouldn't want to risk getting sued by some pompous rich arse who doesn't know how to drive his Ferrari.'

Sam tried to fight encouraging his darker side but he couldn't help but snicker at the comment as the mood definitely needed lightening.

A grand stone fountain made up the centerpiece of the island, surrounded by neatly trimmed flowers and grass that appeared so perfect they must be attended to daily. Sam knew with luxurious places like this, image was everything. And luxury meant two things, besides impeccable service that Sam had already discovered at The Keaton – grandeur and perfection. And that island expressed both. Sam felt his nerves stir as they approached the entrance. The entrance to a place Sam knew he didn't belong, *'not yet anyway.'*

The black cab came to an abrupt halt and Sam almost physically recoiled as a hotel valet opened the door. The sickening feeling gained footing, of not knowing protocol dictated in this situation because he didn't go to bloody posh school and was ignorant as to etiquette. Indecision got the better of him and his opposing sides struck up an argument,

'Pay the cabbie, Prat!'

'Thank the valet first, be polite!'

'Fuck niceties! We've got no time for that shit, pay the man and let's go. We got more important things to do; get your head in the game man!'

Sam knew his alter ego had a point. He needed to be thinking straight and not worrying about being nice like a little girl. He needed to be a man and focus on the task at hand. After all, sometimes niceties had to be sacrificed because time is money in this game so might as well get used to it. Sam decided to listen to his alter ego for once. He forced a twenty on the cabbie and got out before the man could so much as reach for his change.

Sam strode purposefully up the steps towards the revolving doors trying to focus in on his alter ego, harnessing and giving in to its confidence but it was no good. The cage door was shut and his feline friend could offer no more than the occasional roar.

Sam's newfound confident focus teetered and his daydreaming wreck of a self returned. This was exacerbated as two glamorous young women had exited the revolve-way, seemingly aiming right for him, as if they were targeting him for destruction. Their eyes looked him up and down with harsh and unforgiving judgement. Sam could feel them sizing up his cheap suit, his cheap clothes, lack of finesse and even his ancient Casio. It reminded him of the look those young teenage ruffians used to give him every day at work, except this was much, much worse.

'You don't belong here,'

Those harpy eyes said.

Sam hoped they'd lose interest and turn away as he approached, but no, they just continued to stare and walk straight for him, feeding his anxiety. One turned to the other and whispered something before they shared a brief moment of eye contact and both burst out laughing. Then they turned back to him once more. Like they wanted him to know they were talking about him.

Sam had no idea what the girl had said but that didn't stop his vivid imagination from generating examples,

'Probably something along the lines of, "Oh look, it's the paperboy".'

His focus was snapped back to reality as he had to practically dodge out of their way as they steamed towards him like a bulldozer about to flatten an ugly building.

Once more, Sam desperately wished he could stand up to such obnoxious people. Like that large man on the train. These girls were the same kind of people, the kind whose world doesn't exist past their own shallow lives. They completely lacked what Sam had been given too much of, empathy. *'Getting rather judgemental aren't we?'*

In this moment just as he had on the train, Sam found himself wishing he could unleash the lion within him for a reason other than business… So he could forget his empathy and stand up to people and actually call them what he meant to call them, rather than just thinking it quietly. It was moments like this he felt more of a mouse than a man and it sickened him. *'Idiot, you don't know what they were thinking. They may have been flirting for all you know about women.'*

Inwardly snorting at himself, Sam was swiftly distracted from these thoughts as he entered the building. His neck almost snapping off as it swivelled back and around, his eyes scanning the vast space admiringly.

The lobby did not possess the modern grandeur of The Keaton's efficient, minimalistic and yet satisfyingly high quality design. No, this lobby's extravagance demonstrated the original meaning of the word; Magnitude, opulence, boldness and intricate detail.

A completely different experience altogether; instead of the eye-opening bright crystal lights of The Keaton's modern chandeliers, antique chandeliers of delicate design dangled from high ceilings, bathing the space in a yellowy soft but warm light that was very homely. Shimmering white walls were replaced by faded golden wallpaper which merged with marble pillars and intricate stone murals that bulged from the walls.

It was the sort of space Sam imagined royal ballrooms would have looked like way back in the past. In this place, not only did Sam believe he didn't belong there, he also felt underdressed. He remembered he was wearing a suit which rendered that thought ridiculous but the space radiated such regality he felt he should be wearing gentlemen's evening attire… Top hat, cane and the whole shebang!

Still, he was certainly feeling less self-conscious than he had at The Keaton and this equaled if not overtook its grandeur. As Sam approached the long black counter decorated with lines of gold he felt he was becoming more familiar with this world. After all, it was the unknown that frightened. Bit by bit this world would reveal itself to him as he submersed himself in it. His father's words drove through his consciousness again,

'Dive in and take a swim!'

But for now at least, the depletion was only minor and Sam's anxiety still grasped at him. His heart was racing, his hands were shaking and he could feel the all too familiar sweat patches developing under his humid clothing.

"Hello, sir. Welcome to the Dorchester. Are you checking in?" a young woman at the desk asked, her polite yet professional tone somewhat familiar. This time, the undivided attention of her eyes didn't throw him and he replied without hesitation,

"No thanks, I'm meeting Mr Keaton," Sam responded, rescuing the name of his soon to be superior from his memory at the last minute,

"Of course, sir, Mr Keaton is in the restaurant, if you just walk through the archway it's the first room to your right," she explained slowly, gesturing directions with her left hand. Sam was impressed by her confident knowledge,

'How does she know where Mr Keaton is? Could it be possible these staff are so well trained they can locate all of their guests?'

He was tempted to ask her how she knew but then the lion roared,

'Who gives a shit! Stop getting distracted and focus. Head in the game, Keaton is waiting for you!'

This latest comment from his alter ego caused him to spring into shock fuelled action and Sam regained equilibrium, blurting,

"Thank you very much."

'Keaton waits for no one, but right now he's waiting for you.'

The beast was now becoming a little cocky as Sam followed the woman at the desk's instructions carefully.

He tried to ignore the arrogant statement, it wasn't attractive, but once again the brute did talk sense. The billionaire entrepreneur was indeed waiting for him. A smile briefly made an appearance on his face.

Through a wide stone archway Sam entered into an intimate restaurant with no more than fifteen tables. It was ultra-exclusive he supposed,

'How long would it take to get a reservation here?'

'You'll find out soon enough... you'll be able to come and eat here!'

The light was dim but each of the round tables were highlighted by their own individual spotlight which streamed down from the ceiling and reflected off the white linen and silverware, emphasising their purity. The room felt cosy and safe. The tables were islands of tranquillity, like alluring little boats dotted about on a calm ocean at night. The atmosphere was calming.

Sam's gaze was drawn to the centre of the room where countless strands of sparkling beads fell from the ceiling to the floor in a circular wall, a cascade of beaded irridescent light. There was a classic, magic even Disney feel to it. Like something Elsa had created.

Sam stood in the gaping archway looking like a lost lemming, scanning the room for Keaton who he found sat alone near the window. Prime position of course, Sam felt silly for not just checking the best tables as that was where the billionaire was bound to be. That was what being a billionaire truly meant... *'he (or she, let's not be sexist here,) has the best of the best of everything.'*

Carter was standing by over Keaton's left shoulder looking as intimidating as ever, his hands clasped tightly behind his back. But he was not as intimidating as Keaton, not to Sam anyway.

He walked slowly over, giving himself time to mentally rehearse his opening line.

"Good afternoon, Mr Keaton."

Sam was surprised by the casual tone which he wished hadn't escaped.

'That's what comes of over thinking things, prat!'

Once again, Sam mentally bowed to the truth.

Keaton raised his head from the plate of food before him and into the white spotlight, his eyes locked onto Sam's with scary and laser-sharp precision as the deep stare of those black eyes came forth. He looked like the ghost of a glass eyed doll.

The apparition faded back into the dull light and leant back in his chair, fastidiously wiping his mouth with a serviette before speaking,

"Mr Lowell, have a seat."

Keaton turned back to his lunch as Sam eased into the chair, carefully sliding his trusty bag to the floor so as not to disturb the quiet ambiance.

As if on well-rehearsed cue, Carter's solid arms appeared from behind his back along with a black leather briefcase he was holding. He popped the latches and flipped the top over. Sam watched with impatient anticipation, convinced whatever package lay within was for him.

'It's a contract! Slow down, not necessarily!'

The excitement abruptly alerted his Alter ego onto standby mode.

Out slid an A4 sized black envelope bearing some small text in one of the corners that was too distant to make out. Carter walked over to Sam and placed it gently on the linen before him.

Sam was momentarily distracted by the design of the thing… never in his life had he imagined something as plain as an envelope could be so interesting in its design. Upon close inspection he could see it was a matte black and he could now read the small gold text in the bottom corner which read,

'Keaton & Co.
459 Broadway,
New York, NY 10013'

Sam stared blankly at it, now believing it definitely was his contract and found difficulty reigning in his anticipation which bristled with all the possibilities that lay inside that package. Questions erupting like bees from a hive and flitting about in his head.

Then, after wiping his mouth once more, Keaton supplied the answer that Sam wanted to hear,

"That envelope contains your contract of employment."

Keaton's calm monotone voice did nothing to collect Sam's thoughts,

'That's it, that's it right there. That's your dream right there! The golden opportunity to be the man you need to become. No more scraping through life, no more being the doormat, it's time to step up, for yourself and Seren!'

Sam took note; his alter ego's voice was becoming more and more regular but he didn't care. As if on cue, it continued, *'after all, it's only speaking the truth. This is the chance you've been waiting for, the chance to man up and look after your beloved.'*

Keaton studied Sam eyeing up the envelope with a subtle look of curiosity which momentarily broke through the deadpan facade. The man placed his serviette forcefully upon the table causing two forks to chink loudly together. Sam's concentration was broken by the sound, his eyes shot back up to Keaton's.

Sam glimpsed the gold timepiece on the man's wrist, which glinted momentarily as Mr Keaton moved back into the spotlight. Leaning his elbows on the pristine linen he clasped his fingers together. It seemed he was waiting,

'Waiting, yes, for you to open the letter! Open it!'

Sam's thoughts itched with excitement, but the beast snapped against such a hasty decision,

'No, no, fool. You don't read through it now you prat! Stay cool.'

As much as he wanted to grasp the letter and rip it open, his alter ego had once again saved him from an apparent faux-pas providing the calm voice of reason once again. Keaton was not going to sit there all afternoon whilst Sam read through what he imagined to be an extremely detailed document. No, he'd have to wait. A small part of his psyche was relieved to postpone the event and whilst his fingers ached to reach out, he just couldn't do it. However, the busy little bees still buzzed around and refused to settle. The truth was, as excited as he was to find out what lay inside this package he was also afraid to… what if it wasn't what he hoped? The disappointment would be unimaginable – like believing you've picked all the winning lottery numbers, you've won the jackpot! Only to take a second look and realise your 6 was actually a scribbled 5...

He needed a motivational push just to take it and Keaton gave him one, using two fingers to subtly gesture towards the lonely envelope which lay invitingly on the immaculate damask.

Sam slid his hand along the soft linen, dragging the envelope towards himself. The matte paper had a strange rubber-like texture to it. He picked it up, bending over and sliding it into his trusty shoulder bag with the utmost care so as not to damage the edges. For right now, those pieces of paper held more value to him than anything else, excluding family. Sam believed that the unknown contents of that package held the key to everything he desired.

As Sam returned to the table, Keaton explained the package in further detail, as if he were deliberately trying to push Sam's emotions to the edge. This was something the man achieved without even trying.

"In there you will find the finer details; conditions, rights, responsibilities and duties all set out. I will expect a decision before Monday, the number for my secretary is in there."

Keaton referred to the subject as if it were still undecided. But they were both aware of the stark truth of the matter, that Sam was hooked as soon as he'd met the billionaire; that much surely was glaringly obvious to such a worldly and intelligent man. Keaton could have Sam jumping through flaming hoops at a click of his fingers.

Sam had to stop himself from screaming "YES!" without having even opened the package. The notion of someone else having such power over him scared him for a moment. *'Idiot, this is what you wanted, isn't it? Don't be such a pussy!'* The beast having had its say, Sam's full focus swiftly turned back to the hero before him.

Picking up his knife and fork, Keaton's attention returned to his lunch. Sam suddenly saw this as a golden opportunity to strike up an intelligent conversation with the man and, who knows, maybe even impress him. After all, so far their relationship had been rigid to say the least... business, business, business and Sam had a burning curiosity about this mysterious entrepreneur. He wanted to know more about his hero and the only way to find out was to ask,

'Ask him something! Just start a conversation, Jesus the suspense is killing me! This is probably a test! To see if you can start a conversation, to see if you're compatible, come on man if you can't do that, then you're fucked in this game!'

Sam's internal dialogue ranted but the phobia that this could be a make or break scenario was enough to spark Sam's confidence into speaking for fear of failing this man who'd salvaged his dreams,

"I was a little surprised you chose to hold our meeting here... Surely your hotel would have been more convenient for you?"

Sam enquired tentatively, immediately regretting his question which sounded far more impertinent out loud than it had in his head.

However, his regret subsided as Keaton turned from what was a mouth-watering plate of food to flash Sam a subtle expression which conveyed a modicum of respect. The man placed his cutlery back on the table and relaxing back into his chair, made use of his serviette once more before giving Sam his full attention,

"I never eat in my own hotels. I think it unprofessional to carry out anything but business in front of my own staff. Such personal actions would only promote me as a casual figure and not as their employer. One of the main channels of respect is professionalism."

'Ah, good point!' Sam agreed completely and from Keaton's profound response to such a simple question, it was blatantly apparent that this man was the fount of all knowledge in respect of business. He truly was the Professor of commerce and Sam became excited by the thought of all he could learn from this genius.

But then a thought suddenly occurred to Sam as if from nowhere. He'd presumed it had come from his alter ego as it was pretty bold and confrontational but Sam's fascination with this character got the better of him and the words were said before he could call them to heel.

"And yet you sleep at your hotel? That's about as personal as it gets I would have thought?"

Sam was immediately shocked at his own impertinent challenge, the words shot out of him, aimed at the object of his fascination like bullets from a gun, the brute within had somehow managed to escape and run riot for a moment before retreating back and leaving Sam's anxious self to deal with the consequences.

He braced himself for the violent backlash he expected but what Keaton said next surprised him further,

"I suppose I do yes, I don't exactly sleep in view of my staff. Still, I suppose it's somewhat hypocritical of me."

The sudden bold confidence Sam had found seemed to ignite something within Keaton, striking him deep and awaking a part of the man rarely, if ever, seen. He had become far more conversational and engaged. Sam suspected it was a level of respect he had just earned. Possibly it was the fact he'd found the balls to confront the man? *'Or maybe the fact I was right and made Keaton see his own mistake? OK, let's not get too ahead of ourselves here.'* Whatever it was, Sam was glad he'd been brave and wished the beast would burst out of that cage it had been in for all his life right there and then. He was prepared in that moment to fully give in to the marvellous creature.

But of course, his feline friend retreated back as swiftly as it had appeared, immediately replaced by the tension. Sam surprised himself when he came up with the rapid response,

"I think you can afford to be a little hypocritical, sir."

Keaton acknowledged the pithy remark with a fleeting smile. The backhanded compliment seemed to amuse him. Sam believed he may have stumbled upon something… Maybe he was tired of the constant stream of smoke blown up his ass by fake people and had appreciated a more honest and direct approach. *'Perhaps he is enjoying a little healthy confrontation, it may be refreshing to one often surrounded by sycophants.'* The next two words spoken by the man himself seemed to confirm this conjecture,

"Join me."

The tone implied it was more of an order than a request. Not that Sam gave a shit how he said it, a billionaire just asked him to share lunch!

"Carter, a menu."

He continued sharply, turning his head slightly towards the man who still hovered on his left shoulder.

"Yes, sir."

Carter immediately went to do his master's bidding, leaving Sam feeling a little overwhelmed as he voiced his gratitude,

"Thank you, sir."

Sam spoke with a surprised gratefulness.

Silence resumed as Keaton returned to his meal. Sam waited, the beast having retreated, his placid persona returned as he sat stressing about the lengthening silence, *'Think of something to say prat, don't just sit there!'*

Fortunately, the thickening ice was broken as Carter returned with a young man wearing all black. He handed over a menu whereupon Sam had to stop his eyes from watering at the exorbitant prices.

'It's going to be McDonalds for a week if you order here!'

Sam thought in a panic. But refusing to eat was out of the question, it would be churlish to decline. Keaton had invited him… He looked down the list, puzzled by the French dishes whose names meant nothing to him.

He felt the eyes of Carter and the waiter bearing down on him. The anxiety spiked and pressured him into ordering too quickly.

"I'll have the salmon, please,"

Sam concluded that seemed the safest option, though he had no idea what the other words which made up the dish meant. He didn't really care being more focused on other matters, *'How are you going to pay, stupid?'* "Very good, sir."

The young man politely acquiesced, offering a further hint,

"To drink?"

Sam now felt even more stupid. He turned over the menu, panic was taking over again, but before he could choose from amongst the baffling list of whites, reds, pinks and champagnes Keaton jumped in and saved him, announcing decisively,

"Bottle of Dom Perignon, 06. He's celebrating."

The waiter nodded his head slightly before departing.

He hadn't addressed the waiter directly but did flash Sam a brief look which he took as a subtle congratulations. That was the exhausting thing about Keaton, his expressions, if any, were so brief and subtle you had guess what they meant. Your mind was constantly trying to decipher the little details, concentrating so hard that when you left the man's presence you were mentally shattered.

Sam had a new worry, the numbers on the bill this bottle would generate, but the feline beast returned to chide, *'Keaton is right. This is a celebration... After all, how often do your dreams come true.'* But the breaks were then applied by sensible Sam, *'I may be getting a little ahead of myself here!'*

As silence resumed once more Sam's thoughts turned back to the nagging doubt which wouldn't go away, scratching the back of his mind with its subtle, but nagging presence. The question was simple... *'Why me?'*

Why had the billionaire high flying entrepreneur who could have plucked any businessman out of the ether choose Sam, an academic with no discernible business skills whatsoever. It was a bloody good question, possibly the best of all time, certainly one of the most puzzling.

Sam had initially liked to believe it was because Keaton had read him as a person and liked what he saw. But now upon closer examination he doubted that was it. Sam didn't want to second guess himself any more than he already did,

121

his self-confidence was low enough. But he knew there must be something else. Keaton had another angle, surely, such businessmen always had one, there was always a reason and Sam felt determined to find out what it was.

'This man likes straight talking right? So talk straight!'

The feline presence returned to provide another little shove of confidence and Sam went for it,

"Mr Keaton, I'm immensely grateful for this opportunity you're giving me, I really am but… I can't help wondering why, out of everyone, did you choose me for the job?"

He braced himself for the response. Keaton leaned forwards into the light and returned his elbows to the table, clasping his hands together before replying,

"Because, Sam. You possess a very particular trait that is constantly undervalued in this world…"

Keaton was somewhat rudely interrupted by the returning waiter with Sam's expensive bottle,

"Would you like to try the…"

"No, just pour!"

Keaton interrupted back fiercely, as if his self-control had suddenly snapped for a brief moment. Sam could empathise, he was equally annoyed by the intrusion.

The waiter, however, remained professional and unperturbed. He poured two glasses out with care and precision.

"The trait you possess is that of desperation."

Keaton concluded bluntly before bringing the glass to his lips. Delivered from anyone else, Sam would have taken these words as an insult. However, his respect and admiration towards the billionaire's directness prevented this. In fact, all he wanted was to know what the man meant and so he asked,

"I don't understand?"

"There is no man more driven and determined for success than he who has experienced the life that lies at the other end of the spectrum."

Confusion persisted and he continued to push the point further than a smart man should, but he needed to know, why?

"But, I know nothing about the business world."

"There are two types of people in this world Sam. Those that want everything and those that don't give a shit."

Keaton's words flared with passion, he paused for a moment, reading Sam's face which began to convey an understanding,

"I can teach anyone how to be a businessman, but drive and determination, that's not something anyone can teach. You're born with it, a burning desire that lives deep within you."

It all made sense now. Sam was convinced. The caged lion inside Sam that longed to be free, it was the drive, the determination Keaton spoke of. The beast was Sam's true self... All these years he'd been so wrong, this soft outer shell of weakness and anxiety was the fake him. The beast was his destiny. It was who he was always meant to be and Keaton was the key to setting his true self free. Sam took a swig of the champagne which was as expected, sublime.

Sam's thoughts were abruptly interrupted as the waiter returned once more with his salmon. Glancing at the plate he noticed Carter had moved away from the table, he stood, talking quietly on a mobile. Whatever the conversation was it ended abruptly and Carter made his way back over to the table.

He walked right up to Keaton's left shoulder and leaned gently forwards, careful not to get too close to his superior before whispering something Sam couldn't make out. Keaton immediately consulted his expensive timepiece before saying,

"You'll have to excuse me, Sam, but I have some urgent business to attend to."

He stood and Sam politely mirrored the manoeuvre.

"I enjoyed our little talk. I'm sure there will be many more to follow."

Keaton concluded before retrieving a leather pocket book and placed what looked like eight fifty pound notes casually down on the linen. Sam gazed at the money with unabashed hunger, he couldn't remember ever having seen so much cash in one sitting.

Keaton walked around the table and patted Sam firmly on the shoulder as he passed, Carter followed behind, his gaze never faltering from his employer.

With the tension of Keaton's presence gone, Sam could relax and enjoy the best salmon he had ever tasted. As much as he yearned to open that package which lay inside his bag he decided to wait until he was relaxed at home.

Chapter 12

The Contract

Sam arrived back home at around four, walking into the apartment with his bag containing its precious cargo in one hand and a quarter bottle of Dom Perignon in the other. He hadn't meant to drink so much of it but the waiter had kept returning and filling his glass. Well, that was Sam's excuse – he hadn't noticed at the time, far too focused on that delicious meal.

'Those waiters are like fucking ninjas… trained to sneak up on you and fill your glass whilst you're not looking, encouraging you to consume more than you intended.'

Sam giggled at his cynical analysis. You wouldn't say he was quite drunk but there was certainly a nice buzz floating around his head. That Dom was powerful stuff not to mention the fact Sam wasn't used to drinking, but, *'I could definitely get used to this lifestyle.'*

He sauntered over to the sofa placing the bottle and bag on the table before letting his weight go from under him. He dropped like a stone into its soft embrace. Sam had surprised himself by how patient he'd been with regards to his contract. From the moment Carter slid that envelope across the table he had wanted to rip it open with his bare teeth, like a jackal.

Yet, there was also a calmness that had grown within him, a desire to savour the moment. Of course, it might just have been the alcohol mellowing him out. Sam was lying in

Seren's famous position, looking up at the blank ceiling. He turned his head, looking over at his two new favourite items.

The problem with alcohol, particularly good alcohol, was the more you drink the more it seems like a good idea. In the moment, at least, it was addictive, something Sam was just learning as he'd never been a drinker. But that fun side of him, like the beast, had just never had the chance to develop. Whilst everyone at college and uni was having parties, drinking and laughing with friends, Sam had been locked away studying.

Well not any more, that was their time, this was his. Sam the brave, Sam the bold, Sam the hedonist – they would all be unleashed soon enough and he would experience everything he'd been missing out on. *'Then I will be Sam the Invincible!'* Somehow this new mentor had been feeding the beast and every day it grew stronger.

Sam sprung upright into action, wondering what to grab first. He decided on the bottle and downed a large swig, and with a deep, calming breath he turned to his bag. Slowly, with his free hand he pulled his old friend towards him, unfolding the flap to reveal the matte envelope within. His heart was pounding yet his breathing was lethargic as he reached for the package and pulled it out, concentrating hard on not allowing his tense hands to crumple the paper.

Sam moved the bottle to sit in between his legs to free up both hands, then he prized at the seal and bit by bit, it came free. He pulled out what was a substantial wad of pages, at least fifteen he reckoned. Settling back into the sofa he made himself comfortable and began reading, sounding out each and every word aloud to himself. He didn't want to miss anything.

The first section of the contract was called *"Responsibilities and Duties,"* which in itself seemed endlessly detailed. Sam felt more and more daunted as he read down the list, most of which was nonsense to him. This was crazy, he was about to start a job he didn't understand but consoled himself with the fact he'd have the best teacher in the business and he was a quick study. It looked like all those endless hours of study at school, college and uni would come in handy after all. It had all been practice for this – the big game!

Sam imagined this list would have been daunting to any businessman initially, after all it was extensive, but deep down Sam didn't really care how long the list was. It could have stretched from London to New York for all he cared, it didn't matter because he was already resolved to work and work and work.

After an hour or so of rather boring corporate text, Sam's heart rate suddenly jumped dramatically as he came across a paragraph headed *"Salary and Bonus Schemes."* He didn't care if it was shallow, this was the most important part of the contract. This paragraph he was about to read was the foundation of his dream, it was the key to providing himself, and more importantly, Seren with the life they wanted. No more would his girl have to wish and wonder what she could have had if she'd gone for a rich, confident young man instead of a pathetic loser. No, this paragraph was the key to Sam becoming a man. He took a deep breath and began to read,

"The basic salary will be paid monthly into an account/accounts of your choosing…"

Following aloud Sam had intended to read the whole thing through thoroughly and methodically, but he couldn't stop himself and before his voice could sound out the first sentence Sam found his eyes skimming through, searching for that all important number. And then he found it,

"…With a basic salary of five hundred thousand English pounds per annum…"

Sam stopped reading. The pages dropped into his lap, hands to his mouth. A hysterical laugh escaped trembling fingers. The same agitation he'd experienced outside The Keaton after meeting the man himself had returned. The cool headed lion was blown out of the water and unbridled euphoria derailed rational thought.

Adrenaline coursed through his veins with the power of jet fuel. He didn't know what to do with himself, with this sudden rush of energy.

Attention turned back to the bottle still sat between his legs. He picked it up and brought it to his lips,

"Cheers."

He toasted playfully towards the contract before downing the remainder. He fell backwards into the sofa looking up at the blank ceiling once more. All those questions that had been racing around his head like angry bees searching for the answer were finally satisfied. That number, that incomprehensible number gave a resounding "YES!" It was the answer to all his prayers and far exceeded what he'd expected, not that he'd know in the slightest what he should expect from such a position. Apprehension made a brief appearance, further speculating as to the business-man's motives before the alter ego rashly brushed aside all reservation,

'Fuck it, it's just too good an offer to turn down. I will pay the price, whatever that may be!'

And there was no possible force that could have prevented him doing what he did next. His dream job sat there before him only a signature away, so there was only one thing left to do. Sam flicked though the contract to reach the final page where a dotted line stared at him. Any of Sam's reservations had now completely and utterly evaporated, the fact he'd promised Seren they would make this decision together had disappeared. There was no hesitation as he signed and dated the contract.

Then he reached over for the phone on the battered old coffee table and began dialling the number on the bottom of that last page, gazing at the signature that had sealed his fate.

The line only rang once before being picked up,

"Good afternoon, Mr Keaton's office. How can I help you?"

"Good afternoon it's Sam Lowell calling about the job" Sam blurted impatiently.

He recognised that distinctive American accent but didn't stand a chance of remembering a name in his current state. He didn't care, nothing mattered except securing this job.

"Mr Lowell, good to hear from you."

The woman replied before Sam was able to interrupt her.

'No time for niceties!'

Sam's verbal response became more vigorous than he would normally intend,

"Mr Keaton told me I should contact you when I had read through the contract which I have. It's all signed and sealed."

Sam gushed, his words escaping faster and faster, so anxious to make sure this deal was sealed as soon as humanly possible. As if he believed Keaton might retract his offer after all of this. Even though he knew he was being somewhat irrational, Sam knew he would not be able to relax until it was all set in stone and the job was officially in his possession.

"Well congratulations, Mr Lowell, Mr Keaton has instructed me to send on an email outlining his immediate expectations, if I could get an email address I will send the documentation straight over."

The woman explained with practiced clarity.

Sam provided his address then the two exchanged a swift goodbye. The line died and he migrated towards that ancient machine in the corner of the room. Firing it up and waiting.

His leg twitched violently, teeth biting down sharply on his nails. The wait was torture... Sam sat staring at the screen, willing the email to appear.

Finally, he managed to get into the emails, there was one new mail waited for him.

He read,

Dear Mr Lowell,

The purpose of this email is to outline the particulars for the next stage in processing your role of employment within Keaton Enterprises.

You will attend a meeting with Mr Keaton and his Financial Director this Monday at 8:15am. Please arrive with your contract of employment and luggage (business attire) for a week in New York.

Sincerely,

Lynn Fox.
Personal Secretary to Mr Keaton.

'Lynn! That was it.'

Sam rejoiced at connecting the dots before the brute within snapped once more,

'Fuck Lynn! Focus! Eyes on the prize, you're almost there, you've done it. Monday morning you'll be on your way to being a proper businessman, an alpha male!'

The beast was right, after all these years he was finally escaping the bottom of society. Reading over the email once more to double check the detail, the last part in particular stood out,

'*Luggage (business attire) for a week in New York.*'

Breathing another of his imaginative questions into life… Would he ever be going to New York? Turns out yes, yes he would. The Big Apple, the very heart of business itself, a place Sam wished to visit. He'd hit the double jackpot!

Sam thought it was apt that the first order of business of his new job would be to visit the land of opportunity itself. New York, the city. This was where millions of people with big dreams and ambition migrated to.

Slowly, Sam got to his feet wobbling for a moment before he found his balance. The rest of that champagne had reached his head as he sauntered gingerly back to the sofa and launched himself onto it. All the adrenaline and excitement began to die down and exhaustion took over.

Logic and reason were allowed to surface once more as Sam looked back over what he'd just done with newfound insight.

His predominant feeling now morphed into apprehension as his thoughts turned to Seren and the conversation they'd had when he told her about the job. Yes, she had definitely said,

"Take the job."

Sam remembered that clear as day, but of course he did. We always remember what we want to. What his mind had stubbornly chosen to brush aside was what Seren had said prior to that,

"It's just, you're nearly there sweetheart, I... I don't want to see us throw away everything we've been working so hard for when you're so close."

But the real remorse hit him when Sam seemed to recall he'd promised, PROMISED Seren that they would discuss this contract together before he went and signed it. So, what had he done... gone ahead and signed it without so much as even considering her opinion,

'Shit, you're supposed to be a team, a team!'

Sam's thoughts abruptly detoured from this onto another point, which concerned him further still. It wasn't just what she'd said it was how she'd reacted to his news. Rather than the excitement and pride he thought she'd feel for him there was only trepidation. Why wasn't she happy? Sam was becoming the man she deserved, a man of success and status, she could finally give up that hateful job of hers.

Sam now found himself confounded as a new question came into play,

'Why wasn't she happy about this?'

But the combination of his exhaustion and the alcohol now devoured any concern, distorting his focus and he began to drift away into a deep sleep before he could ponder the thought further.

Seren arrived home at her usual, depressingly late hour. She sauntered into the living room and smiled widely at the sight of Sam, passed out on the sofa looking like a child with his limbs randomly sprawled out.

She crept towards him, ready to curl up beside him. But, her smile and warm feeling quickly vanished as the contract on the table came into focus, signed and dated. Disbelief stole her rationale and blatant anger boiled to the surface.

She stared at the piece of paper, she couldn't believe he'd signed it, how could he? After everything she'd discussed with him, about Nina's husband, George and her own father... The raw emotion of betrayal trickled through her system and she felt sick as she stared down at this man whom she considered to be her best friend. Happily for the oblivious form on the sofa, exhaustion finally took over and she joined Sam on the saggy old sofa, finally drifting off into a deep sleep. When she awoke some 30 minutes later, her thoughts violently returned to the crux of the matter. She was seriously pissed off. Sam had promised her they would read that contract together, as a couple, as the team they were supposed to be!

Her deep blue eyes bored through Sam with a white hot fire of purest rage. Seren wasn't one for getting angry and losing control but no amount of yoga or meditation or counting numbers could put out this inferno,

'He said we would decide this together
He promised
He lied to me
He said no decision was made but it was, wasn't it
He'd already made up his mind all autonomously
My opinion doesn't count for shit!'

Finally, Seren lost control completely, the fire exploded and she saw red! A wild, angry and betrayed woman erupted from the sofa, grabbed the empty bottle of Dom Perignon, which still lay in between Sam's legs, and launched it as hard as she could at the brick wall in front of her.

The red mist ebbed and Seren watched in shock as the bottle struck the unforgiving surface and smashed into a thousand tiny pieces, scattering like artillery shrapnel about the floorboards, a few of the larger pieces almost reaching the sofa.

Sam shot up to see Seren standing over him. Her long blonde hair streaming in front of her face like a wild banshee, she was panting heavily and those electric blue eyes were targeting him. She was the image of a beautiful wild animal about to attack.

Sam was instantly aware that she'd seen the contract and he remembered his final thoughts before passing out. The large side order of guilt returned.

Seren was taken aback by her own actions, immediately regretting the drama of it. That had been dangerous and completely out of character. But every woman has her limits where patience is concerned and Seren had finally found hers. She'd simply snapped, that was the only way she could describe it. Like an elastic band that's been used one too many times.

Any regret was soon forgotten as Sam's eyes met hers. The rage returned in abundance and her words struck Sam sharp as a butcher's knife,

"So, when did OUR future become yours, Sam?"

He froze for a moment, stunned. Sam had seen the love of his life mad before, of course he had, but never like this. She had taken it to a new level and he was genuinely fearful… She looked as though she might launch something else, this time right at him. He knew it was the bottle that had been used as a missile, but didn't dare take his eyes off her.

Never before had a clever response been needed more. However, under pressure to provide an acceptable and appeasing answer, the best he could come up with was another question which was just about the stupidest thing he could ask,

"You saw the contract?"

He'd barely finished before Seren's spoken words lashed back at him, unleashing yet more vitriol,

"Yes, Sam. I saw the fucking contract!"

This violent and totally out of character outburst complete with expletives relieved most of her rage and, shocked at her own use of inappropriate language, she stopped to take a deep, calming breath before continuing in a less aggressive tone,

"What happened to discussing this together? What about all that work you've done?"

Seren now sounded more disappointed than upset, which in many ways was worse. Though at least Sam could have a conversation with a disappointed woman. No man stood a chance against the power of an enraged female.

"I was going to tell you baby when you got home. Look, I'm sorry. I know I shouldn't have signed it without you. That was fucking stupid! I just got over excited about what this means for us, I was going to talk to you about it when you came home, I swear, I just… fell asleep."

Sam's explanation was heartfelt but pitiful in its logic, in that it didn't contain any.

"Us?"

Seren's tone became more belligerent, the banshee was back in residence.

"Yes of course – us. This is my chance to make something of myself! To be the man you deserve!"

Sam explained with deep feeling.

But Seren just stared back at him, perplexed. She had no idea what the hell he was talking about or why he would have felt this necessary,

"What about becoming a doctor? Helping people? That's not making something of yourself? Three years Sam. Three fucking years we've struggled so that you could study to become someone that really matters! That makes a difference… Now that you're so close you want to throw it all away, and for what?"

"For something better!"

Sam exclaimed excitedly, the beast was going to have its say.

"Better… How is you becoming some businessman's bitch better than helping people? I thought you didn't care about any of that superficial crap!"

Seren did not understand Sam's reasoning and her bewildered expression looked through him as she tried to gain some understanding of what was going on in his head. They had shared a common goal up until this point. Together they had a dream to help people who needed it most and now Sam wanted to throw in the towel so he could go into business? BUSINESS? Where was this coming from? It was like the Sam that she knew was rapidly morphing into a completely different character…

The lion within Sam wanted to scream,

'The money!'

But he reigned the beast in, knowing that was wrong way to convince Seren this was right for them so he consulted his empathetic self, got to his feet, and walked over to Seren, placing his warm hands softly on her shoulders and replied,

"This is the right thing to do, I need you to trust me on this honey, it's going to change our lives for the better, you'll see."

Sam tone had become soft and gentle, and very persuasive. He squeezed Seren's shoulders firmly and this seemed to sooth her. No matter how she tried to stay mad at her man, as soon as those big brown eyes and his smooth deep voice spoke, she couldn't help but mellow, her soft, forgiving heart working against her head. Sam's cunning manipulation had done the trick.

The long day at the hospital suddenly caught up with her, rage having drained the little energy that remained. Like always, all she really wanted to do was fall into his warm arms and sleep through till morning, but she was determined to have this out and stood strong, fighting off her exhaustion. She rallied her defences,

"I just don't want to see you throw all those years of hard work away for something else just because it's here in front of you now."

135

Seren tried once more to change his mind. She hoped in her exhausted state that this was all just down to the sudden temptation of a job that was within his immediate reach. She'd always understood the long gruelling years of studying to become a doctor must be hard. Years of his life gone without so much as a secure job at the end of it. All those years of work and the constant stream of exams hanging in the balance.

Seren was under no delusions about the pressure he must have been under. But she didn't understand, this decision he'd made had nothing to do with his previous ambitions. It had simply blown it out of existence,

"Seren, I just need you to trust me on this, okay?"

"You know I do."

She didn't want to fight any more, not having the heart for it and the two collided in a healing, comforting hug.

"I know this is scary, but I just know it's what I'm supposed to do. Bumping into Keaton was not a coincidence – it was fate – this is OUR fate."

Sam got his point across as he squeezed Seren's slight frame even tighter.

Then, Seren's muffled question escaped and sent his stomach churning. She had raised the subject his mind had blocked out all this time,

"What about your father? This will break his heart."

Sam knew his father would always love him no matter what and that there was never any danger of losing that love, but he could certainly lose his respect. Sam knew this decision would make as little sense to his Dad as it had to Seren. His father was never driven by money or success, only family and responsibilities, things he'd drummed into Sam and he was grateful for that.

This job would provide security for both Seren and himself and they could get married, even think about starting a family of their own. What man ever had more motivation to be responsible towards his family.

This is how Sam imagined he would explain all this to his father. All he could do was hope Dad understood that his

136

son was not him… but his own man who wanted to stand on his own two feet carrying his own dreams.

After a long silence Sam simply said,

"I'll tell him this is what I want and he'll understand."

There was another long pause as the two remained in their tight embrace, Sam now slowly rocking from side to side. He tilted his head to look at Seren, who was practically sleeping as she leaned her insignificant weight upon him. He indulged himself as he remembered her fury, like an exotic wild animal, and now found the memory of this wild tigress strangely erotic.

Skilfully he swept her legs up into his left arm and carried her into the bedroom where he lay her down as gently as he could. He sat beside her, fixated on her angelic state as another practical thought crossed his mind,

'Oh and one more thing honey… I'm going away for a week. Don't worry I'll only be across the Atlantic.'

It sickened him. Sam knew he'd have to tell her tomorrow… Another conversation to look forward to. Sam knew this constant reel of little or no notice news couldn't last forever. Seren was a patient girl but even her tether had its limits and Sam had already witnessed it snap momentarily today.

He felt like a cat running out of lives.

Chapter 13

Blind Ambition

It was early, Sunday morning and Sam had decided last night it would be best to get 'the conversation' out of the way so it was done and dusted. He knew there would be a stream of repercussions throughout the rest of the weekend; of course there would, Seren's feelings weren't going to vanish overnight no matter how much Sam would have wished them away.

But this was a far better option than telling Seren at the last minute on Sunday night just before he left the country. It was already short notice and he had no desire to make it any shorter.

And so as soon as Sam woke, at around eight, he tiptoed quietly to the kitchen where he made a tactical full English of bacon, fried eggs, black pudding, tomatoes and even eggy bread. Sam was pulling out all the stops, hoping a delicious meal in bed might soften the blow… It was worth a shot, anything was at this point as his nine lives were surely on the brink of running out.

There was no real danger of Seren waking of her own accord. Friday night her internal clock shut down and she'd sometimes sleep right through till twelve even if left to her own devices, her body recuperating all that mental and physical energy that her full-on fifty-hour week at the hospital robbed.

Sam topped up the large plate with a mountain of the greasy delicacies, placing it on a tray with salt and pepper and carrying it carefully towards the bedroom. The smell wafted up his nose as he walked, leaving his mouth watering.

'Here goes.'

He approached this sleeping angel who had the capacity to transform into a terrifying flesh eating animal at any moment.

Sam moved around to her side of the bed and sat on the edge beside her, placing the tray of goodies on the bedside table. He pondered for a moment on the best way to wake her, considering sliding between the sheets and her legs before wisely settling on shaking her softly. Food could be classed as a relatively innocent apology whereas sex was a different matter and would in the current circumstances be construed as crass with underlying ulterior motives.

Seren began to stir, her eyes fluttering open in brief interludes, squinting as they adjusted to the bright morning light. She shuffled under the sheets from her snug curled up position onto her back and more upright.

Her eyes were now fully open and she stretched her limbs out, her eyes honing in on the source of the wonderful smell which filled her deep breaths,

"Good morning."

She smiled quizzically, apparently all the troubles of their lives had been washed away by a refreshing night's sleep, though Sam intended to bring things right back down to harsh reality.

"Here you go."

Sam sang as he lifted the tray and waited for Seren to pull herself into an upright position before placing it lovingly in her lap.

She said nothing. Just flashed that angelic smile at him again which conveyed more than enough gratitude. Sam retook his position beside her, hesitating tentatively as he didn't want to disturb this hiatus of hostilities. But he had to, there was no use putting it off. His anxiety was ready to burst out of him, whilst contrition fought to rule in its place.

Sam decided on waiting at least until she'd finished the plate of cholesterol, until the hot food and cutlery was out of her grasp. He was now much more wary of pissing her off after the incident with the bottle. Sam now knew he wasn't the only one with a raging beast.

He took his place back on his side of the bed and waited patiently for Seren to finish the food which she gobbled down like a starved cat. Then she placed the tray back on the table and leaned over to kiss Sam gently on the cheek,

'Now! Now's the time, there won't be a better one.'

Sam made the decision to rip off the bandage and went for it,

"Seren, honey there's something I need to tell you, it's about the job."

The temperature of the room dropped as Seren's electric eyed stare settled upon Sam. He could feel her burning into the side of his skull. Reluctantly he faced her and the music,

"I was going to tell you last night, but you were so exhausted and then you fell asleep and…"

Sam gabbled but stopped himself as Seren's gaze burned even hotter and he received the message loud and clear.

'Just fucking man up and tell her straight!'

The lion was right as usual. Not even the best lawyer could sugar coat this news.

He rebooted,

"I have to go out to New York this week… For the whole week, until Friday."

Sam explained, feeling rather proud of himself and glad he'd just come out with the brutal truth. A substantial weight of relief lifted from his shoulders. However, that positivity was short-lived as Seren's eyes began to water and her head hung low. Some of her golden hair falling forwards and hiding her face, but Sam could tell from the subtle tremble of her quiet voice that she was upset,

"This is how it starts then, just a week here, a week there."

Her tone conveyed a hopeless resignation.

Sam was confused, understandably, he had no idea what she was talking about and wasn't going to resort to the classic guessing game men often played in these situations. He

140

continued to follow his alter ego's advice to man up. So he simply asked her,

"What do you mean?"

Sam shuffled closer in preparation to comfort her but he stopped as she suddenly raised her hand and started at him.

It was then that Seren shared her feelings. Everything she'd wanted to tell him the night before, she spilled it all. She explained all about her father; how bit by bit she had lost her connection with him courtesy of his high-powered job, how the role had consumed and left him the mere ghost of his former self and most importantly, how she feared losing Sam the same way, her fear of history repeating itself.

Of course, Sam did his best to convince her he was not the same man as her father, which resulted in her sharing the story about Nina's husband, George and how Seren knew she needed to let Sam follow his dreams and discover the realities for himself and how she wanted to support and believe in him. Believe that he would always come back to her in the end. The couple had been talking for around two hours before the conversation finally ran out of steam.

Sam was taken by surprise when Seren opened up about her father as she'd never been willing to give any more than a few vague details before. Sam never pressed the matter as he soon learned the subject raised negative feelings and was not up for discussion. It didn't really matter to him anyway, he had never been given the opportunity to get to know Seren's family and for the time being at least, Sam was contented, never one to pick at old wounds.

He'd always just assumed they were never close and that she had no interest in the man, but the truth was much deeper. Sam couldn't help but feel a tad ashamed for not sensing it before. After all they'd lived together for more than three years, Sam thought he knew everything about his partner but he guessed everyone kept secrets… even from the ones they love.

Anyway, he was glad she'd told him as now all of her negativity towards this brilliant new opportunity made sense, and he realised her fears were perfectly justifiable. At least to her and, of course the poor girl was going to worry history would repeat itself, it often does!

But Sam was confident that in their world, Seren would always come first. He remained true to the belief that he was not doing this for his own selfish reasons but for the team. Yes, he wanted to become the confident and successful man but that was so that he could look after Seren... Wasn't it?

Glad the dreaded deed was over and done with and that there was a rational cause for it in the first place, Sam allowed himself to relax. If it had not been for the New York trip, Seren would not have been pressed into opening up about her father and her true feelings. So this had been a positive thing, right?

Of course, pushing Seren to her emotional limits like that was the last thing Sam wanted to do, but sometimes only absolute necessity will lead people into true confidences and the couple were certainly better off having shared that conversation. Now they were back on the same page and had what they needed; Sam had Seren's love and support, and Seren had Sam's word he would not become her father, that he would always put her happiness first.

As lovely as the morning's end result was, this bliss couldn't last for long as Sam had a busy day's schedule ahead. He needed to head into the city to get some supplies for his trip; a new business suit, travel bag and various other bits and bobs.

But there was another far less appealing task he had to take care of first. Sam had phoned Mr Phillip Patrick and arranged to meet him at his home. The man was always very accessible and had been an excellent mentor and the favourite of Sam's university lecturers.

Sam was a medical student at the University College London, having gained his place at the prestigious setting thanks to his outstanding GCSE and A-level results. All that studying and missing out on teenage life had paid off academically. Sam's ambition, originally a brain-child of his father but quickly adopted as a personal goal, was to become a GP.

A unique alliance had quickly formed between this one particular lecturer and his student. It was not unusual for Sam to gravitate towards his teachers, in fact it had always been the case throughout his studies. He'd had very few close friends and spent most of his time alone. His teachers had always been nice to him, paid attention to him because he was a particularly bright boy and such a pleasure to teach. Sam would often stay behind after classes to ask questions, always hungry for knowledge.

But in this case, the relationship was much more intense. Sam had arrived at university where thousands of strangers co-existed and he was completely alone in an alien part of the city. For an individual who suffers from anxiety and a lack of confidence, this had been his own personal hell on Earth.

Sam's induction lecture had been given by none other than the highly esteemed Consultant, Mr Patrick. What an inspirational speech it had been. The man spoke with such fiery passion for his subject it was hypnotic. Sam had decided that was how he wanted to feel about his own career. Sam was captivated and as the auditorium emptied at the end of the delivery he just sat there. His vivid imagination racing with so many questions he wanted to ask this awe-inspiring figure.

After a few minutes Philip had noticed there was still one young adolescent sat in the lonely stands. It was clear from Sam's young eager face he wanted to talk and so the educator walked up to sit beside him and the two chatted for a good half an hour. A new friendship was instantly created.

The consultant had seen something special in this young man and it wasn't just his intelligence, all the students at medical school possess that. No, there had been something more. Something more palpable. It was his determination to succeed which drove his constant thirst for knowledge, and he absorbed it like a sponge. Whilst the rest of the class would be following on with the teacher on chapter 8 of their medical text book Sam would have read ahead at least a couple of chapters in his spare time, always ahead of the game. He had an insatiable thirst for knowledge.

And now Sam had convinced himself of the true reason for his unmatched work ethic, he was destined to push himself to the limit and the only way to do that was to join the only profession where the possibilities are limitless and boundaries don't exist – the world of business.

Sam had asked if Seren fancied a trip into town, even offering to buy her anything she wanted (He'd be able to afford it soon enough) But it was no good. She had taken her favourite position curled up on the sofa, hugging a hot water bottle to her chest in one hand and reading good old Stephen King from the other. It would take an enticement Sam had yet to discover to drag her away from such a happy place.

Sam grabbed his keys and of course, his old leather bag before kissing Seren firmly on the forehead, so as not to obstruct her concentrated vision.

He whispered,

"Love you."

Then strode purposefully towards the door. Ready to face the busy day ahead.

Sam took a taxi straight to Primrose Hill, he'd told his mentor he'd likely swing by round about midday. This was not going to be a pleasant meet, Sam hated disappointing people and there was no doubt Phillip would be disappointed. They had even talked about working together when Sam graduated. Philip had said there would always be a spot for his protégé in his department.

Sam hadn't mentioned why he needed to meet the Consultant who didn't ask. Phillip had simply presumed it was just for one of their semi-regular friendly catch-ups. Not suspecting even for a moment the truth. No one would have guessed Sam would be one of the many to drop out early. He'd always been such a committed studier.

But that would have been the title of Sam's life story and he was sick of it. He'd spent most of his life in a room, alone, studying and he'd had enough. It was time to go out into the real world and experience life. Real life, that exists beyond the classrooms and books. It was time to "Dive into" the ocean of endless possibilities.

"Just pull over here!"

Sam exclaimed to the cabbie as they approached a street of neat London houses. He fancied a little walk and some fresh air to think about what he might say, how exactly he would unburden his revelation.

And this was a lovely place for a thoughtful stroll in a secluded little street with three story residences lined up on both sides. The houses themselves reminded Sam of the street from Mary Poppins… the one where Mr Banks and his family lived. This wasn't quite as grand; the houses were certainly smaller but of identical design; white stone encased large rectangular windows with Roman style borders. The frontages fenced in by intricate iron railings of pure black.

Sam sauntered along the path, talking his time to admire the homely atmosphere. He didn't really want to arrive at his destination, he could have walked up and down and around this neighborhood all day had time allowed. Alas, at some point he had to arrive at number 19 and he dutifully walked up to the gloss black door and knocked twice. Waiting in apprehensive anticipation for the muffled sound of footsteps approaching the door. Sure enough they came, louder and louder until they stopped and the lock clicked, the door swinging free.

"Hi Phil"

Sam said with a faked positivity that the middle-aged academic standing in the doorway read immediately. The undertone of regret was not subtle. The Doctor knew as soon as he opened that door and saw Sam's bleak expression this was not a social call. Philip extended Sam the same faked curtsy as for this brief moment the two men ignored the negative undertone of this meeting,

"Sam! Good to see you friend, come on in, I'll put the kettle on."

The doctor waved Sam in, walking back down the long hallway towards the kitchen. Sam carefully closed the door before following.

Philip had always given off a very casual vibe even in the classroom, like he was just one of your mates and not a teacher, there was no high or mighty side to the man, he was grounded. That was probably one of the reasons Sam had warmed to him, he had the rare ability to make even the most self-conscious of people feel at home.

Sam would often go to him with personal problems, he'd been as much a psychoanalyst as a teacher of medicine to Sam. It's likely that's what he suspected this last-minute meet was about... Sam had something he needed to confide or talk about. After all, sometimes you just wanted to confide in someone outside your family.

Sam entered the kitchen, a small yet well designed space with sleek granite counters and slate grey cupboards, all very chic. Sam sat at the closest of three bar stools which surrounded the small island.

"How's Seren?"

Philip asked with genuine interest. Making small talk as he leant back on the counter, waiting for the kettle to boil.

He'd never met Seren in person, but Sam had shared plenty about her, so he felt he had.

"She's fine... I mean, aside from being constantly exhausted."

Sam replied with an honest dismay. The more his mind returned to his girl and that hateful job the more he raced towards his new career so that she could leave hers behind. Philip came back with empathy born of experience, knowing full well the working life of a hospital nurse,

"Tough profession, nursing!"

Philip turned back to the kettle as it bubbled happily, retrieving two cups and tea bags from the top shelf and setting them ready before he continued, the edge of sincerity apparent,

"Real saint, that girl, you make sure you hold onto her!"

Sam smiled in agreement. Philip was always giving him little pieces of fatherly advice; it came naturally as he was just that sort of man. The father figure with bags of experience and wisdom... Like Nina. It never bothered Sam anyway, he respected the man and a man respected was a man taken seriously. The kind of respect Sam aspired to radiate.

The tea was poured carefully before being transported over to the island where he sat on the closest stool to Sam. At around fifty-five with silvered short hair and rounded frameless spectacles, the man could have passed for a pretty good Steve Jobs look-alike.

"So, what did you want to talk about? Sounded a tad strange on the phone"

That was the other thing about Philip, he always dug straight into the heart of the topic, no dodging the point no matter how awkward the subject matter. He was a straight shooter but managed to do it in a way that wasn't intrusive or aggressive thanks to his charismatic and gentle persona.

Sam froze for a moment… he had now reached the point of no return but didn't know how to say it.

'Just tell him!'

The courageous lion always returning when he needed it most, but before Sam could take its advice Philip was helpful as ever, using the medium of a joke as a lever,

"Not getting cold feet are you?"

He smiled widely before taking a sip of his tea.

"Not exactly."

Sam tone splintered as far across the spectrum of severity as it could go. Philips playful expression suddenly mirrored Sam's. He placed the tea back down on the table and queried, hopeful his suspicions were wrong,

"What?"

"I'm quitting."

Sam answered bluntly with no hint of remorse and the ammunition hit home.

"I hope you're joking?"

Philip gave a concerned chuckle but Sam's vague expression didn't falter, *'no going back now!'* it could almost rival Keaton's poker face. It was as if he were already mirroring his new mentor.

"I wouldn't joke about something like this, Phil."

"But I… I don't understand you're my best and brightest, you'll be qualified in less than a year! And there'll always be a place for you in my department. "

Philips words were tempered with disbelief. He, like Seren before him didn't understand where this was coming from all of a sudden. It was as if Sam's less endearing twin had walked through his door this morning, a character he hadn't met before.

The man seemed quite upset. He had garnered a paternal awareness of responsibility towards Sam over the three years as his mentor and like Seren, didn't want to see him throw it all away at the last hurdle.

"I'm sorry Phil, I really appreciate everything you've done for me I really do, but this is not something you're going to be able to understand, I can't explain it but there's just something else I'm meant to be doing with my life."

Sam's explanation was vague but he knew it wasn't worth going into the real details of 'why,' because it was true that Philip wouldn't understand at all, how could he. All these years Sam had believed they had been kindred spirits, but the truth was they were entirely different species and Sam saw it now.

Philip gave one last attempt to sway Sam but he knew it was futile. The newfound fire of determination blazed in Sam's deep brown eyes. Philip could see it, this was a new man. He had one last verbal stab,

"Won't you reconsider?"

Sam gave a slow almost disturbing shake of his head, the inscrutable facade still standing strong.

"I can't say I'm not disappointed… I'll hold your placement as long as I can, just in case you change your mind."

Philip continued resignedly, he had been completely deflated, realising there was nothing he could say or offer to change Sam's decision or appeal to his better nature. It was game over.

Sam's former persona had left the building and this provided him with the strength he needed as he hammered in the last nail with hollow diplomacy,

"Thanks, I really do appreciate everything you've done for me, I'm sorry to let you down like this."

The two men sat generating small talk as they finished the tea, both knowing they would likely never see each other again. Secretly, the lecturer harboured a wish that Sam would see sense and change his mind but Sam was more resolute than ever.

By the time Sam arrived back home from his shopping expedition he was spent. His knees screaming out in agony as he summited the two floors up to the apartment. Never had he wished for an elevator more.

At the door he managed to wrestle the stubborn bags into his left hand so he could play 'find the keys' with his right. He struck gold, skilfully shuffling them in his hand, forcing the front door key into the lock, his arms aching under the weight of clothes and sundries as they sensed the end was near. It took a good five seconds of bodging to get the rusted lock to give in but eventually it relented. Pushing the door wide with his toe, he took one victorious stride inside and let his arms give in. The bags hit the hard floor with a loud rustling sound.

Sam smiled to see Seren was exactly where he left her, curled up on the sofa reading her book, a cold cup of tea on the table remained untouched. It was as time had been suspended and she hadn't moved. This was nothing new to Sam as with the right captivating book it was normal practice for Seren to read all day, from sunrise to sunset.

He closed the door with his heel and walked over to her. He snuck up, like a cat searching for warmth, and lay beside her, resting his head on her lap. Seren automatically started running her fingers through his thick brown hair but didn't miss a beat, choosing to remain in her fictional world.

Sam closed his eyes and relaxed, letting his body sink into the sofa and Seren. He could feel the warmth radiating from her legs, it soothed his aching neck.

Sam's body wanted to drift away into a deep sleep but his racing mind wouldn't let him as bravado fought with reason. There were far too many complex emotions wreaking havoc thanks to his big day tomorrow… The biggest day of his life loomed, it was show time and the curtain was about to go up leaving Sam naked and exposed on the stage in from of the world, at least that's how he felt.

There were too many emotions racing around up there; excitement, anticipation and determination but also dread and fear of the unknown world that lay behind that thick curtain that had been drawn all of his life. Just about every emotion it was possible for a person to feel was in there somewhere.

Sam wanted to communicate his deepest darkest fears, he needed to talk, needed some solace. Serena's comforting and sensible advice always managed to soothe him. She could make it all go away, at least for the moment.

His first attempt at conversation was feeble as he skirted round the issue,

"What a day."

Punctuated with a long sigh.

All Sam received in response was a gentle hum. Seren still completely enveloped in her novel.

He'd need to do much better to gain the undivided attention he was after, Sam wanted more than that soothing voice, he wanted to see those calming ocean blue eyes focusing upon his own. In that moment Sam felt a bit stupid, *'I'm like an immature child pining for his mother's attention when she is clearly busy with something else.'*

This thought vanished rapidly as he didn't care what he was being like. He needed to be distracted from the doubts and fears that grew and grew inside. He needed his partner to tell him everything was going to be alright, he needed her now more than ever, he needed his anchor.

So, he decided for once to open the door and speak his mind, normally he would wish to protect her from his negativity but he had no choice, it needed to be said and so he asked the question which haunted him,

"Seren, honey… I'm not going to drown am I. I mean, I haven't bitten off more than I can chew?"

Sam couldn't have chosen a better question or even words to grasp Seren's attention. The book dropped to her knee and she turned to him. It was the most surprising and welcome question he had ever asked her. Sam had never opened up like this before. Like most men he preferred to keep his feelings bottled and corked rather than open up and admit doubt.

Seren was so overjoyed to see that nervous and shy guy she met all those years ago, so much so she had to force back a wide and totally inappropriate smile.

No, Sam needed her right now and she was glad of it, it made her feel like they were a team once more and right now Sam needed his teammate to back him up 100%, just like Nina had said.

So Seren replied in a soft, yet firm tone,

"Sweetheart, this is what you really want, isn't it?"

Sam replied with immediate instinct,

"Yes, of course."

"Then everything will work out for the best, you have to trust yourself."

But that was far easier said than done for a man with such low self-esteem. Like many over-achievers, Sam never felt anything was good enough – always reaching higher. How could he trust himself if he had no confidence in himself? It was a vicious and never ending loop.

Where was that lion now? At the crucial moment, it had disappeared back into the depths of his mind, oblivious in its cage.

Sam said nothing and Seren could read the distant yet sickened look on his face that conveyed the unspoken truth – he was not convinced.

Seren would need to up her game and did so,

"I believe in you Sam. You have the ability to achieve anything and everything you want to, there's not a single doubt in my mind about that. You're intelligent, you work hard and you're a good person... No one deserves their dreams more."

Seren had knocked it out of the park. J.F.K's writer couldn't have come up with a better speech. Sam didn't need to reply he just smiled back and Seren knew she need say nothing more.

Of course, it wasn't enough to restore the beast, only Keaton seemed to possess the ability to coax him out of hibernation. However, his optimism was liberated as normal service was almost resumed. The most important thing was that Seren was behind him and she couldn't have provided a better incentive. All of the doubt and fear drifted into the background as her uplifting words rang out as church bells in his ears and Sam drifted away into a deep and blissful sleep.

Chapter 14

The Dotted Line

Sam was rudely awoken from his deep sleep at precisely six-thirty by two simultaneous sounds; his phone alarm's deep siren-like bellow, alongside his old reliable alarm clock with its high pitched rattling bell. Once upon a time he had left his mobile on silent and the alarm had failed to sound. Today he was taking absolutely no chances and utilised all the tools at his disposal. The two devices together made for an impressively loud cacophony that even a comatose teenager would be hard pressed to ignore.

For a man heading into the most important day of his professional life, Sam had slept rather well. Certainly much better than he had done that night before his meeting at The Dorchester, his head filled with thoughts of drowning and being torn apart by sharks. Sam believed the key to his restful night was down to the culmination of his utter exhaustion juxtaposed with Seren's supportive words. Every time Sam felt his mind slipping towards doubt and fear he regurgitated five restorative words, "I believe in you Sam." His self-belief was somewhat revitalised as he rolled over to the inside of the bed, immediately registering the empty space beside him, she had already gone. Rejuvenation quickly followed on the heels of disappointment as ink on paper drifted into his line of vision, he snatched at the message,

"Sam,

Sorry I had to leave early, I didn't want to wake you.

Have a wonderful week in New York. I know you'll be great!

Love always, Seren

xo"

Sam sprung from the bed, eager to face what promised to be a memorable week.

After a quick shower to wake him up and breakfast to keep his mind sharp, Sam mentally checked with military precision the contents of his luggage, which he had placed in pole position by the front door the night before. Everything was in its rightful place.

He made one final check of his physical appearance in the round hallway mirror before concluding he was presentable. Then, as if on cue the muffled but unmistakable horn of a car sounded from outside. The taxi which he had also organised last night had arrived.

As instructed, Sam arrived at The Keaton before 8:00 with minimal delays thanks to the taxi driver's use of the backstreets. His local knowledge helping to avoid the bulk of the notorious London traffic. Sam gave the cabbie a twenty and waited for a moment in anticipation of the doorman he knew was about to open the door for him. Sam was enjoying the idea of becoming used to these customs of luxury.

Flashing a smile of gratitude to the man, Sam jumped out with his two bags; the large duffle which he carried in his right hand and of course, his old leather 'friend' which was slung over his back.

The doorman offered to take the bags and store them for him. Sam's 'OK' was automatic, his mind focused on other things. He paced up the steps and through the door to be greeted by a familiar face,

"Good morning, Mr Lowell, Good to see you again. Mr Keaton will be joining you in Conference Room 1."

Thomas explained before leading the way.

Though Sam was indeed beginning to get to grips with the customs and increasingly comfortable at being submerged in the grandeur of this world, one thing he couldn't get his head around was how seamlessly everything worked. There was no waiting around, no difficulties such as those he usually encountered. Everyone always seemed to know what was going on and the goings on always ran like clockwork. Although this did cut out all the time wasting it also meant there was no time to stop or pause. He just had time for a quick thought, *'This is exhausting'* before being led to one of the open elevators. Thomas reached inside the doors and pushed the 3rd floor button.

"There you go, sir; it's at the end of the corridor, to your left."

Thomas explained before moving to one side and gesturing politely for Sam to enter. He did, and the doors closed effortlessly.

It was mere few seconds before 'Joanna Lumley' gave the floor number and the door opened revealing a long corporate corridor. Floor 3 was filled with conference rooms and Sam counted at least five as he made his way down towards the end, large rooms walled with frosted glass either side of him.

'This is where all the high flying businessmen staying in the hotel come to thrash out their deals… how much money had passed through this floor?'

Sam's overactive imagination speculated about the contents of those mysterious opaque rooms.

He reached the end of the line and an open door, *"Conference room 1"* conveniently labelled on the glass wall. Sam froze for a moment, peering through the doorway which revealed part of a large table with many chairs. Sam wondered if the man was already in there, sat just out of sight. The thought retrieved his anxiety, his hands began shaking and his stomach churned. Like ripping off a plaster he took a deep breath and marched into the room.

But the elongated space was completely empty. A long glass table dominated the centre surrounded by twelve leather office chairs. For a moment Sam wished Keaton had been there already. Another stretch of time in that empty stage of nothingness would allow his anxiety to breed.

He sat for a torturous fifteen minutes. Gazing up at the large round clock above the door every 30 seconds wishing away the time whilst in between swivelling in his chair like a bored child, chomping on his nails until some fingers bled.

Sam desperately willed that courageous lion to break out and consume him but the brute lay conspicuously dormant. He was left in silent contemplation with his self-conscious, anxious self until Keaton arrived at, no doubt bang on, quarter past the hour.

Sure enough, bang on eight fifteen there was movement from the hitherto silent mouth of the doorway and Sam's eyes darted towards it. He was filled with concern as a gentleman of mid-sixties walked through the doorway. Sam wondered if maybe he'd got the wrong room and began to panic. A split second later his angst was abated by the sight of Keaton, who followed the elderly gentleman inside. Carter brought up the rear and closed the door behind him.

Sam shot up to his feet as the three men approached him and Keaton moved around the stranger to introduce him,

"Morning, Sam. This is my Lawyer Mr Antolini," he said gesturing his right hand towards the old man. Sam didn't know whether to initiate a handshake or not so he did nothing, just smiled politely and prepared to speak, but Mr Antolini beat him to it.

"Please, call me Carlos."

The man was definitely Italian, the distinctive accent just surfacing above his professionalism. He was a short stocky man and Sam's first thought was *'just like a stereotypical member of the Italian Mafia,'* Sam continued his mental evaluation – bright silver hair, meticulously styled with a generous helping of product and the careful use of a comb, pinstriped suit with red tie and matching handkerchief. Sam's conclusion was not very flattering, *'He definitely looks the part of a lawyer, friendly on the outside, but slippery.'*

"Pleasure, sir,"

Sam mirrored professional politeness, immediately embarking upon his act of trying to fit in, it was like putting on a mask. Something he wouldn't have to do if that god damn beast would just take over!

"Shall we."

Keaton's impatient statement made it blatantly clear he did not have the time or patience to dawdle.

The billionaire's sharp words had cut the friendly atmosphere like a knife, reminding them all why they were there.

'No time for fucking niceties Sam! Down to business.'

The lion was back in residence for which he was grateful. Keaton's presence seemed to somehow provide the beast's sustenance. Sam had suspected as much and was glad of its support.

The three men sat quickly and Mr Antolini got down to his job, adroitly delivering his explanation with a concentrated stare,

"So, Sam, I am here in a professional capacity to ensure all is in order before you proceed with your new employment. There are a few other documents for you to sign, all boring paperwork but it has to be done, and of course, to answer any questions you may have?"

The question mark hung in the air and Sam finally nodded and conveyed an understanding smile as he sensed the man was about to continue,

"You brought the contract I presume."

"Yes, yes. It's all signed and everything."

Sam's voice betraying his eagerness. Still hadn't quite mastered that inscrutable facade.

He reached for his bag which he'd placed on the floor and removed the contract from the battered leather. Carlos held out his small, dry wrinkled hand and grasped it tightly. Removing the papers from the matte black envelope Sam had reused (it seemed too nice to throw away) he flicked straight to the back page with the practiced skill of a man who'd done this countless times, studying it minutely before speaking,

"All looks to be in order. Congratulations on your new position."

"Thank you."

Sam replied impassively, on this occasion managing to reign in his emotions much more effectively. His eyes and attention swung towards Keaton as he sensed the man was looking at him. The two shared a brief stare and the billionaire gave one of his subtle appraising smiles.

Carlos slid the contract into his own leather folder which was bulging at the seams, leaving the envelope hollow on the table. He then retrieved a wad of even larger papers from the same leather pouch, spreading them out in front of Sam before explaining,

"Now, these are just some other documents that require your signature, like I say all boring corporate stuff, health insurance and alike."

Carlos spoke with vague disinterest as he pointed to one of the three documents that he'd laid out alongside an n expensive looking fountain pen.

Sam's eyes widened at the daunting wad, it looked about fifty pages and he wasn't going to sit here and read through it all whilst Keaton waited; the man wouldn't wait, he'd be in New York before it was read through.

Sam's logic sounded an alarm,

'I really shouldn't sign this without reading every detail.'

But then his concerns were blown out of the water by the raging return of the rebel forces,

'Just fucking sign the thing! This is your dream remember, the opportunity of your lifetime, you only get one of these so don't fuck it up now! SIGN, SIGN YOU PRAT!'

Sam looked at Mr Antolini who offered up his black Mont Blanc. Sam took it and scrawled along the dotted line. The old man smiled before continuing to the second document,

"This one is a non-disclosure agreement; it simply means you can't discuss any details regarding Keaton & Co."

Sam signed again without hesitation.

Mr Antolini's sleazy smile grew wider still as he turned to the last document,

"Finally, this section is for your keeping. In it you'll find all the details of your employment, offshore bank account, business numbers etc etc."

Sam was reminded of the crocodile in Peter Pan but hastily pushed the thought away as the pages were pushed towards him. The smile quickly faded as the lawyer collected up the other two documents with Sam's freshly inked signature and slid them back into his folder, where he saw something that jogged his memory, rather casually remarking,

"Oh yes, I almost forgot, New business phone and computer."

The Italian placed a brand new iPhone and MacBook on the table. Sam eyed the goodies. He had not expected such luxuries, not really having considered such details or that there may be more to come,

"… And of course, company car."

Finally, the man pushed a set of car keys towards Sam who stared wide eyed at the unmistakable Audi logo. His imagination fired into life as he wondered which model it was. He settled on an A4 or A5 but gave nothing away, too busy concentrating his attention on remaining professional and calm in Keaton's presence.

"I believe that's everything sorted then."

The lawyer concluded definitively before turning to Keaton.

"Well, Sam."

The billionaire announced, turning to face Sam.

Sam stared back, mesmerised.

"We have business to conduct."

He flashed that subtle smile as briefly as ever before vacating his seat and turning his attention to Carter who had remained in his 'go to' position, guarding the door.

"Have the car brought round, we're going straight to the airport."

Sam heard Keaton order, watching as Carter complied with alacrity.

Mr Antolini briskly stood up and Sam followed politely but the elderly gentleman turned and walked back towards the door without so much as a goodbye. It would appear professional pleasantries were no longer necessary.

'The slithering lawyer has the required signatures. Not all old men are gentlemen.'

Sam's attention returned to Keaton and they were left alone in the space. Keaton moved closer,

"Ready?"

The lion found its voice and replied in a calm, collective tone, "Absolutely."

Chapter 15

'G650'

The two men strode out of the hotel in unison, the billionaire leading the way with Sam closely shadowing at his right shoulder. They could almost have passed for twins but for the vast contrast between Keaton's pristinely tailored three-piece business suit, and Sam's chain store trousers and jacket that fitted him about as well as could be expected.

Luckily Sam was too distracted by the deep purple Rolls they approached to notice himself. It was a beautiful machine, the perfect culmination of style, elegance and power.

'Rather like its owner.'

Sam noticed one of the valets carefully placing his duffle bag in the boot whilst the other stood by with the eyes of a hawk, alert and ready to serve anyone requiring assistance.

Carter was standing by the rear door of the car which he opened wide with perfect timing as Keaton stepped in without hesitation.

Sam slowed his pace, hesitating, unsure if he was meant to get into the other side and sit beside his new employer.

Carter closed the door and, flashing Sam a quick glance moved around to the far side of the car. Sam quickly caught on and followed the subtle guidance, the rear door was opened and the newly signed employee entered cautiously. Sam now felt an inexplicable reluctance to enter such a small space with the entrepreneur, who at this moment had the air of a dangerous and unpredictable coiled viper.

161

'Man up, your imagination is working overtime Prat!'

The white leather surrounded Sam's body in luxurious comfort. He fought hard against the sudden urge to fidget. He wanted to ask where they were going but then remembered he already knew and a surge of adrenaline shot up his spine.

Carter took his place in the driver seat and they pulled away. The beast of an engine purring into life.

"How do you feel?"

Keaton asked, breaking the tense silence.

The question suggested interest, yet it was delivered in the man's classic deep, emotionless voice.

Sam had already decided honesty was the best policy when it came to Keaton. It had become crystal clear that the man was a human lie detector and able to read you like a book. Sam wisely summoned a plain and blunt one word response,

"Nervous."

It would have been the name of the first chapter of his life story, right underneath the title, 'An exemplary student.' Sam looked forward to escaping his old world, eager to welcome his new improved situation.

Meanwhile, Keaton played the one-word conversation game naturally,

"Good."

Sam's expression conveyed his request for further elaboration. Keaton's attention seemed to be engaged elsewhere but the businessman somehow sensed an explanation was needed,

"It's your body's way of telling you that you care."

Sam was a little unnerved at this insight into human emotion but brushed it aside,

'That's just part of being a great businessman.'

After all, business was largely about people. If you could read their thoughts and feelings that must be a benefit?

'Another lesson to learn, reading people.'

Sam made a mental note.

He hadn't replied to Keaton's profound comment, unable to think of an intelligent response. He was sure silence would appeal more to Keaton than stupidity…

'If you've not got anything good to say, don't bother to speak.'

The remainder of the journey was spent in silence. Keaton's attention focused in on his phone, sending all manner of emails about important business stuff, Sam suspected. Whatever it was he wasn't about to distract the mastermind's focus.

Sam turned his attention to the window, gazing out at the bustling streets of London. He was encouraged by an egotistical thought which ascended from deep within him,

'All of those people would give anything to be where you are.'

It was right, this was, just about the pinnacle of existence, the top of the word. Sat in the back of a Rolls Royce, driving through the greatest city in the world whilst heading for the city of dreams, with a billionaire at your side. The only way this moment could have been improved was if Sam was in the other seat,

'One day… one day, you will be.'

Sam hunted for clues, a sign or landmark that would give away which airport they were heading for. Minutes later the answer came as the word "Gatwick" caught his eye. Sam's attention was turned from the world outside by a loud vibrating noise. Searching the cabin for the source of the intrusion he suddenly felt stupid as his guru answered his phone,

"Keaton."

There was a pause as the man listened intently, Sam was held in suspense, wondering what was being said.

Keaton continued,

"No, I want the board assembled at the office at twelve thirty, I'm coming in."

This arbitrary instruction was delivered with regal authority and the call was ended. Sam couldn't imagine a conversation where the man wouldn't be in charge.

Sam realised Keaton was a powerful man but was only just beginning to grasp how influential a billion pounds made you.

They reached the airport and Sam soon began to recognise familiar structures, having been through Gatwick twice before. The first time was when his father took him to Italy as a surprise for getting into medical school. The second trip was a year later when Sam took Seren to the same place, Lake Como. The trip had practically bankrupted the young couple but the memories were worth it.

They approached the bustling entrance, and Sam prepared to get out, but the beast drove straight past. He quickly settled back in his seat resolved in the knowledge he'd find out what was happening soon enough.

The car carried on down the road turning left, then right, then right again until they were on a narrow, one-way road which seemed to tunnel under the main gate as it dropped down into darkness.

Sam leaned right so he could peer through the centre console of the cabin, he could see daylight at the other end of the short tunnel. They stopped just before it at a security gate, heavily guarded by armed security. Sam studied with intrigue as Carter opened the window and appeared to hand a laminated ID badge to the nearest guard. The ID was scrutinised before being handed back with a firm nod. The gate rose and they drove back out into the daylight and onto the runway. Sam glanced over at Keaton who blithely continued to consult his phone. They sped along the smooth surface, Sam gazing out the window, fascinated as he watched huge aeroplanes pass by. Just another little something to add to his rapidly growing list of interesting experiences!

The car came to a steady standstill, Sam lowered his head and looking out of Keaton's window he could see part of a white wing. The billionaire beside him didn't even look up as Carter opened the door and he exited the vehicle. A rush of kerosene fumes and engine noise flooded the car.

Sam opened his own door, too excited to sit and politely wait,

'Fuck protocol!'

He jumped out, turned to see a sleek jet dominating his eye-line; "Keaton & Co" scribed elegantly across the tail. Sam walked slowly round the car, his eyes remained fixed on the winged beast. The idea of a 'private plane' had never even crossed his mind. Of course, it made sense, in Keaton's crazy world of luxury and excess.

'No billionaire should be without one.'

Just when Sam thought he was adjusting to this unknown new world, it had kicked up another notch. He followed Keaton and Carter towards the front of the jet where a man dressed in smart aviator uniform waited to greet them.

"Good morning, sir. We are all set."

The man found it necessary to bellow in order to be heard over the powerful engines. He addressed Carter, witnessing Keaton's attention remained elsewhere.

"Mr Keaton wishes to depart immediately."

Carter instructed as Keaton ended his umpteenth call of the day.

The man offered a curt nod then he and Carter stepped aside to invite Keaton aboard first. Sam followed his new tutor walking closely behind. Sam felt the Pilot's eyes appraising this new passenger, discomfort returning as once again he had the feeling he shouldn't really be here.

Sam entered into a tube of opulence he would only expect to find in a top hotel. Self-assurance flew out the window as the backdrop edged up another notch. His eyes feasted on the tasteful mesh of white gloss walls, tables and sideboards in pale knotted birch, modern cream leather armchairs were dotted about the cabin facing each other. A soothing ambiance was created by track lighting in the ceiling. Keaton sat in one of the six chairs, Sam dawdled, agonising about social etiquette,

'Should I sit facing the man or give him some space? Dammit man, just choose a seat!'

Settling on the other side of the cabin, the awareness Sam had encountered upon first entering The Keaton recurred,

'I don't belong in this lavish world.'

Sam was distracted by the powerful vibrations of the engines surging through his seat as they now began to creep forwards. The stewardess lifted the door and closed it firmly. Sam gulped,

'Trapped, no turning back now.'

There was a definite feeling of finality to that door rising and closing. The typically attractive young stewardess moved down the corridor towards Sam, she smiled politely enquiring,

"Can I get you anything, sir?"

No doubt presuming the eye contact was a communication that he wanted something. Sam was caught off guard by the solicitous question and fumbled a rushed response,

"No… thank you, I'm, er, fine."

She smiled once more before carrying on towards the rear of the plane and Sam turned his attention back to the space he was in, having a hard time getting his head around the fact he was inside a plane. It felt more like an apartment. He was abruptly pulled back from his musings as Keaton's deep voice penetrated,

"Sam."

He turned to see Keaton had discarded his phone and was staring right at him. The man's head resting on his left hand that was supported by the armrest. Sam again noticed the beautiful timepiece glistening on his wrist. Keaton continued with a request,

"Join me."

Gesturing towards the lonely seat facing him. Sam got up and darted over to the chair where he sat upright like a meerkat, looking very uncomfortable.

Keaton studied Sam's nervous ticks, the shaking hands, quickened breathing and flushed expression before he spoke as bluntly as ever,

"The nerves will pass."

"That's what I'm hoping."

Sam replied honestly in the hope opening up would help relax him as it had done in the restaurant. He desperately wished the beast would wake up but for now it remained dormant.

The jet reached the runway and came to a halt. The entrepreneur offered up some advice,

"Soon enough this world will become your world. Lock a man in a skip long enough and eventually he'll start calling it home."

It was an oddly dark and incongruous illustration, yet it made perfect sense to Sam and the thought calmed him. After all, the man was right, as always, it was all just a matter of familiarity,

'Soon jetting to New York in a private jet will become as common-place as taking a cab.'

The cocky alter ego was back, resurrected as always by Keaton. Sam was glad to see it's revival buoying him up, with the confidence, drive and determination he needed to succeed. Sam's nervous ticks had now disappeared and his thoughts were clear. He looked forward to the day this character took over completely.

Sam was yanked from his thoughts as the engines surged into powerful action and the jet began to accelerate with brutal force down the runway. Keaton continued, not at all distracted by the sudden rush of power,

"You know why I chose you Sam?"

Both men were now completely oblivious to the brutal force of the planes acceleration.

Sam replied with forceful surety, recalling in his crystal clear mind the strangely inspiring words his employer had said to him at The Dorchester,

"My desperation for success makes me driven and determined."

Keaton's immovable features gave way to a fleeting smile of agreement before he replied,

"When I look into you I see myself."

The plane lifted from the ground and soared up into the clear morning sky. Some ten minutes later they reached cruise altitude and levelled out whereupon a voice disrupted the silence from the intercom,

"Good morning, gentlemen. This is Captain Edwards speaking, just to inform you we should have a nice smooth journey across the Atlantic with clear skies, arriving at our destination in approximately seven and a half hours. The weather in New York today is clear with temperatures reaching around 21 degrees, thank you and enjoy your flight."

Keaton had spent the ten intervening minutes predictably glued to his phone as if his life depended on it. Sam imagined that would be the level of devotion required by him soon enough, but for now at least he could sit back and enjoy the journey.

He had been gazing with fascination out the window at the world below. The buildings, the cars, the people all so small and insignificant a mile down below his feet. A feeling of power washed over him as he flew in the clouds, heading for his dreams… His ego expanded.

Sam's attention was directed towards Keaton who turned from his phone to the console on his right, pressing one of the many buttons firmly. Mere seconds passed before the stewardess reappeared from the back of the plane and stood over the men wearing a beaming and inviting smile.

Keaton spoke,

"Black tea."

The two then turned to Sam, expecting his order.

"Same."

He blurted, then remembering his manners,

"Please."

The thought of a hot cup of tea now reminded him he was in fact very thirsty. This incredible journey he was on was so important to him it even sidelined his basic human needs. Sam believed this was a good measure for telling when you really, really want something.

As the young lady walked back up the aisle the two men turned to each other. As always, Keaton orchestrated the conversation, delving into the details he wanted to know,

"Girlfriend?" he inquired, safely having assumed that no wedding band meant no wife.

Sam was still not quite used to the billionaire's unique way of speaking, his questions and statements were so blunt and seemed to come from nowhere. As though he only had the patience to discuss what he wanted precisely when he wanted. There was absolutely no time wasting, it was more like conversing with a cyborg than a human being.

"Yes, Seren. We've been together since college."

Sam explained with pride as he thought over how lucky he was. But Keaton didn't seem to care, in fact if anything the man seemed a little perturbed. Sam reflected,

'Perhaps he senses Seren could be a possible saboteur to this new alliance. Well, he's bang on the money there!'

Somehow Sam guessed the next question, sensing the entrepreneur's sudden interest in her

"How does Seren feel about your new career?"

As much as he'd have liked to fib he couldn't do that to his mentor,

"Concerned at first, she was worried she was going to lose me, but she came around."

Sam explained. Keaton sat forward, emphasising his response with some brutal advice,

"You have to do what's right for you Sam."

Whilst nodding in agreement, Sam's mind was conflicted, his more chivalrous side shouting loud and clear,

'No! You have to put your partner first!'

With the other argued,

'No Sam! Listen to your mentor, YOU and YOUR dreams come first!'

On this occasion – no contest – his ego won the battle.

The two men relaxed back as the stewardess returned with a silver tray holding two glasses of steaming back tea, no milk, no cream. She politely enquired,

"Can I get you anything else?"

Receiving the synchronised reply,

"No thanks."

Having taken care of her passengers, she retreated to the back of the cabin.

Sam decided to reanimate the conversation by returning Keaton's question, hesitating for a brief moment before plucking up the courage to ask,

"What about you, sir? Wife? Or girlfriend?"

Even with his newfound confidence the question seemed a tad intrusive. Sam now squirmed inwardly, his innards summersaulting,

'Oh my God. You've pushed your luck a bit too far this time, Prat!'

Keaton's lack of discernible reaction settled the tension and an explanation was supplied,

"No. Business and women are not a productive mix. Both require time and dedication and I chose a long time ago to focus mine on my company."

Sam was astonished at this candid statement. But as always, the more his mind mulled over Keaton's words the more sense they made.

He imagined owning a business was like creating a great piece of literature. To build something truly successful, you must completely submerge yourself in the world without any distractions to hold you back. Sam decided to risk another intrusion into his mentor's affairs,

"So, how exactly does a thirty-three-year-old become a billionaire?"

Sam couched the question in a casual tone, his courage now fully charged, having deduced this top dog didn't exactly invite questions, but didn't dissuade them either. Sam was driven by his insatiable thirst to acquire knowledge of his mysterious hero who was everything he wished to become.

Keaton took a long slow sip of his tea, as if pondering where to begin and which parts of his personal story to share. Slowly replacing his glass on the table, the reply was given, with his signature straight to the point bluntness,

"When I was seventeen my parents died in a car crash,"

Sam was immediately captivated, yet disturbed at the brutal and emotionless statement, but this feeling swiftly vanished as he reconsidered,

'Such a horrific thing would either break or harden a man.'

"I took the insurance money and decided to make something of my life. I started my own business, sixteen years later here I am."

Sam was completely transfixed and his respect for this character skyrocketed. So inspiring that a teenager could lose everything and somehow find the strength to not only go on living, but to build an empire from the ground up. Now utterly convinced that this man was everything he should aspire to be.

He longed to have such a strong heart.

"That's incredible... Truly, you put everyone else to shame, sir."

Sam's awestruck reply was quickly brushed aside,

"I'm not interested in anyone else Sam, and neither should you be. Your focus should be on you and your dreams. That's it."

The advice was reiterated as Keaton urged his protégé to look out for number one. Sam failed to notice the somewhat brutal message, focusing solely on taking his superior's advice and turning it into action. Subconsciously ignoring the negative, vigorously nodding his agreed response.

The rest of the flight remained mostly silent. Keaton religiously tending to his phone, making and answering call after call and email after email. It was a never-ending bombardment of media. The man never stopped. Sam was reminded of 'The Terminator'. It was exhausting just watching and Sam began to appreciate what running your own business really means in terms of its reality. It was the hard work and dedication Sam knew he possessed deep within, that beast within that was determined to break free and conquer the world. He sat up straight, poised for action,

'I'm ready!'

The protégé decided to use up the long hours getting to grips with his new phone and laptop. Like a child playing with his brand new toys. He figured he'd be spending a lot of time using them for the foreseeable future, so he'd better educate himself.

As the East coast of America appeared on the horizon there was just time for a light sushi lunch as they crossed the last few miles of the shimmering Atlantic.

Sam had tried sushi once before but had never used chop sticks, and stared at them with the perplexity of a child when first presented with cutlery. He studied Keaton who picked them up, split the divide and rolled them between his palms. Sam mirrored the process with far less grace and clumsily ate what was one of the best lunches of his life.

As the plane began to descend Keaton gave his new employee some more instruction,

"Sam?"

The protégé turned from the stunning view of New York city below, giving his undivided attention,

'I want you to watch me this week, learn from me."

"Of course, Sir."

Sam replied with feeling, already having planned on studying the man's every word, every movement.

The two men enjoyed the inspiring view of the city of dreams which lay right at their feet. A thought grasped at Sam's consciousness as he gazed at the view below,

'This is where I belong.'

Chapter 16

New York

The jet touched down at JFK midday local time. The beaming sun burst through the door as it opened, the humid 20-degree air hit Sam like a warm blanket as he exited the plane to see yet another, identical, Rolls Royce awaiting them on the tarmac. Standing by was young man in black suit, tie and a cap, ready to transport them into the concrete jungle.

Carter had now materialised – Sam had not even noticed his presence on the jet – opening the rear door for Keaton whilst the young chauffeur opened the other for Sam. The two men then got in the front and they drove away. Sam watched the jet recede behind them and if their destination had been any other he would have been sad to leave it.

Eyes glued to the window, Sam was immediately drawn into that initial curiosity of visiting a new country, absorbing its culture. Driving out of JFK the landscape was not much different from back home; moving along a winding motorway with small crammed houses and businesses lining the road, the odd graffiti and boarded up building dotted about. It was completely underwhelming; Sam didn't know what his alter ego was expecting but right now he was not impressed, his expanded ego now had bigger expectations.

However, this all began to change as they drove further and further into Brooklyn. Sam's interest in the view shifted. As if from no-where, the buildings had morphed into monsters. Some of them rising up six or seven stories rivalling many of the buildings in central London which tickled Sam's interest slightly, but still failed to match up to his expectations that New York had conjured up in his vivid imagination.

Along with the red stone buildings Sam had also noted the perfectly engineered grid system which had now materialised. The road stretched forwards, a perfect 90 degrees left and the same right, and that was it. Sam found it completely bizarre whilst his mathematical mind loved its geometry.

But not even Sam's cool newfound confidence could prevent his awe as they began the journey across the Brooklyn Bridge. An engineering marvel; two brick walls rising out of the water and up into the sky, suspending the steel cage containing an endless stream of traffic, a spider's web of steel cables stretching up to the brick walls.

And Sam could see it up ahead, Manhattan. A jungle of shimmering glass, sitting on its concrete pedestal. It was bold, it was brash, and Sam's ego fell completely in love with it. This was the place befitting his high minded ambitions.

Manhattan. Sam had never seen anything like it and even if he were to travel the rest of the world he doubted ever finding its match. A grid of perfectly straight roads closed in by magnificent skyscrapers reaching up impossibly high. So high Sam's neck could hardly strain to see the tops. He had lived in London for much of his life and was used to city sights, but this place was on another level. What really captivated Sam was the magnitude of everything; the buildings, the cars, the roads and even the pavements were wider than back home, because they needed to be. Sam had never seen so many people, they moved around the buildings, a seething mass of hectic liquid.

The Rolls turned left onto a road which would have rivalled a motorway back home. Four lanes all heading into the heart of the city.

The traffic seemed endless but moved at a good pace, traffic lights at every intersection made for a smooth transition. Yet still it seemed like chaos as the closed-in atmosphere was filled with the music of beeping horns and people shouting, the sweet sounds of the city. Sam was accustomed to the car horns but was rather shocked when his ears picked up some of the comments from other drivers, windows wound down so their words could reach out to their hapless recipients,

"Come on, asshole."

"Let's move it!"

"You could get a fuckin' bus through there!"

Sam found the irritable phrases spoken in their strong American twang quite comical.

Soon came the stage which made every single person who saw it feel as if they'd fallen into a movie. They entered Times Square, Sam recognising it instantly from the countless movies and pictures it had featured in. The huge space buzzed, people penned into the centre by the surrounding traffic. Strikingly bright billboards surrounded the seething mass, advertising everything from Coke to the latest blockbusters.

"Quite something, isn't it?"

The bemused businessman's comment invaded the silence that had endured since leaving the airport, watching Sam's head as it swivelled erratically, taking in the energetic scene.

"It's unbelievable."

Sam forgot for a moment who he was speaking to, his attention remaining mesmerised on the City, apparently ignoring his superior. But Keaton didn't care, the subtle smile once more flitted across his blank face, openly relishing the sight of Sam becoming more and more hooked on this city of dreams.

"This is it Sam, my world. Soon it will be yours too."

Keaton's black eyes remained fixed on Sam, like a shark targeting his prey. It was clear this was the billionaire's home, this was where he belonged. He was in love with the electric pace, the competition, the ruthless and unforgiving nature of this brutal city that never sleeps.

175

It was a drug. The drug of obsession, obscenity and power. The most addictive of all because it rendered no visible side effects, it just made him rich. It was the drug Keaton wanted to get Sam hooked on and it was already taking effect.

Forty minutes after leaving JFK they reached 459 Broadway 10013. The Rolls had turned off the main artery of the city and stopped on a quaint little one-way street. The two men in the front got out and opened the back doors in unison. Sam exited, scanning his new environment; the skyscraper had been replaced by eight or nine story office buildings packed tightly together. This scene was more down to Earth, like home, but Sam's ego remained aloof. The drug of more, more, more already taking a hold.

He and Carter followed closely behind Keaton as the three men walked along the pavement, the chauffeur returned to his mundane role of waiting in the car.

Sam's eyes were drawn upwards to a black plaque, the words "Keaton & Co" etched in gold letters. They entered.

Up one flight of stairs the space opened up to a wide corridor. Walking briskly past the welcome desk where two women sat typing vigorously and past a string of glass offices they eventually met with imposing double doors situated at the end of the corridor. As they approached, to the right was an open office. A gorgeous young lady looked up at Sam and their eyes met for a moment before she turned back to the computer screen. Sam suspected this was Keaton's PA, Lynn Fox.

As the three men reached the door, Carter moving ahead to open it, Keaton suddenly stopped in his tracks and turned back to address Sam with an air of deadly gravity,

"This is a board meeting, so when we enter this room, you don't say anything. You're here to observe and learn."

"Yes, sir."

Carter flung the doors wide open in a somewhat theatrical gesture and the trio walked into a room almost identical to conference room 1 back in London. The occupants all sat to attention, taking note of the new arrivals.

"Apologies for my tardiness Board, thank you for convening."

The Chair made his apologies as Carter exited, closing the doors behind him. His protégé followed obediently as Keaton took his seat at the Head of the table, observing his mentor's immediate effortless dominance over the room with his overpowering presence.

The seven board members consisted of six elderly men and one woman. All present had been playing the game of business for decades and all now under the rule of a man in his early thirties. Each one of them took turns gazing at Sam, their silent query apparent to Keaton who immediately provided an explanation,

"This is an associate of mine, Mr Lowell."

The mentor gestured towards his new apprentice. It was a vague explanation with no real detail but Sam knew it was safe to assume none of them would dare question the man, and they didn't. Six just looked up at the billionaire now wearing the same gormless faces. However, one man didn't follow suit. Sat at the other end of the table, he consulted the papers laid before him with scrutiny. As if he were preparing to question Keaton. Sam stood at his shoulder as Carter would, taking in every detail. The orchestra was silent, everyone anticipating the conductor's imminent instruction,

"Board, I have gathered you today to enlighten you on my plans for a new hotel in Singapore."

The sea of features remained unfazed, except for that one man sitting opposite Keaton who continued to inform,

"I already have the design and construction plans in place, it's all been arranged. Now, I have a meeting with the bank tomorrow morning whereby I will acquire the necessary funds. Next week, there will be a presentation, after which you will all cast your votes on whether to proceed… or not."

There was a brief silence as everyone took in this bombshell which Sam had no doubt was as unexpected to them as it was to him. Sam's confidence returned at this point and, having noticed a chair close by, he made use of it and prepared to be entertained. The gentleman at the other end of the table gruffly voiced his opinion,

"Mr Keaton. I am, vexed by the sudden and late delivery of your, plans. I'm wondering, why it is you didn't include us, your Board, in these plans of yours sooner?"

The question was valid but Sam was surprised it had been asked, this was the first time he'd witnessed someone with balls large enough to challenge the billionaire. You didn't require a degree in psychology to see these two titans were not kindred spirits. Keaton's expression turned sour as he replied,

"My plans are my own Simon. I built this company myself and do not feel it necessary to consult you, my Board, until my plans are fully formed and ready for application."

Sam totally sided with Keaton,

'Why should he divulge his plans until they are ready to become more concrete.'

But this skirmish wasn't over and following another brief pause, Simon upped the ante,

"Agreed, we are all indebted to you. However, collectively we own forty-nine percent of this business and therefore, have a right to be informed about any developments that are being pursued."

Sam had to admire the old boy's integrity and guts,

Keaton's dead eyes fixed themselves upon their hapless target. The spectators were suspended in bitingly cold tension, witnessing these two men who stood a cut above, on a higher level of power and determination, the level Sam wished to join.

"You have a right to know?"

Keaton slowly repeated the seemingly rhetorical question and the atmosphere of the room fell a few degrees. At this point the Chair directed his gaze around the room surveying every occupant one by one,

"Let's put it to a vote. Every person who believes they have the right to each and every one of my plans raise your hand."

All arms remained firmly planted. Except Simon who raised his defiantly, but it was to no avail, he had lost. Keaton's hold over the rest of the board was clear to Sam. It couldn't have been any more obvious if he'd had them all suspended on strings. The Board saw fit to side with their Chair.

Simon had no choice but to retreat and accede to his CEO's reign.

"As I said, the opportunity will be presented to you all next week."

One more, he flashed a forbidding look around the table. Sam knew, as everyone else did, that this "vote" next week was a foregone conclusion. When Sam really thought about it he didn't understand why anyone would object to his mentor's judgement… He'd given them no reason to, had he?

"Meeting adjourned."

Keaton directed tersely and on cue, the seven seats were vacated and the room emptied, leaving only the apprentice and his mentor.

Sam remained mute, his intelligent mind running through the events that had just transpired, analysing, but he was soon pulled from his thoughts as Keaton turned his chair got up and walked towards one of the many large windows. Gazing down at the street below as his tension drained and his calm cool self returned,

"What did you learn?"

Keaton had the air of a university professor.

Sam's mind raced once more over the events, trying to form an intelligent and concise conclusion,

"You have an authority over people, a presence I've never seen before."

Sam answered honestly. Keaton continued to gaze out at the world,

"Authority is a culmination of respect and fear, Sam. How you dress, how you speak, how you carry yourself. This is what builds your character."

Sam's intellectual mind decrypted the code before he replied with certainty,

"I have to change my character."

Keaton turned from the window to face him,

"You have to become me, Sam. Then, one day you too will command the same authority. And conquer the world."

Keaton gave a wide mirthless grin at the prospect of his creation, which Sam duplicated. They could have almost passed for twins if not for Sam's cheap suit.

"Are you ready to become a businessman?"

The mentor was instantly rewarded,

"I was made for this, sir."

Keaton patted him firmly on the shoulder before moving towards the door. Sam watched, frozen with respect for this creature who indicated it was time for action,

"Let's get started."

The two men exited the room, picking up Carter as they walked back down the corridor.

Keaton suddenly stopped and spoke,

"Ah, before we head out, this is you."

He turned towards the door to his right. A door to one of the glass offices, Sam's eyes happened upon the label, deciphering the gold lettering that read,

S. Lowell
Business assistant

Sam grinned his approval,

'My own office. Yessss!'

This was a small detail – his name on the door – but it was a physical confirmation, solidifying his new reality.

Keaton and Carter quickly moved on. Sam lingered momentarily, savouring this moment of personal triumph, his growing ego further inflating.

Chapter 17

New Suit, New Man

"717, Fifth Avenue."

Keaton directed as the three men settled back into the Rolls, the driver nodded and they moved away slowly.

"What's at Fifth Avenue?"

Sam inquired, becoming ever more comfortable around the tycoon as their relationship developed. He not only saw the billionaire as his mentor but also his confidant, his friend, not in the regular sense of the word of course but Sam liked to think he was the closest thing Keaton had to friendship.

Still, he would have to hold the suspense as he received a cryptic answer,

"Everything."

The regular silence was back but Sam didn't mind. He was becoming accustomed, it no longer inspired tension or fear within him. The confidence that Keaton had brought forth from the darkness was now a constant presence as the alter ego held centre stage with absolute authority.

Anyway, he was perfectly happy to gaze outwards, feeling a surge of adrenaline as the bold, brash, rush of the city returned; the rising skyscrapers and the seething mass of humanity and cars.

As the car turned onto Fifth Avenue Sam understood that when Keaton had said "Everything," he meant it. His head pivoted right and left to see the unmistakable brands, Chanel, Gucci, Givenchy, Bulgari, Rolex. Every designer brand you could conceive lined this amazing stretch of road where you

181

could buy anything from a £25,000 timepiece to a £200,000 sports car, assuming you had the money of course. Sam tried to imagine what it would be like to come to such a place in the knowledge you could have it all. As he looked upon the very world he craved, his determination was electrified into overdrive.

The Rolls pulled up outside a large black frontage,

"Wait here. Come on Sam."

Keaton simultaneously directed at the Chauffeur, Carter and Sam before he went for the door. Sam immediately followed, forgetting he was walking out onto a main road. A yellow taxi honked aggressively, the driver yelling,

"Watch where you're walking, ASSWIPE!"

But Sam's attention was elsewhere, fixed on the building before him. He paced swiftly round the car to walk beside Keaton. The building was guarded by two large men dressed up in black tie and matching sunglasses, reminding Sam of 'Men in Black'. They both glared at the approaching men but Sam wasn't fazed in the slightest. That insecure and anxious young man was now someone to be reckoned with. He simply stared straight back.

As soon as they set foot in the cool, air conditioned building, Keaton was greeted by a small and immaculately dressed man who was clearly attired head to toe in "Dolce & Gabbana".

"Good afternoon, Mr Keaton, how lovely to see you again."

Even Sam's vivid imagination could not have conjured up a more typical salesman.

"Afternoon, George."

Keaton replied, the mask remained in place.

"What can I help you with today?"

George replied expectantly, sparkling eyes darting towards Sam.

"My associate here, Mr Lowell, is in desperate need of some new business suits."

It finally clicked, the suspense was lifted. Another of Sam's wishes was about to be granted, the prospect of a properly tailored suit.

"Ah, Mr Lowell, sir, anyone associated with Mr Keaton is a firm friend of mine. Did you have any particular style in mind?"

Sam's expression remained blank, his cynical persona now in the driving seat,

'No doubt he's imagining all the commission he's about to get!'

Keaton quickly intervened,

"Some three-piece business suits, charcoal wool I think would be a good place to start."

"Very good, sir,"

George began, clasping his small, well pampered, hands together energetically. This was a man who truly loved his job.

"If you'd like to follow me."

He continued, leading them to the back of the store. The tailor pulled a thick black curtain gracefully across to reveal a private room and stepped aside, inviting the two men to enter before drawing it closed.

It was relatively cosy yet spacious with a mirrored wall sitting opposite a long cream leather sofa which lounged upon a sumptuous sea of royal purple carpet. The smell of fresh material wafted upon the air.

"Please gentlemen, make yourselves at home, I'll just go and fetch some samples, is there anything I can get you?"

George asked, as Sam followed his lead and sat.

"Two expressos, extra shot, thanks, George."

Keaton instructed casually.

Sam's gaze shot to Keaton in perplexity.

'Did he just order coffees in a clothes store?'

George appeared unphased,

"Of course, sir."

Sam sat in silence, more used to bargain basement service.

183

Keaton sensed his protégé's discomfort and pivoted on the soft leather to face his apprentice,

"Sam, you're an intelligent man, after all you've seen you must understand how the world works by now. In this ruthless world we live in there is but one king. And if you have it, you have everything."

'Ah yes. Cold hard cash! Cruel and unjust but so is the world.'

Sam dipped his chin in acknowledgement, the point having been driven home.

The next fifty minutes spent in that cosy little room were amongst the best of Sam's life up to that point, as he perused materials and styles, fashioning his own personal suits from scratch. He had never enjoyed shopping before, like most men, but this was something else. This was recreating your own image!

He stood in the centre of the room drinking excellent coffee whilst a tailor measured every inch of him to ensure everything fit with comfortable ease, with George offering obsequious guidance and advice.

Sam had a new wardrobe; five new beautiful charcoal suits accompanied by five crystal white shirts, three pairs of leather shoes, two belts, silk ties in a variety of designs and matching handkerchiefs.

It would be by far the most Sam had ever bought and he was so completely caught up in this new world he'd completely forgotten about the one thing you needed to be a fully paid up member – cash.

Keaton called Carter who arrived promptly to pick up the elite bags, the remainder of the order to be follow. Sam meandered back into the public store, privately fretting,

'How are you going to pay for all this?'

George meanwhile lurking about like a vulture, waiting for payment. Keaton's words immediately put Sam at ease as the two men walked towards the door, directed casually towards the diminutive shopkeeper,

"Charge it to my account, George."

Sam wasn't sure how much had been charged – no price-tags, of course,

'If you have to ask you can't afford it.'

Hazarding an educated guess, it would be in excess of his yearly food bill. He felt very uncomfortable that Keaton had picked up the bill and as he followed Keaton out of the building pride spoke up,

"Sir, I…"

He paused, waiting for the man to turn and address him,

"I didn't expect you to be picking up the bill, if I'd known…"

The mogul sharply interrupted,

"Who else? You've yet to receive your first salary!"

Before returning his attention to the car, whereupon Carter opened the door and he jumped in.

The man was right, of course. Sam had begun his life in this world of everything but had not earned it yet – he was only living here because of his mentor's charity. He began to believe there was another side to Keaton, the evidence backing up his personal theory,

'Look at how far he's brought you and all because he believes in you!

Keaton is the one who gave you a chance

Keaton is the one who rescued you from that pitiful life

Keaton is the one who set the beast free and gave you confidence

Keaton is the one who's turning your dreams into reality

Keaton is the man who's allowed you to become the man you were always meant to be!'

Sam's fealty was now absolutely unconditional and he gratefully got into the car.

Chapter 18

Reality of Ambition

The Rolls arrived back at "Keaton & Co." The mentor said he wanted to talk to Sam so they made their way up to his office.

"Have a seat."

There was a moment's silence, Sam waited patiently,

"Sam, I didn't just bring you to New York for a makeover. The Singapore project that's going to be presented to the board next week, I want you to present it."

Sam had suspected this trip wasn't going to be just about shadowing his mentor. He was here to work too and if Keaton uttered those words yesterday it would have probably given him a heart attack. But that was the old, weak Sam.

This newly reinvented creature was ready and raring to get started on whatever was thrown at him, he relished the opportunity to finally prove himself to the man who'd shown so much faith. It was time to show he was a businessman destined for success and he replied firmly,

"Yes, Sir. I won't give you cause for regret."

"I know you won't."

Keaton replied with surety, his inscrutable countenance revealed a micro smile before returning to default status and continuing,

"Miss Fox will bring you all the files."

The impeccable timepiece was consulted as he rose energetically to his feet, Sam following.

"Walk with me, I have a meeting in Atlanta."

Keaton instructed, patting his apprentice on the shoulder, Sam followed him into the corridor where Carter joined them. Reaching the elevator, Carter pressed the last button simply labelled "R." Keaton continued the conversation,

"This pitch next week is not for the board, I have them in my pocket. It's for you Sam, your chance to prove to me you can play the game. In a world of sharks, you have to be one too, or get ripped apart."

"I understand; I'll show you that you made the right decision hiring me."

The tycoon merely nodded.

Exiting the elevator at last, a surprised Sam found himself standing on top of the building where before him stood a white helicopter perched upon a green pad. Its razor sharp blades slicing effortlessly through the air. Keaton and Carter continued towards it, leaving Sam with the distinct impression that Keaton's presence was becoming more and more pivotal in sustaining his powerful new persona. As the chopper flew up and away across the New York skyline, Sam felt slightly bereft. An addict whose drug had been suddenly snatched from him. The despondence soon subsided as he realised he had a job to do,

'Come on man, you have been assigned an important task, you can't let Keaton down!

Sam entered his office for the first time, closing the door firmly behind him, glad of a brief respite. Sauntering around, he savoured every moment, admiring all the details of HIS space. Upon a glass desk was a large Apple display screen, three black notebooks of different sizes and a selection of fountain pens.

He moved to the leather office chair and let his weight go. Swivelling playfully around for a 360 degree look at his large room, he happened upon the glass screen behind him showcasing the view of the street below. He looked across at the building opposite and the countless windows, each telling its own modest story. Sam's peeping was interrupted by a knock at the door.

"Come in."

He answered instinctively.

The door opened wide and in came the beautiful Miss Fox. A smile dressed her face, deep blue eyes penetrating as she sashayed towards him. Sam felt a rush of instant attraction quickly followed by guilty contrition.

"Afternoon Mr Lowell, I'm Miss Fox. Mr Keaton asked me to bring you these files on the Singapore project. I've also got your room card as Mr Keaton has you staying at our hotel. I've written the address down for you."

The distinctive soft twang was more adorable now he set eyes on the whole package.

Sam had been so focused on her he'd failed to notice the dauntingly large wad of papers she held to her chest.

He adroitly sprung into manly action,

"Here, let me grab those."

Sam had to get up close and personal as he grappled the burden from the delightful secretary, eyes popping as her voluptuous breasts were revealed. Sam couldn't help but sneak a peek at the black lacy bra.

Immediately sensing he had overstepped social boundaries, Sam's eyes quickly darted back to hers as he registered her stare. Both were aware of his cheek but she simply smiled. Sam broke the awkward tension by turning to place the papers on the desk, the solid weight already causing his arms to ache. He turned back hoping words would find him, but they didn't. His focus remained fixed on her attributes and for a split second the thought of bending her over his desk touched his consciousness.

Lynne intervened politely,

"Is there anything else I can do for you, Mr Lowell?"

This unfortunate question added fuel to the fire as a boyhood fantasy of the manager and his secretary sprang to mind. Thankfully, Mr Sensible now stepped in,

'Yeah, as if!'

After another moment's tense silence Sam managed a reply and a sheepish smile,

"No thank you, I, I best get started."

Sam glanced at the daunting pile once more, spotting the black key-card resting on top.

"Well I'm just outside if you change your mind."

Sam's body couldn't deny he had an instant crush and he watched her retreat, admiring her long sun-kissed legs, elegantly enhanced by sexy high heels. However, there were papers to read and he now turned his attention wistfully in their direction, spending the next few hours reading through extensively detailed plans for the new Singapore build, determined to read the whole thing before retiring. Thanks to years of practice, studying complex text books on mathematics and medicine Sam read rapidly but even with these well-honed skills it was dark by the time he'd finished the mountain outlining everything including figures and marketing strategies.

As the last couple of pages finally approached his eyes were fighting to close, stinging and exhausted. The ocean of small printed words were beginning to move and rearrange themselves in a dyslexic dance.

Finally, the marathon session was over and Sam fell back into the comfort of his chair. Consulting his battered Casio which read 9:43, he reflected it had been the longest, most tiring day of his entire life. He had crossed an ocean, created a new wardrobe and read a novel on business in Singapore.

Sam rubbed the back of his neck, gently massaging it in an attempt to relieve the painful crick developed courtesy of the hours hunched over his desk. That was it, he needed to find this hotel and get some sleep if he was to be of any use tomorrow. He grasped the piece of paper that Lynn had jotted the address down on, along with the glossy key-card, making his way sluggishly out of the office and along the corridor. The place seemed deserted, all the lights were off and silence prevailed. Sam imagined he was the last one there, save security and he pictured Keaton leaving under the same circumstances every night, suspecting the entrepreneur was always the last to leave. Only a workaholic could have built such a company by 33.

As Sam walked out into the refreshing night air he suddenly realised he was alone, with no dollars, in an alien city.

'Why didn't you bring some dollars with you, Prat?'

His nervous side dredged up some panic but this was quickly stamped out,

'Stay calm! You have the address and this city works on a grid system.'

Normal service resumed as he recalled the city's mathematical system which was manna to his mind.

Sam concluded it would be wise to retrace his steps back to the main road that ran like an artery up the centre of Manhattan, locating the address from there should be relatively straight forward.

After ten minutes of retracing, his fantastic memory returned and he found the main road, sign-posted "7th Avenue." It was even more striking in the darkness than in daylight. Sam was suddenly glad he'd walked as such a sight should not be missed.

He sauntered along the great canyon; the endless line of traffic lights constantly flickering from green to amber to red and back again, the animated bill boards and illuminated shop signs all adding to the rainbow of colours. Sam gazed up into the black sky where countless windows reflected in the darkness, disembodied entities which appeared to be floating.

The streets were still bustling with people and cars, filling the canyon with consistent noise, the blood of the city still flowing; it never stopped or even slowed down. This city truly never slept and it revitalised Sam, firing up his adrenaline and pumping newfound energy into his system.

This was New York's signature trick, its hectic chaos so switched on all of the time it radiated vast amounts of energy. It reminded the Londoner of the tube back home, absorbing and radiating the negative energy of its commuters, the city seemed to be what Sam had always imagined it to be – the city of his dreams.

Another thirty minutes of sauntering passed by when he reached the right street and turning off, Sam reluctantly left that magical street behind, the hotel being only two hundred meters down the less inspiring street.

The hotel presented much the same as The Keaton back in London although this building was far wider and taller. Sam estimated at least thirty floors but couldn't be bothered to count them as the adrenaline of 7th Avenue had ebbed and exhaustion had once more settled in. Strolling into and towards the elevators Sam's eyes were drawn towards the left of the front desk. The scenery was luxuriously magnificent but Sam was far too focused on getting into his soft warm bed to pay it the attention it deserved. He checked in and was relieved to find all had been meticulously pre-arranged by Keaton's efficient assistant.

Matching the colour coded floors with the purple bar on his key-card he made his was up to the thirtieth. Dragging his feet along the carpet Sam was now half asleep, moving towards his room with the slow pace of a zombie. He slid the glossy card into the lock and scanned the large, dark space. He stumbled about and eventually located the bed in the third room. Expensive mattress broke his fall as he crashed out upon soft linen, immediately diving into a sleep so deep a hurricane would have had a hard job disturbing him.

Chapter 19

Power of Money

"Knock... knock... knock."

The sound was weak but ignited Sam's consciousness into feeble life,

"Knock, knock, knock."

The second time was louder and more rapid, penetrating his mind with clarity. Someone was at the door.

Sam's mind changed up a gear and remembered where it was. His eyes shot open, rapidly retreating to a squint as the bright early morning light hit his retinas. He crawled across the linen towards the edge of the enormous bed, feet just catching him as he slid abruptly off the edge.

"KNOCK, KNOCK, KNOCK."

The persistent knocking now carried a hint of impatience. Moving out of the room towards the door Sam felt himself to make sure he was decent, realising he was still dressed in his chain store suit from yesterday. But that was irrelevant, it could have been Keaton at the door and Sam wasn't going to keep him waiting any longer.

He opened the door to reveal a bemused Carter taking up his usual military stance, sardonic smirk barely concealed as he relayed instructions,

"Morning, Mr Lowell. Mr Keaton wishes that you join him in his office at eight."

Sam stood up straight appearing as professional as he could, both men trying to ignore his sleeping attire.

"Thank you, Carter."

Upon Sam's polite response, the man strode back briskly down the corridor and Sam's inner bitch couldn't resist a sarcastic remark,

'No doubt rushing to get back to his master in case a door needs opening or something.'

He closed the door, glad his mentor had sent this human alarm clock. He may have slept through the entire day he had been so comatose. Sam consulted the battered Casio hoping eight O'clock was not imminent, relieved to see it was only seven thirty. Plenty of time!

After a rushed but revitalising waterfall shower, a refreshed Sam was suddenly consumed by the horror of a child who had got undressed only to realise they'd forgotten their gym kit.

'Shit… where are my clothes? And where is my luggage!'

He realised the last time he'd seen his duffle and shoulder bag was yesterday when they got off the plane. Frantically searching the suite, horror was replaced with relief as there in the corner of the sitting room sat one duffle bag, one leather bag and several labelled "Dolce & Gabbana."

'Phew, the new suits are here!'

Carter must have brought his baggage over yesterday afternoon.

'The man is like a ninja valet, dispatching all the boring and mundane chores so well you completely forgot about them. But that doesn't explain how my new suits got here so quickly. How did that happen?'

Sam was impressed.

Quickly remembering he was now in the city that never sleeps,

'The tailors must've worked through the night!'

In his new world of luxury it appeared there was no carrying luggage, no checking into hotels or waiting at the airports; everything you needed was instantly taken care of. He didn't have to consider anything but business.

Sam unpacked his new wardrobe and dressed with meticulous care before walking over to the walled mirror in the hallway. He smiled widely as for the first time his appearance reflected the new man within, clean cut, professional and confident, his new improved persona was complete.

Sam strode out of the elevator and down the corridor with purposeful energy. He gave three firm knocks on Keaton's door, waiting for the response,

"Yes."

The door swung wide and he burst through. Keaton looked up from his desk to discover the character he'd created.

The billionaire offered a rare spontaneous smile prior to speaking,

"You look the part. How do you feel?"

He asked, knowing full well the answer as it was printed across Sam's smug face.

"Fantastic."

The calm, emotionless reply replicated that of his mentor's,

"Surprising the difference a proper uniform can make. Have a seat."

Keaton instructed and the two men sat in opposite symmetry, both protagonists gazing at reproductions of themselves.

"Any minute now a Mr Prior, our new bank manager, is going to walk through that door and we have to persuade him to lend us twenty-eight million dollars."

Keaton explained casually, but with a hint of arrogance, as though the billionaire expected the bank to just lend him the money at the click of his fingers.

"Sounds like a hard sell."

Sam replied in the same blasé tone. The two were actually discussing $28,000,000 as if it were petty cash.

"The previous manager was a longtime acquaintance but he's retired so now we have to deal with this new fucker."

The hostile emotion in Keaton's voice increased and Sam was surprised at the expletive. He was just about to add his own comments but before he could formulate any,

"Knock, knock, knock."

"Yes."

Keaton bellowed, clearly emotion was now getting the better of this enigmatic character.

The door opened slightly and Lynn's face popped through the gap,

"Mr Keaton, Mr Prior is here."

"Show him in then."

The billionaire stood up and buttoned his jacket. The apprentice mirrored, pivoting in line with Keaton as he moved round the table and stood marginally ahead of Sam in order to confront their guest first.

The door opened and an overweight man with thick black frames and carrying a hefty briefcase walked in.

"Hi! I'm Mr Prior, manager of BNY Mellon."

Now, this hulk was loud and brash and had entered the vicinity with an arrogant overconfidence, his body language demonstrating zero respect for the ego he was addressing.

"Mr Prior, pleasure,"

Keaton fabricated cool politeness and continued,

"This is my associate Mr Lowell."

He gestured towards Sam who stood fast,

"Hi."

Prior said in the most disappointingly casual tone, dismissing Sam before shuffling past him towards the desk where he now sat. The mentor & apprentice shared a glance. Sam took his seat beside the fat man but continued to observe the CEO as his black eyes burned into the insolent banker, but the warning swiftly disappeared as Prior turned to him and spoke,

"So, I have looked over the details of your company's request for funds. And there are a number of concerns."

His delivery was patronising and Sam felt the room temperature drop a few degrees.

The billionaire placed his elbows on the desk and linking his fingers, brought his hands to his mouth with a calculatedly calm exterior. He disdainfully looked down his nose at Prior, speaking in a disturbingly slow and deep tone.

"You have concerns…"

Sam felt a freezing tension descend, and was reminded of the Board's meeting.

"Yes, after all twenty million is a large amount of money, Mr Keaton and I have to make sure all investments are solid."

Prior had not picked up on his client's negative body language. Hints that Sam, the fast study, was becoming accustomed to.

Keaton's reply was immediate and biting,

"Not nearly as much money as I have personally invested in the bank which you work for, Mr Prior."

"What exactly are you saying?" The room temperature plummeted still further.

Still the naive young Prior pushed his luck, Keaton's response searing the atmosphere like a guided missile,

"Seeing as you clearly need it spelling out, I will do so,"

The powerful billionaire rose from his chair and leant forwards in an intimidating manner,

"I hold hundreds of millions in the bank that you merely work for. You are an employee, Mr Prior, disposable and there are hundreds more like you! Now on what side do you believe your employer's loyalties lie?"

There was a long pause as the conceit was stripped away, swiftly replaced with humility as the banker abruptly came to terms with the realities of life.

"If you do not proceed swiftly with this deal, I will be contacting your superior to inform him of how you seem to lack any ounce of professionalism, and that I'll be taking my money to another bank!"

Keaton's gaze held that of his quarry, awaiting a response.

"I did not mean to offend you Mr Keaton, I apologise,"

The fat man's voice finally found itself and croaked out a reply as he bowed his head in embarrassment. His career hung in the balance and he waited for the fat lady to sing.

Keaton held for a moment with sadistic intent before finally putting the poor man out of his misery,

"I expect the deal agreed by the end of the week. Now get out of my building."

Prior rose quickly and waddled towards the door, tail firmly between his legs as he made his hasty exit.

"That's sorted."

Keaton spoke casually, the calm exterior having returned in the blink of an eye. It was almost robotic the way those emotions only surfaced when absolutely necessary. All actions had a purpose, even his emotions, and the rationale was always the same. Business.

Chapter 20

Night out in New York

Following the intense meeting, Sam had returned to his office where he spent the rest of the day getting on with his job. Dissecting the dense text of that mountain of paper into manageable bullet points he could use in the presentation. Every fact, every detail had to be checked, double checked and learned. There would be no chances taken on this, no stone unturned. Sam was determined to enter that room with a fully functioning, loaded gun that would protect him from any questions.

Once again Sam had forgotten about his basic bodily needs as he ploughed through the work and the day. He would have gone without so much as a drink if not for the lovely secretary checking in on him every couple of hours. This behaviour was not normal and his driven mind was aware that pushing this hard could not be healthy. But he was not a part of the normal world anymore, this was a different place with different rules and he accepted the consequences,

'In order to gain everything, I must first donate everything. That is the price of absolute success.'

Sam was distracted from the reams before him by three rapid knocks at the door and before he could gather his scrambled thoughts to answer, it opened, and Keaton entered, walking in a couple of steps before asking,

"You ever been to a steakhouse?"

Sam's stomach lurched violently at the mention of food, realising it had not been fed all day due to his brain's dedication to his new role.

"No, I can't say as I have."

As always, Keaton's presence invigorated Sam.

"Come on, let's eat!"

The billionaire turned back towards the door and out of it. Sam dropped what he was doing and loped after his mentor,

'I'm like a dog chasing a bone. A very rich and powerful bone!'

The Rolls awaited them and the two men entered the car in sync.

As they pulled away Carter spoke from the driver's seat as blunt and instructive as always,

"Jet landed ten minutes ago, Mr Keaton."

The wristwatch was consulted before the reply was given,

"Good."

And diplomatic silence resumed. Sam soon disrupted it with his newfound bold confidence,

"This isn't a social dinner, is it?"

The question was spoken more as a statement as Sam was sure he knew the answer. If he knew Keaton as well as he believed he did, there was no such thing as sociality in his world. It was all business and he soon got the answer he expected,

"Of course not."

The two men shared a glance and Keaton smirked,

"I flew out some of my new connections from Singapore, were going to show them a night out in New York."

Sam hazarded a guess,

"Local investors?"

"No. The success of our new hotel requires more than just money. Singapore is a rich economy but it's also crowded, so we need influential connections. It's all about marketing. "

Sam caught on,

"So journalists?"

"Precisely. Eight of them spanning across all media, newspapers, magazines and even a young 'You Tuber'. Each one of them holding the potential to reach out to thousands of customers. So it's our job to make sure they have the time of their lives in New York, no matter what the expense."

Keaton shot Sam a look that demanded acceptance of the situation with the unspoken implication that anything could happen. Naturally, the apprentice responded appropriately,

"I understand."

Essentially, it was sugar-coated bribery. They would throw the best New York had to offer at these influential people with the objective of snagging a five-star review.

It was wrong – immoral even – this game, but Sam had committed himself and his principles would have to be put aside. This realisation was dawning that Sam's idol was prepared to twist the rules to suit his own needs. Keaton's proclamation spoken out loud in Dolce & Gabbana reverberated,

'In this ruthless world we live in there is but one king. And if you have it, you have everything.'

Whilst Sam's own moral sanctity was disturbed by the blatant lack of ethics, he understood that the world isn't fair,

'It isn't just, it's a dangerous and turbulent ocean and to reach the pinnacle of success, you have to become a shark.'

Sam was now at the top of the food chain and intended to play the part no matter the costs as his dream was hurtling towards his reality.

Carter drove another couple of miles before pulling over on Park Avenue. The three men entered a quaint little frontage of dark wood and glass with the words, "Wolfgang's steakhouse" printed in modern font upon the deep cloth canopy.

They walked into a room unlike any Sam had ever seen before. The floor was dark and well-worn wood, square pillars in symmetrical formation rose up to the low ceiling which was made up of small cream and black tails generating contrasting patterns and creating perfectly formed domes. All was bathed in warm yellow light streaming from the Victorian styled lights suspended from the centre of each dome. It was cosy and old fashioned, yet its pristine upkeep gave the illusion it was built only yesterday.

Sam's other senses were enticed as the sweet smell of barbecued stake filled the air with such thick potency he was sure he could taste it. His mouth watered and his stomach rumbled as he imagined the juicy melting meat. Sam was cultured enough to know no one did red meat better than America, except maybe Argentina.

A waiter showed them to a large reserved table in the centre of the space and it wasn't long before their guests arrived. Everything timed, as usual, to near perfection and Sam was reminded of another pithy expression,

'*Time is money and cash is king*!'

Sam silently watched as all the formal introductions were made with methodical and efficient accuracy, standing at his mentor's side, waiting to be introduced whilst Keaton worked the room and – with the appearance of selflessness – enquired solicitously about their journey. No doubt to remind them he'd flown them out on his private jet – such generosity. But this would be no free supper, everything had a price.

As all took their seats at the round table, only Keaton remained standing and as the group settled he announced,

"Welcome everyone, to New York. I hope you all have a very pleasant stay, as we intend to show you all this great city of ours has to offer, but we do promise to send you all back in one piece,"

At which statement, there was a collective comradely chuckle. Sam marvelled at the man's brand of instant charisma, the effortless speech which flowed out of him with grace and elegance in that deep voice. He had everyone at that table spellbound. The billionaire always seemed to know exactly what to say to draw people to him, as if his whole life were a rehearsed act.

He continued,

"I look forward to talking to each and every one of you during this fine evening and am sure we will all part firm friends. Welcome to the party, gentlemen!"

There was enthusiastic applause from everyone, besides Carter, who maintained his professional vigil in the background.

What was so genius about Keaton's opening speech was how he enticed and intrigued them with the promise of a spectacular evening. The party were already on the hook, all that was left to do was reel them in.

He orchestrated the conversation immediately with one question so fantastic in its simplicity,

"So, who's got the most readers?"

A web of competitive, light hearted banter burst into life and Sam observed how this genius used vague yet calculated questions to stir the pot whilst maintaining optimum temperature. And this cunning spider did it with such aplomb that he alone directed operations from his command centre. The apprentice appreciatively watched and learned.

For a while Sam latched onto the main flow of words, constantly absorbing information as he studied his superior and how he controlled the flow using questions. Then Sam branched out on his own and began sub conversations with those closest to him, mimicking the mogul's techniques to good effect.

The meal forged a sea of conversation and newfound friendships, or at least that's how the guests saw it. But Sam knew these foreigners were no more Keaton's friends than that insufferable little bank manager. They were just useful tools; puppets providing opportunity and the billionaire intended to play them like a fiddle until they served their purpose, whilst he moved onto his next mission.

A couple of hours had passed and everyone at the table was full of champagne and red meat. Except Keaton, who Sam noticed had not touched a drop of alcohol all evening, sticking surreptitiously to his healthy black tea.

"Everybody having a good time?"

The host asked, getting to his feet to address the room. A slurred and positive chant came in unison from his guests.

Now, gentlemen, it's time to show you how we do a night out in New York City!"

Keaton raised the glass of champagne he'd poured just to make the toast. Sam was in awe at how his employer had turned a group of professional strangers into his groupies in a few hours, with nothing more than conversation and mild intoxication. It was staggering and Sam's admiration blinded him from how terrifying the notion was. He, like the guests from Singapore was hooked on the drug that is Alexander Keaton, who now placed the glass of champagne back down on the table without having touched a drop.

The rest of the night was a sea of obscene spending in the top bars and clubs down town Manhattan had to offer. As the group migrated from bar to club and club back to bar again Sam noticed a pattern emerge from the chaos.

Every so often, Keaton would split off from the main group taking one of the guests with him. The billionaire would find a quiet corner and talk privately, at the bar or outside. Sam could never tell what was being said, far too intoxicated by this point to do any more than notice vague anomalies. Keaton would talk and talk with passionate gestures whilst the receiver just sat and nodded continuously, left full of positive energy.

Then, Carter would be called over and pull out a sheaf of papers from the briefcase he always carried. Keaton repeated this process with each and every one of his guests, one by one as the night drew out until all of them had apparently signed and agreed in ink whatever was written on those pages. Sam imagined those poor intoxicated fools had as little idea about what they had just done as he did.

From then on the night was a complete blur of colour and sound.

"Knock. Knock. Knock."

Sam's stiff eyes slowly parted, stinging at the bright light the blurred room slowly came into focus. His consciousness delivered an immediate and throbbing headache and he rolled out of the ray of light. Gingerly, his aching muscles raised him up against the headboard.

"Knock, knock, knock."

He'd passed out in his clothes again, for the second night running and in that moment of early morning clarity he hoped for a day that didn't leave him completely spent, a day of work he could come back from and have an ounce of energy left for some TV, or maybe even just to read a couple of pages of a book.

Sam glanced over at the Casio still clinging to his wrist, it read "7:30." The last time he could consciously recall was 3.45am as they ascended in the lift. Therefore, he calculated the earliest time he had arrived in the pit was 4:00am and possibly much later.

'Crap!'

"KNOCK, KNOCK, KNOCK."

As Sam got to his reluctant feet and sauntered over to the door his old self teetered on the brink of his lucidity and attempted an escape from his exhausted ego,

'I'm not sure I can do this'

This doubt was summarily dismissed by his alter ego who was determined to beat his former self into submission. He opened the door to see his expected visitor,

"Morning, Mr Lowell. Mr Keaton asked for you to join him downstairs out on the veranda."

"Thank you Carter, I'll be right down."

Sam felt a sudden wash of shame at having wished for easier days, his thoughts turning to his mentor who was already up and ready to face the day, having experienced the same night as his apprentice,

'Minus the booze, Prat!'

But still the man was up and must have been for a while as he'd travelled to the hotel from wherever he lived to fetch his apprentice. Sam was convinced the man wasn't staying here as they had not come back together, he was sure of that. He presumed the billionaire had some incredible apartment in one of the many skyscrapers,

'That's where billionaires live, at the top of the world.'

Now that Sam really thought about it, Keaton was extremely gracious to go out of his way to come and effectively be his alarm clock, knowing full well his new apprentice would require a strong kick up the behind at first. This man truly was a great mentor.

Sam darted out of the elevator and up to the front desk where he addressed one of the very approachable young ladies,

"Excuse me, where is the veranda?"

"Just through there, sir."

She replied with a ready smile, her right arm pointing towards the back of the hotel. Sam smiled back and darted away again, he'd already kept his mentor waiting seven minutes, which was a record time to get up but still seven minutes and time is money!

Sam reached the back of the hotel and a glass frontage hidden behind thick black curtains that closed in, leaving only a doorway's width of light. He walked through it and out into the fresh morning breeze to find a tranquil open veranda with a beautiful old iron banister running along the edge. A riot of beautiful blooms dangled gracefully from hanging baskets.

The apprentice scanned up and down the long stretch – where guests sat eating breakfast – in search of his mentor. As he scanned more and more frantically, a dread crept at the edges of his thoughts at the unlikely notion that the temperamental billionaire may have left. Relief struck when his weary eyes finally spotted the man's meticulously unmistakable hair – Carter standing by like a hawk – at the far reaches of the space, peaking out over a large newspaper. Sam's confidence was restored as he approached.

Sam was about to introduce himself but as he prepared his verbal announcement Keaton beat him to it, drily announcing,

"Sleeping beauty's with us."

The words, whilst conveying a joke were simultaneously delivered in his signature emotionless voice.

"Sorry, last night hit me hard."

The sheepish explanation delivered with professional sincerity.

Keaton lowered "The Wall Street Journal" which he folded twice before placing it on the linen beside his half-finished French breakfast, the sight and smell of which left Sam nauseated.

The man gestured towards the chair opposite and his apprentice quickly obliged.

Sam felt improperly dressed in his three-piece business attire. The billionaire wore a contrasting cream summer suit finished with a grey silk shirt and matching handkerchief. A pair of tortoise shell sunglasses resting on his manly nose.

"I can forgive you after last night's performance. They all spoke very highly of you."

Keaton explained and though once again the words seemed on the surface to be a joke Sam got the distinct impression that if he hadn't delivered last night such tardiness this morning would have resulted in a coach class ticket back to London.

The apprentice cunningly changed the subject with a question,

"Where are they now?"

"Should be getting back on a plane about now."

Sam felt a gust of shame at the thought he'd been the only one to sleep in. He realised in that moment he was still the inexperienced rookie in a world of pros. His determination would have to step up to the plate.

This thought swiftly passed, replaced by a tantalising question he recalled from the only real memory he had of last night,

"We got what we were after, I presume. They all signed?"

Keaton's attention was grasped,

"You noticed, I wondered if you would. Another key aspect of business, Sam, observation,"

Sam suddenly felt as if the whole night had been a game devised by his mentor as another test. But he didn't care, the important thing was he'd passed and his ego glowed.

The conversation continued,

"Yes, they all signed."

"What did they sign?"

Sam asked with intrigue, longing to be let in on whatever the tycoon had planned. He wanted to be more than an apprentice to this man he respected and was now prepared to follow with religious devotion. He wanted to be the man's equal,

Keaton paused for a moment, the black eyes conveying their shark-like stare as he judged how much to divulge before answering,

"Contractual agreements for prime reviews in respect of our new hotel."

The explanation was vague and Sam knew the man wasn't telling him everything but he was just glad to have some detail. It was enough to satisfy him and his mind adroitly contemplated the disingenuous intelligence of the whole plan,

'Plenty of lessons to be learned.'

And Sam intended to absorb them all.

Before the apprentice could collect his thoughts and reply, the CEO continued as he consulted his wristwatch,

"I have to fly out to LA for a couple of days. I'll leave you in the capable hands of Miss Fox, make sure that presentation is ready and polished by Friday."

The man got to his feet and Sam followed,

"Counting on you!"

He finished, patting Sam firmly on the shoulder as he passed and disappeared back through the curtains, Carter following closely behind. Leaving him alone with nothing to do but work.

Chapter 21

Acid Test

Friday. The big day Sam felt he had been waiting for his entire life had finally arrived. The chance, the opportunity to prove that this world of fortune and luxury was in fact where he belonged, not just to his mentor but to himself as well. He had dived head first into the ocean and survived, now came the tricky part of staying afloat.

The last two days had been a mountainous struggle of work the likes of which he had never experienced in all his years of studying. Throughout the days, and much of the nights, he'd polished and perfected his pitch plugging all loopholes and doubts. Breaking only for the absolute need of bodily sustenance and last night when Seren had called to check in, but the conversation had been extremely brief. She could hear the distraction in his voice, almost as if Sam wasn't present; his subconscious's natural reaction to her questions providing stunted answers, just going through the motions whilst his consciousness remained fully focused on his arduous task.

Sam still held onto the belief this was all really for Seren, so she could quit that hateful job, so she could have everything she wanted from life. So that he could become the man she deserved, but of course, that's not what Seren saw. She was beginning to see her father.

He had poured his heart and soul into this presentation. His determination, his pride and even his inflated ego rested on today's outcome of the simple decision of the board who would vote for, or against.

Sam arrived at Keaton & Co suited and prepared at 9:50, having managed to get plenty of practice runs in beforehand. So many in fact, he'd lost count, it had all become a blur of automatic words.

Making his way down the corridor, the precious laptop that contained the accompanying slide show held tightly between his hands, he reached Keaton's office. But the door was left open and the room was empty.

"Mr Lowell!"

The distinctive twang sounded from behind.

Sam turned 180 degrees to see the familiarly welcome sight of Miss Fox, sat at her desk bearing that heartwarming smile.

"Miss Fox, I was supposed to be meeting the board at ten, I'm sure."

Sam's bewildered response was delivered whilst checking his Casio to confirm it was now 9:52, his exhausted mind second guessing itself. But his creeping concerns were put to rest by Miss Fox and her soothing explanation,

"The board are already convened, sir in the conference room. I'll inform Mr Keaton of your arrival."

She reached for the black office phone on her desk, pressing a couple of buttons before placing the receiver gently to her ear and waiting.

The waiting, it was mere seconds but the nothingness Sam dreaded had come and his nerves found him. Heart racing, sweat forming, he began to pace up and down, twitching the cold aluminium laptop from one hand back to the other all in an attempt to distract himself, distract that old familiar part of himself he so hated and was desperate to escape.

"Mr Keaton, Mr Lowell has arrived."

Miss Fox broke the tense silence, listening for a moment before she placed the receiver back down and returned to Sam,

"He said for you to come in at ten."

Sam nodded once in dazed response.

He twitched back to his Casio with wishful hope it was 9:59, but reality gave him 9:56. The nerves hit an all-time high as for the first time since meeting his mentor in Conference Room 1, his mind was given the chance and energy to stop and contemplate the importance of what lay beyond those imposing double doors. This was it, the make or break moment. As they say,

'This is where they separate the men from the boys.'

He responded with a deep calming breath that held the raging tide back for just a moment before the relentless battering of crashing waves continued to pound.

This building dread was now clearly on display, printed in glorious technicolour as his body twitched and shook. The American secretary took pity on him and spoke kindly,

"You go in there and then you knock 'em dead!"

Knowing all he needed were a few words of encouragement. Of course, in the past Seren had always been around to carry out such niceties.

"I've never done anything like this before, everything's riding on it."

Sam let himself go, confided in her,

"Then you go in there and you own that room. You don't let this opportunity slip away!"

Her worlds were strong and sharply delivered and exactly what Sam needed to hear. She had re-motivated the beast within him, that violent push out the door that we sometimes need.

Sam smiled and replied with forceful determination,

"I won't."

"Here, I'll come in with you, set it up."

She took the laptop from him.

"Thank you Miss Fox."

Sam replied in a professional tone, his eyes and expression conveying a more personal gratitude.

She flashed that gorgeous white smile again and replied, "Please, Lynn."

He checked his watch, it read 9:59.

They walked up to those imposing doors and Lynn Knocked three times as they both waited for the voice of Keaton,

"Yes, come in Sam."

Lynn opened one of the doors wide and stepped aside.

Sam entered, scanning the room he noticed the table was scattered with papers, many of the board members had relieved themselves of their jackets and a few had rolled up sleeves. It looked like they'd been there all morning, discussing some urgent and important business.

There was a tense and expectant atmosphere, that Sam egotistically presumed was down to the presentation he was about to give and the big decision each of them would have to make. But he'd failed to recall no such burden existed as Keaton's influence over all of them had already fabricated their decision. No, there was something more going on and whatever it was had everybody besides Keaton tense.

As Sam made his way over to the far end of the room, where the projector had been prepared, he noticed the chair at the head of the table, opposite Keaton was empty. Simon was not there. But Sam's racing mind didn't have time to play find the missing Boardman. Now was the time for focus and professionalism,

'Head in the game Sam, SHOWTIME!"

He stood, his gaze directed at the dull floor so as not to be distracted by those piercing eyes whilst he calmed himself and gathered his thoughts into ordered formation. He waited, waited whilst the generous secretary connected the laptop which she did with practiced efficiency before walking back to the door and closing in firmly behind her. The sound reverberating eerily into the silence.

Sam was ready, he raised his head proudly and went for it,

"Gentlemen, as you all know I am here this morning to convince you of why Singapore is a worthwhile investment,"

Sam struggled for a moment to find the right volume in such a large space but once he did he was off,

"Today I hope to install your confidence in our Singapore venture with solid facts and figures that as you know, never lie."

Sam's confidence flourished as he became submerged in a trance of concentration. The religiously rehearsed words flowing from his lips with effortless ease to the point he lost himself within the speech, almost as if someone else had taken over and he had become a mere spectator. Sam was in the zone.

Losing himself and his nerves he began gesturing with enthusiasm, walking around the room and making eye contact with the skill of a true public speaker.

"And so I personally believe this is a great opportunity for us to exploit a growing market of customers after a luxurious experience, which we will provide. Thank you for listening and I'd be happy to answer any questions?"

He finally concluded after about an hour of in depth analysis and projections.

Silence fell, and predictably not a single hand rose into the air. Sam turned to his mentor, looking for a clue as to his next move. He was frozen in anticipation and hope as the trance had passed and his consciousness had returned him to the reality of this defining moment in his life.

Then, Keaton gifted what Sam imagined to be the greatest praise he had ever bestowed. The billionaire brought his hands together and sent three loud clatters of applause throughout the void. Sam's confidence peaked as he'd now reached the summit of his mentor's approval. His idol, the man he viewed upon the highest pedestal had shown his respect, illustrating that he knew Sam was everything he'd hoped he would become.

"For… for, for… for."

The voices sounded out one by one, in unanimous agreement and Sam couldn't help a smug smile cross his face as his ego was fed up to the brim. He made his way round the table, receiving praise from each and every one of them personally before eventually getting to his mentor at the other end but before the two men could exchange words the door opened and the missing Board member walked in.

That tense and expectant silence resumed as Crow's vacant expression swiftly turned to confusion at the sight of everyone convened, but him.

"What the hell is this?"

He blurted, the question directed at the head of the table where he knew the orchestrator of this situation sat. Sam moved to the side, out of the path of these two heavyweights who were locked in a battle of wits.

"Simon, you made it. Have a seat."

Keaton instructed, completely ignoring the old timer's valid question. A question that Sam silently seconded. Reluctantly, the late-comer made his way over to his vacant seat. All the while keeping his eyes fixed on Keaton, as if the man were a dangerous predator that would strike as soon as you turned away.

The silence was palpable and what Keaton uttered next with such cold bluntness shocked Sam,

"Simon, you're out."

"What?"

The response was perplexed.

"You're out. The board has obtained evidence you have been embezzling expenses from this company. If you sign the contract before declaring your resignation from this board, then no further legal action will be taken and you will retain all your shares but no longer contribute to the decision making of this company."

Crow gazed down at the contract and readied pen laid before him. He smiled widely and gave a mirthless laugh before replying with a tempered passion,

"You jumped-up son of a bitch! I always knew you were cold Alexander, but I underestimated just how pure fucking evil you really are."

The room was packed with blood curdling tension so thick Sam could hardly breathe through it. Everyone in that room was horrified with the exception of these two monstrous bastions who locked heads in this violent clash.

"You're trying my patience. Sign it."

Sam could not see Keaton's face as he stood to the man's side, and was glad of it, for he could hear that terrifying rage that was ordinarily buried deep within.

"I knew you had friends in high places Alex! I didn't realise they extended all the way to the government, at least now we know what you were doing out in LA!"

Upon this accusation, Keaton's full fury forced its way to the surface and Keaton snapped, shooting up from his chair, voice raised in blood curdling rage,

"SIGN IT! Or I swear by the time I'm finished with you you'll be living in a cell with no windows!"

Even the great Simon Crow was now humbled, for he knew Keaton was not only powerful but also a man of his word, He was not in the habit of making hollow threats.

Reluctantly, he signed away his job and career. After which his body sunk into the chair, the man had been defeated and left completely deflated. And even though Sam was bound to Keaton's side, he couldn't help feeling sorrow for the old man who warranted respect for his integrity. In that moment, he honestly couldn't have decided in his own mind whether the man was guilty or not, torn between the mentor who had given him everything and the old timer. Sam suspected this was a decent man.

The switch abruptly toggled back and the calm collected exterior resumed with unnatural ease, whereupon he dismissed the room of uncomfortable souls who swiftly scattered. Sam automatically followed his mentor towards the door, darting back briefly to see the disgraced ex-employee still sat in seemingly stunned horror.

'Doesn't seem like the behaviour of a guilty man?'

Sam's overdeveloped sympathy escaped for a moment before being barked at,

'He's just sorry he got caught! You stick by Keaton, that loser is nothing to you, a stranger. Alexander Keaton is your saviour your mentor; remember!'

In a simple choice of which side to take, most rational men would have their feet firmly planted on Keaton's shores.

But Sam still didn't feel quite right about this, there was something about Crow, something he'd noticed the first time he saw the man. He had a positive aura which kind and generous people just seem to radiate. You couldn't make sense of the insight, it was just a gut feeling. There was something about this whole thing that didn't sit right with Sam's conscience and his ego had not quite managed to bury his disquiet.

"Miss Fox, cancel the rest of my appointments for today."

Keaton instructed as he emerged from the room. Lynn verbally complied,

"Yes, Mr Keaton."

The secretary did her utmost to retain her professional exterior and hide her personal feelings. She'd never known the man to cancel anything.

The billionaire turned back to address his recently proven apprentice,

"I have to make a quick business call, then there's something very important we need to discuss."

Keaton's serious tone now garnered Sam's undivided attention,

"Yes, Mr Keaton."

The respectful and professional response held fast whilst the dizzy heights of euphoria found Sam, his recent achievement began to permeate through the disbelief.

But what Keaton uttered next sent professionalism out the window,

"It's Alexander now."

He patted his apprentice on the shoulder before walking away towards his office.

Sam's euphoria merged with a sudden burst of adrenaline that seethed up into an uncontrollable emotion that he needed to release upon the nearest person. He darted round to Lynn's desk, where she sat typing obliviously, and kissed her firmly upon her warm cheek. The tastefully sweet perfume she wore captivating his senses as he pulled away.

Briefly stunned, her surprise was swiftly replaced by that gorgeous smile as their eyes met. Sam stood tall and took a step back for fear her blue eyes and red lips were too enticingly dangerous to be in such close proximity.

"What was that for?"

Lynn broke the short, tense silence,

"Thank you."

He replied, emanating blunt sincerity, backing away a couple of paces politely before turning towards his own office.

Sam entered the comforting seclusion of his office in search of a much needed moment of solace to absorb, but before he could close the door behind him it was forced back out of his lose grip and swung wide. The unsuspecting apprentice now saw Mr Crow appear through the crack as, wild eyed and frantic the man slammed the door before pulling Sam back away in hurried concern, Keaton could return any moment.

Crow spoke with a rushed urgency incongruous in a man of his stature,

"Sam, listen to me. I know you don't know me but I know you and you don't belong here with these money grabbing demons. I've met enough people in this world to know the difference between those who belong in hell and those who don't, get out whilst you still can!"

Sam was a little freaked out by these fire-fuelled pious words but managed to stutter a forceful response,

"Mr Crow, I, appreciate your concern for me but this is exactly where I belong."

"Alexander Keaton is not the sort of man you want to get close to kid; he uses people, you're no more important to him that the gum on the pavement. He falsified evidence against me because I found out who he really is, but you can't fight the power and connections of a man like that, he is into everything and he always wins…"

The old man was beginning to ramble, he seemed genuinely terrified and it awoke a warning deep within Sam who interrupted, one comment in particular disturbing him,

"Wait, wait what do you mean who he really is? What are you talking about?"

Sam attempted to reel in the conversation with calmingly slow words. But his curiosity had been provoked by this sudden bombardment of concern for his wellbeing from a man that deep down he knew would not be scared without reason. This was a powerful businessman and possibly even a criminal.

Simon took a moment to compose himself before replying with a crazed look in his eyes,

"Alexander Keaton does not exist, Sam. He's just a phantom, come with me and I'll…"

The old timer stopped dead in his tracks as his heightened senses clocked the click of the door handle behind them. Both men turned with apprehension, still caught in their tense moment which was amplified at the sight of Keaton, now standing in the doorway. With menacing eyes burning into Crow's, he spoke in an ice cold tone,

"Get out of my building."

A threatening *"or else"* radiated from his expression and Simon took the hint which hit him like a wrecking ball. He'd dared not even finish his sentence and walked in a dejected trance towards the door, out, and down the corridor. Keaton's eyes fixed on him all the while like a predatory hawk.

Sam's head was left spinning with newfound and unanswered questions whilst he tried to answer them rationally.

'Keaton's not real, what does that mean?
Old codger is losing his marbles!
How could the man not be real he's standing before you!
That's not what he meant and you know it!
The man could be a fraud!
That's ridiculous, Alexander Keaton is a businessman and has been a mentor and friend to you, this is how you repay him, with doubt?

He didn't doubt you – he believed in you – time to return the favour, Sam.'

Before his indecisive mind could really get into its confrontation he was pulled back into the now, by the man to whom his allegiance still lay,

"Let's take a drive."

Chapter 22

Road Trip Revelations

Keaton steered him to the elevator and down into the bowels of the building to a small underground car park. Well hidden from the public and for a good reason. Sam soon discovered why as they walked across the cold concrete floor towards two beautiful monsters.

"Here."

Keaton said, turning back to throw something small at his apprentice who adroitly caught at it with both hands.

Slowly, Sam unclenched his tight fists to see a glass key with "Aston Martin," written across it sat in his palm.

"Are you serious?"

Sam inquired. He had only driven two cars before; The first being when his father taught him to drive in his old VW beetle which Sam actually thought was pretty cool, but then again to a first time driver anything is pretty cool really, perhaps even a Reliant Robin. The second and last time was when he had taken Seren to Italy and they had hired a little Citroen out of necessity, a poxy one litre thing that only just made it up the mountainous landscape of Northern Italy in first gear. Regardless of his abysmal experience he had just been handed the keys to a 6.0 litre 568 horse power 200 MPH black English monster.

Keaton answered Sam's question with another question,

"Do I strike you as a joker?" the billionaire asked rhetorically as he approached and unlocked the second vehicle, a black Italian monster in the shape of a Ferrari 458.

"Try and keep up!" he continued, stepping into the low prancing horse with practiced skill.

Sam walked over to the door of the Aston, gently he pulled at the handle and stepped into a luxurious cabin of leather. Pushing the key into the console the engine sparked into thunderous life, sending a shiver down his spine. Nervous anticipation washed over him as he'd suddenly become well aware of the power and price tag of this masterpiece of machinery. Cautiously, he trailed his employer towards the entrance as a symphony of horsepower echoed through the enclosed space. Sam opened his window to enhance the experience.

As they pulled out onto the sunbathed asphalt almost immediately stopping at a set of traffic lights, Sam noticed a young teenage boy in the taxi beside him. The kid stared in jaw-dropped awe at the two monsters.

Sam smiled widely, finally privy to what it feels like to be on the inside looking out rather than the outside looking in. It was an ugly feeling of smug pride and added yet another dimension to his ego.

Keaton led them out of Manhattan along the coast as minute by minute Sam felt more confident behind the wheel. And he needed to be in order to keep up with the Ferrari in front which certainly was not going to hang about for him. If you couldn't keep up you'd be left behind.

They drove for an hour, racing along the wide and twisting coastal roads until eventually the tycoon pulled over at a small restaurant on the seafront. Sitting at a table overlooking the stunning view of blue ocean as far as the eye could see, Keaton ordered a bottle of Champagne, but of course didn't touch a drop which didn't bother Sam in the slightest as he drank glass after glass.

"Sam, you've proven yourself to be everything I knew you would be, I look at you and I see myself. Now it's time to tell you why you're really here."

Keaton began as he retrieved a pouch of cigars from his inside jacket pocket, handing one to Sam who took it gratefully before replying,

"What do you mean?"

The billionaire's mask gave way to a vague smile,

"You didn't really think I spent all this time and effort to train up an assistant."

Sam didn't know how to respond as that's exactly what he'd assumed but would have felt stupid to admit it now, now he'd found out he'd been so blindly mistaken. Whilst he now dared to hope that he might be the bastion's equal one day, he'd never initially presumed to expect anything more.

"There is a very specific reason for your presenting the Singapore project, Sam. You're going to run it."

Keaton instructed casually, turning to the cigar in his hand, lighting it before chucking the gold lighter over.

Sam caught it and took a much needed moment to compose himself as once more his mind burst into debate,

'*We've done it! You're going to be master of your own destiny!*'

In Singapore? I'll have to move to Singapore?

'*It's a beautiful place of luxury and glamour, it's where we belong!*'

In Singapore? Leave New York, leave London, my home!

'*One day you will return a rich and powerful man, a respected businessman!*'

I don't know… This might be too big for me!

'*This is it! Remember, Sam, you're one and only chance to have everything you ever wanted. There won't be another one. Are you willing to go back to that store? Back to being nothing and leave this world of everything behind… Well?*'

NO! I can't go back.'

The cigar sparked into life and Sam had made his decision,

"I won't let you down, Alexander."

His employer didn't speak or even gesture in reaction; he sat still, enjoying his Cuban. He appeared so secure it was as if the man had known he had Sam hooked the day they met.

"Before I hand over part of my company, there is one final aspect I need to know you can handle."

Keaton interrupted the bliss, just as Sam was just beginning to settle down to the sweet taste of his cigar and the soothing crashing of the waves upon the beach below.

"What is it?"

Sam, filled with intrigue wanted to know what his final lesson would be.

"The only other thing besides your drive I can't teach. Ruthlessness! I need to know you can be calculated, Sam. That you can throw your empathy out the window, because it has no place in this world."

"I can, Alexander. I understand it's all just business."

"I know you do, but understanding something and doing it are worlds apart, it's the difference between thoughts and actions. One you can change, the other you can't. You have to prove to me you can handle this harsh and unforgiving world. So, Monday you're going to fly out to our hotel in LA and fire the manager. I want you to look into his eyes and tell him he's lost his job. Then, I'll know you're ready."

"I'll get it done," Sam replied.

"There is only one way to conquer this world and that is to look out for 'numero uno'. Money and a clean conscience are not well matched, it's one or the other. And it is for each of us to decide which is more important, we all have our individual drives in life."

Sam digested the words before replying,

"What's yours?"

"I'm driven by the single most highly-prized condition that has been fought for by humanity since civilisation began. Freedom! Used to be the biggest, the strongest man who owned it, then it was the man with the strongest religion, then the biggest army, now it's the man with money... We are just animals, Sam, hurtling through an infinite void on a rock at seventy thousand miles an hour, completely alone. I make no apologies for the selfish life I lead, and neither should you."

Sam was completely seduced. Poor Crow was forgotten and Sam was once more hanging onto every word Keaton said, the man's philosophical point resonating eye-opening revelations within his own psyche.

He was resolved to throw his conscience out the window and put himself first, along with his beloved Seren of course. He would forge himself a life of freedom and make no apologies for doing so, such ruthlessness was just the way of the universe.

Chapter 23

Home

Sam arrived home at 10:17 PM on the Friday night. Keaton eventually letting his apprentice return to London after he'd been through most of the Singapore project's eye watering details. The strain of which the billionaire more than made up for by lending a private jet for a smooth and comfortable trip back home.

Entering the apartment with the pathetic enthusiasm of a zombie, Sam dropped his bags and dragged his feet directly towards the sweet salvation of bed. Seren was there, passed out on her side, an empty bottle of red wine on the dresser.

He desired with longing desperation to wake up the sleeping beauty and stay up all night to explain in infinite detail everything that had happened and how there would be,

'No more worries.'

That calmingly long journey home had finally allowed all those long days and nights to catch up and Sam slept like he'd never slept before.

Saturday morning the couple exchanged affections that Sam now realised he'd missed, having been far too busy the past week to realise he was missing anything. However, the remainder of the day was uncharacteristically strange. It was clear from her wincing expressions and the avoidance of conversation that Seren was severely hungover. Her drinking had slowly crept up on her as the week rolled by, first it was one glass, then two, three and by Friday it was a bottle. Self-medicating to help her sleep with that cold empty space beside her.

Seren could do just fine without the affection and even the conversation, it was the fact he simply wasn't there anymore that unsettled her. Every night for over three years they had slept together, over 1,000 nights of regularity and comfort had just suddenly vanished. She had been suffering the symptoms of withdrawal.

Of course, Sam was only in New York but even so that was an ocean away and during those long dark nights he could have been in Chelsea or China, it made no difference it still felt like he'd evaporated into thin air. And that magical elixir we call alcohol just helped settle her; that was all, she saw no harm in a glass of wine in the evening, many people do it. However, like all drugs it doesn't mix well with unhappiness and the dosage required had swiftly increased.

Sam had no inkling about any of this. Like many people who have been gifted everything they desire, he'd become completely complacent and blinded to any negativity. In his mind, which had now become irrational thanks to the irrational world he'd become accustomed to, everything was great.

Everything was not great, at least not from Seren's point of view. Not that she was thinking about it at this point, far too spent from a hectic week at work to be bothered to delve into psychoanalysing her feelings. All she wanted to do was sit in silence and read one of her books which had the power to take her away to another, happier world.

This, like everything else, had recently worked out perfectly for Sam who could spend the day working through endless piles of paper pandering to the Singapore project which was now his responsibility. He had also carved out a little time to pop down to the local jewellers, also arranging a romantic evening where he then intended to share everything with Seren.

There was a cold aura about the cramped apartment, as if both of them were leading separate and unconnected lives. Ignoring their problems for completely different reasons;

Seren, because she was too drained to think about them, let alone fight. Sam because he was completely oblivious they were even there. But it was obvious they were out of sync.

Chapter 24

Night out in London

Sam consulted the Casio, "6:15." It was time to start the show. He approached Seren, still curled up on the sofa, book in hand.

"What's this? Some kind of role-play."

She joked, her enthusiasm revitalised thanks to her favourite pass-time of reading. Yet, the laughable atmosphere gave way to intense attraction as she looked upon the regally suited man before her. He appeared so unattainably gentlemanly.

As the two remained locked in sexually charged eye contact, Sam replied with confident authority,

"Later! Right now I want you to put on that little black dress because I'm taking you out."

"Out? Where?"

Seren exclaimed, dropping her book as a sudden rush of excitement ran through her. It had been so long since they'd been out, it was a special treat reserved for birthdays and anniversaries.

"It's a surprise. Go on."

Sam teased, gesturing back towards the bedroom and she scampered quickly away.

Pacing up and down the short hallway Sam impatiently waited, looking forward to seeing that tight black dress which had always been his personal favourite. He wondered if they'd even make it to the restaurant as it had been almost three weeks which might as well have been a year he was so hungry for her. His inflated ego and confidence had released a gigantic surge of testosterone, the likes of which Sam had not experienced since as a nineteen-year-old virgin he'd experimented with Seren for the first time. Except now he considered himself a pro and intended to hit on her like a raging bull.

Some fifteen minutes passed, which Sam noted as a record time, before Seren emerged from the bedroom and his jaw almost hit the floor. She was a vision of elegance; Long hair arranged so that it cascaded like a golden waterfall over the right shoulder, eventually resting at a small yet perfectly shaped breast, thick black eye liner enhanced her electric eyes and deep red lipstick painted plump lips like a target, the thin dress following her feminine curves down to smooth legs whose length was enhanced by black laced heels.

Sam had to fight off his animalistic urge to help her straight back out of that dress, able to delay his gratification thanks only to his equalling and more important longing to tell her that after all these years of struggling he was finally going to do his job and look after her.

"Well?"

Seren asked seductively, the hungry expression on Sam's face already giving her so much pleasure but she wanted to hear him say it. When it came to sex she had always known exactly what she wanted and how to get it.

Sam tried to construct a sentence that wasn't dirty, a laugh escaping as he spoke,

"This is going to be a great night."

Not only was he confident that tonight he'd be setting her troubled mind to rest but he'd also be having the best sex of his life. A winning combination of physical *and* mental satisfaction.

Then, as if on cue a car horn sounded from just outside,

"Our carriage awaits."

Sam concluded with a wide smile and the couple made their way down.

Inviting Seren to get into the back first was a gentlemanly yet also tactical move, engineered so that he could check one last time that the small velvet box was indeed in his jacket pocket. Pressing the thin jacket material firmly, he felt the outline and relaxed.

That morning Sam had seized the opportunity provided by Seren's complete immersion in her book to run down to the small jeweller on the high street which she loved. There was a specific treasure, a bracelet of small yet powerfully shimmering diamonds that had sat boldly in the window, waiting patiently for an owner.

Sam recalled Seren pointing it out months ago, her eyes drawn to the stones which sparkled in the morning light as the couple made their Sunday morning trip to the deli.

"Such simple elegance, it's almost criminal such a beautiful thing should go unloved."

Seren had commented as she regarded it with child-like awe.

It was a memory that had been firmly embedded in Sam's mind as he longed for her to have it, wishing with all his heart he could buy it for her, and hating himself for being unable to do so. Every Sunday morning, week after week they walked past that jeweller's and that beautiful piece had haunted him. Acting as the symbol for how pathetic and unworthy he felt. Sam tried and tried over the months to squirrel away enough money to eventually buy it. But every time the money rolled in, it rolled right back out again.

But now everything had changed, that pathetic and unworthy boy was long gone and in his place, a man of commerce; confident and successful.

Making his way down the bustling high street with purposeful enthusiasm Sam stopped abruptly as an ATM caught the corner of his eye, accompanied by the realisation he hadn't actually checked his new account yet, and oh how the endless possibilities of what the number might be consumed him.

Reaching for the black card, Sam approached the machine. He pushed it into the slot and punched in each number with hesitant force brought about by apprehension.

229

In the moment of blinding tension even his mathematical mind had no clue what the screen would read,

"Please Wait"

The machine taunted him for glacial seconds before it revealed all with abrupt understatement.

Sam took a step back and laughed in shock at the number,

"£26,849.31"

Approaching the glass frontage, to his delight Sam spotted that the treasure was still there, where it always had been, as if it were always meant to be Seren's.

As the salesman retrieved the item, Sam instructed,

"I don't wish to know the price... It doesn't matter."

The man was perplexed by such an illogical statement but Sam didn't care. Wishing to experience what it was like to buy something without knowing its price tag. A luxury he could never have afforded in his past life. It was the pure, unparalleled feeling of complete freedom, just as Alexander had said. It was as if having money made the whole concept of the economy disappear. The never-ending worries of money had disappeared. This mathematical reality that had run and consumed his life for all his years had become immaterial. Sam discovered in that brief moment that freedom isn't just about being able to go wherever you want, do whatever you please. To experience true freedom is to have the immense weight of poverty removed.

The car took them into the heart of London whereupon Seren's tantalising question,

'Where are we going?"

Which Sam had been refusing to settle, was finally answered as they pulled up outside a skyscraper of angular glass, it was The Shard. They took the elevator up and up to the restaurant on the 31st floor. On arrival, they were quickly settled in at a table beside the wall of glass which gave way to a stunning bird's eye view of the night lit London cityscape. Sam having been able to reserve such prime real estate thanks to the power of name dropping.

All he'd needed to say down the line were the magic words,

"Mr Alexander Keaton."

And suddenly, as if by magic, a table was available.

Having ordered a bottle of his new favourite drink, Sam turned to Seren, whilst bearing an expression that asked her opinion of it all; this new world of luxury he was introducing her to.

But all she was really interested in was that view. Her eyes unable to stop darting back at that breathtaking sight. More than four years she'd lived in London but never had she seen it like this. From such a distance the city seemed so peaceful, so gracious. All the noise and chaos had dissolved; it could have been the kingdom of heaven itself with millions of fireflies floating upon an ocean of darkness.

"Sam this is…"

Seren began, but was interrupted by impatience born of an ego-filled seeking of approval. Sam longed for it; still he persisted in his belief that deep down this had all been for her, to make her happy.

"You like it?"

"It's… wonderful,"

Came the hesitant reply. Her eyes darting around the room in an uncomfortable twitch.

"What's wrong?"

Sam quickly read the subtle ticks he knew so well.

"Nothing, it's nothing I'm just a little shocked I suppose,"

Seren lied. She didn't want to disappoint him, knowing full well the consequences of his realisation that this was not the sort of place she felt at home. To her it wasn't so much luxury as it was pretentious. Truly she intended to enjoy the evening, making the most of her time with Sam, she being under no illusion and that their recreational time would soon be compromised.

"I wanted to wait, until after the meal… Never could delay gratification."

Sam explained, reaching into his inside pocket and retrieving the black velvet box. Sliding it across the soft cream linen until it sat before Seren, who gave a wide smile of surprise and anticipation. Sam watching her developing expressions with devoted focus. Enjoying every moment of the pleasure he inflicted.

Parting the reluctant latch, a gasp escaped her lips before swiftly composing her girly glee at the sight of the sparkling gems,

"When did you…"

She began, the answer arriving before the obvious question was finished,

"This morning, you were so ensconced in your book, sneaking out was easy."

Sam explained, a cheeky smile of pride written across his face.

"Very sneaky. Can't believe you remembered."

Seren was genuinely taken aback, it had been months since she had pointed out that little treasure. Considering the last two weeks he'd had, such an impractically kind gesture was heart-warming to her. It was enough, even if he was away all week and their time together was sliced down to the weekends she felt she could handle it. Seren was a strong and simple woman, all she needed was the occasional reminder she was still there, that she still mattered, and this selfless gesture of love said exactly that.

"I wanted you to know that this is all for you, Seren."

Sam's words felt genuine to him, but sounded somewhat lacklustre as they left his mouth. Because, deep down, he knew they weren't true. Having been fed by the best, his ego radiated such selfish greed it blinded him.

Seren had heard Sam's words but missed their subtle message, distracted as she arranged the accessory with delicate care upon her wrist. She was unconvinced,

"You have changed Sam and what's more, you are completely unaware of it. Our brain constantly adapts to our environment whether we like it or not and there is no mirror with which we can reflect it."

Seren was right, Sam had quickly become accustomed to a world where he was the master's right hand man, of indisputable importance and now, everything that had been important to Sam had become inconsequential.

"There's something else as well…"

Sam continued, his voice became almost creepy in its vague distance as he attempted to build the suspense as high as he could, in anticipation of an even greater hit of gratitude which his ego now craved like a drug,

"Alexander has entrusted the new hotel we are building in Singapore over to me. I'm going to be the executive director of the project."

Seren experienced a moment of biting shock, at Sam's stark revelation and the casual tone in which it was delivered. As if he'd just informed her of some mundane and daily information, rather than this life changing scenario. And she knew, just as she had when he told her about the job Keaton offered him that the decision was already made, there would be no discussion, no compromise.

"… You're going to work in Singapore?"

Seren required confirmation of the nonchalant statement.

"Well, yes of course I'll have to go out there but I'll be back for the weekends I suppose, the details haven't been hashed out yet."

Sam's explanations grew rapidly woolly and blasé. It was suddenly so clear that it didn't matter to him if he could make it back home every weekend or even monthly. The job – that's all his mind was focusing on – like a scratched vinyl stubbornly running over the same phrase again and again with no other melody to play.

"I'm sorry I don't understand! You spent a week in New York and now *you're* moving to Singapore?"

Seren's voice became querulous. The couple were equally upset by each other's reaction.

"I thought you'd be happy for us?"

"I'm happy for *you*, Sam. And I'm glad to know what's really important to you. I finally see who you really are."

Seren faked a smile.

"What do you mean, happy for me? You should be happy for *us*. It's *our* future we are talking about. We can have everything Seren! I'm finally going to provide you with the life you deserve."

Sam rambled, sidestepping any negative undertones.

"Where is this coming from? There is nothing wrong with my life! Sam, I love you, truly I do, but don't ever make the mistake of thinking I'm so pathetic I need you… I'm not some fucking soccer mom!"

Seren's emotions gathered thunderous momentum; a storm in the making.

"I just want to look after you! We don't have to worry about money anymore, you can quit that job you hate so much and relax."

Sam desperately explained those intensions he had so blindly convinced himself were for her benefit. But he'd only succeeded in salting the wound.

"I don't hate my job. What are you talking about? I'm not quitting!"

"You're always complaining about how understaffed the hospital is. You're constantly exhausted."

"Everybody complains about their job, Samuel, it's a reality of life, we all struggle sometimes. I love my job, it's important to me, helping people is important to me – it's who I am. And I thought it was who you were too."

"What's that supposed to mean?"

"We shared the same dream, you used to want to help people, to become a doctor and make a difference! You've changed Sam, and I'm sorry but I don't recognise the person you've become."

"I'm the same person Seren, I just want a better life for us!"

"No, no you're not. That man has changed you, warped you into someone else, selfish and only driven by money!"

Seren couldn't bring herself to say what she dreaded to be true. That Sam, the sweet, innocent and shy boy she met had been twisted and moulded into a character she'd always despised. With inflated pride and conceit, just like her father who had also been sucked into the corporate machine, generating money without consideration of the consequences.

"Yes! Okay, fine so I've changed a bit. Alexander helped me find my confidence, my self-belief, he pulled a nervous and pathetic boy from the gutter and made him a man."

"That's where you're wrong. You may have lacked self-confidence and may have even been a nervous wreck, but you had principals, Sam. You had empathy, you cared for others. And that's how you define a real man, not by how much money you have."

"Money is the world Seren, it's the only thing that matters, when you have it you have everything! Alexander has shown me that, and you'll see it too!"

Sam passionately proclaimed the truth he was absolutely sure of, but Seren's distant expression warned him that he'd gone too far.

"No I won't. Maybe you're right, maybe the world does revolve around money, but that's not a world I want to live in. I can't follow you down that road Sam."

Seren's words were determined and dignified and she fought hard to hold back the tears that welled up in her eyes. Needing desperately to hold onto her strength, because she knew what she had to do. It was the toughest decision of her life but she was resolved that walking away was the only card left to play. Leaving was the only weapon Seren had that could force an ethical decision from this man that she loved and admired.

"What are you saying?"

"I'm saying you and I don't work anymore."

Sam should have said something, anything, he could feel her slipping away but his lips wouldn't part. He couldn't construct a sentence, his ego refusing to believe her apparently irrational reaction. In his mind he'd worked so hard for her, to provide her with a better life, to become the man she deserved and now he had made it Seren had thrown it all back in his face. And he couldn't understand why.

Seren waited for an answer, hoping with all her heart he would break out in apology as the realisation of who he'd become hit him, but of course it didn't and the silence prevailed.

Accepting the reality of the fact that Sam would not be having an epiphany – at least not today – she spoke one last time as she got up from the seat. Struggling more than ever to hold back her emotion with a quaking voice,

"I tell you one good thing that's come out of your success Samuel. Now you can afford to stay in a hotel."

She turned, and walked away.

"Seren."

Sam called after her but her course didn't deviate an inch. He should have gone after her, fought for her. But he didn't. Sam just sat there, his mind swimming with disbelief and trying to figure out what he'd done wrong. The dream that had become his reality clouding his judgement about all else that really mattered to him, in the deep reaches of his consciousness where that anxious little boy still clung on.

Chapter 25

More Wisdom

"Knock, knock, knock."

Sam was distracted from his corporate calculations, confused as to who on earth could be at the door. He rose cautiously from the desk where countless papers were scattered, still feeling the generous helping of alcohol that last night's events had created. His ego refused to accept Seren's reaction to his news, and so he'd turned to the only thing he knew anymore – his new grounding – work.

Upon opening the door, Sam's drowsy state was rejuvenated by the familiar face before him.

"Dad?"

He spoke, his mind doubting his eyes for a moment.

"Morning Son."

Year by year ever since Sam left home it seemed the two got together less often. He supposed that was natural and accepted his son had his own life, not that that made it any easier.

"What are you doing here? And how'd you find me?"

"Well I'm no detective, but I like to think I know my own son better than anybody."

Mark Lowell flashed a wide grin, teeth complimenting his dull grey hair.

"Was that an answer?"

Sam murmured offhand, not sure whether that was a joke or not. He turned and walked back into the generous suite, his father following quickly, closing the door behind.

"Seren called. Said you were in need of advice."

Mark stated, a hint of concern revealed as his eyes scanned the room, alerted to the mountain of papers on the desk and the two bottles of champagne on the bedside table. It was clear from the creaseless sheet and dark circles around Sam's eyes that his son had not slept.

"Well I don't. Everything's fine."

"Fine, I see… So she just kicked your ass out for a laugh then. I know some people got a strange sense of humour, but this steals first place."

"How much did she tell you?"

"Oh, just that you quit school because of some fancy new job, that you were staying at a hotel, figured it was somewhere local and up market, this is only the third I checked."

"Should have called."

"I did."

Sam recalled he'd never given his father his new number when he received the shiny new model. This didn't click as odd in any way as Sam continued to employ the excuse,

'I was just too busy, no time for niceties!'

"Anyway, this is not a conversation I wanted to have over the phone Sam."

"Conversation?"

"Yes, the one you and I are going to have right now."

Mark stated with unyielding force, making it plain he would not be leaving until they had a reciprocal conversation.

"Look Dad I know you're pissed about medical school but I couldn't go through my li…"

"I'm not pissed about that!"

Mark objected.

"I mean I'm not exactly farting rainbows over here, of course I'm disappointed you couldn't finish after having been so close. But I'm not here for me, this is about you."

"Like I said, I'm fine."

Sam persisted. He didn't want to talk about it. He never wanted to talk about it, he just wanted to work.

"The love of your life just threw you out and you're fine. Sam, if that's the truth it disturbs me."

Realisation hit home – Seren's words, "He's changing, Mark" were in fact not an exaggeration at all.

"What do you want from me, Dad?"

Sam asked, as irritation festered, and his annoyance travelled on an upwards trajectory.

"I want you to be a man and step up! Talk to Seren, go back home where you belong."

Mark summoned the most fatherly tone of wisdom that he could muster, its only affect adding fuel to his son's now ill-concealed irritation. Its reply took on a petulant edge,

"She made it perfectly clear that she doesn't want me there anymore. You know what she said to me, Dad? She said she could happily live without me, she doesn't need me, she doesn't want me!"

"That's not true and you know it! You're twisting her words, God knows why, it's as if you're trying to push her away… You and that girl are meant to be together Samuel, I've seen the way you are. You're a team, you look after each other."

Mark's persuasive pitch tried to gather a foothold whilst remaining calm; trying to maintain a delicate balance between delivering his point whilst remaining neutral. He felt like a referee in a Sumo match.

"That's exactly what I'm doing! Trying to making something of myself! To be the man she deserves! To build a life worth living!"

Sam's irritation ratcheted further, anger seeping in as his point of view was still not being seen.

"That's not what I mean, Seren isn't some shallow teenage girl Sam! She doesn't need a piggy bank, she's a grown woman. She doesn't care about money, she never has. It's you she wants here and now, not away all the time across the ocean. That's not looking after someone!"

"How do you know what she wants?"

The inclination for self-righteousness stubbornly held fast.

"Samuel, don't be so bloody naive that girl could have had any posh toff she wanted… Seren didn't choose you for money, she chose you because you hadn't been corrupted by it… Money is a dangerous thing. It changes people and often not for the better."

The derogatory tone in which Mark mentioned money awoke that great ego now dwelling within Sam and he burst into passion-fuelled might.

"Oh wake up Dad! Money is the reality of life. It's what makes the world run and if you don't have it, you have nothing. I'll be damned to hell before I go back to a mediocre life!"

"My God. If your mother were here."

Mark's voice held a mixture of exasperation tinted with profound sadness as he achieved bulls-eye on an exposed nerve.

"Well she isn't, is she Dad!"

Sam spat out his retort. Anger at Seren's response had merged with his overtired frustration and finally escaped, the full force of which had now directed at his unfortunate father. Sam's muscles were tensed, laser eyes protruding from a psychopathic face.

Mark was stunned into frozen shock for a time, he couldn't believe this was his son. Eventually collecting his feelings, he uttered words that would have hit home in happier times.

"Where's that caring boy we raised? The principals? What happened to you?"

"I woke up. Finally, I see the world for what it really is. It's just chaos Dad, there's no justice, no right no wrong. And in such a world principals are not a valuable commodity, they're just an anchor. And I am not going to be dragged back down to the bottom."

Mark nodded in hopeless acceptance that it was too late; whatever had hooked Sam held him prisoner and it wasn't about to let go. The defeated man sauntered back towards the door and turned, his parting shot delivered in a last ditch attempt at penetrating the hardened exterior.

"You know, I always knew you had a drive for success, you always worked so much harder than everybody else, it was clear. But I never imagined you'd go so far for it. I love you Sam, and I'll always stand by you, it's my job. But it's also my responsibility to tell you if you continue down this path, you won't like what's at the end of it."

Mark turned his back one more and made it to unhinging the door before Sam's witticism hit him right in the gut.

"And what would that be Dad, Money? Freedom?"

His father turned his head back and flatly uttered one word.

"Loneliness."

Chapter 26

Package

It was Monday morning, Sam was up and at the day well before dawn had a chance to catch up. The ungodly hour becoming an ever more regular occurrence in his life. Last night had been much the same as Saturday, work and alcohol to numb the long span of darkness. A suffering within him boiling up, accelerated by the developing troubles in his life, troubles his ego kept locked in the depths of his soul. Still, he had himself convinced everything would work out, that this path was still the dream, it had to be. Just keep working, work was the key.

Sam arrived at the strip at 5:00 AM on the dot, just as Keaton had instructed. The concept of time as an ever more valuable commodity occurring to him as there seemed to be less and less of it every day. Stepping up into the tube of luxury ready to enjoy an eleven-hour power nap, Sam's drowsy thoughts of sweet sleep, another increasingly unobtainable commodity, were forced away by curiosity as he noticed a black duffle bag, sat boldly upon one of the cream chairs. Approaching it he noticed a white envelope fed through the handle, bearing an inked marking,

Sam

The word casually written in the unmistakable old style font of Alexander's elegant hand. Sam reached for the letter, opening it whilst his true intrigue honed in on the mysterious bag whose plain exterior gave nothing away.

He read,

This package is to be locked in the safe at the back of the closet in your room, code 667459. Tomorrow morning, 7:30 AM a man will come to collect it. He will introduce himself as Mr Bodach.

P.S The watch is yours, a token of my appreciation.

Sam dropped the paper, quickly turning to the duffle bag as curiosity nibbled.

Snagging the zip across, he spread the dark crack open and the contents into the light. Sam took a step back in shock at the sight. Money, lots and lots of it, far more than he could have visualised. Thick wads of hundred dollar bills, Sam's mathematical mind speculated at least $100,000. But this was a wild guess, it could have been more.

As the shock slipped away, his attention turned to the square jewellery box that sat like a boat upon the sea of green, the familiar branded lettering, "Cartier" stamped in gold letters. Caressing the smooth leather Sam savoured the suspense for a moment longer, enjoying that burst of adrenaline Keaton had gotten him addicted to with this extravagant lifestyle.

He popped the lid to reveal a gold timepiece unparalleled in stunningly intricate design. The inner mechanics all visible, showcasing the red ruby jewels within.

Sam was overcome. He was convinced Alexander Keaton was a generous man, after all he'd done for him. But he would never have imagined the man being the gift giving type. The billionaire continued to surprise and Sam conveniently forgot all about the bag full of money.

Eleven hours later Sam stepped out of the air-conditioned plane, hit by a wave of eighty degree California heat.

The Keaton hotel had sent a driver who waited on the strip.

"Mr Lowell, it's a pleasure, sir."

The young go getter spoke with forced confidence as Sam approached with a presence almost equal to Keaton himself.

"Straight to The Keaton," he commanded.

No time for niceties! Sam needed to be focused on the important job he'd been assigned. The beautiful California coastline with its golden sands leading out to sapphire blue ocean passed Sam without so much as a glance. Too many emails to answer and notes to write, this was a business trip – he was no tourist.

Sam was greeted by the manager of the hotel personally as he entered the lobby. This man's curiosity was stamped out by a devoted professionalism. Sam felt no pangs of guilt,

'Ah, just the man I wanted to see.'

"Mr Lowell, it's great to meet you. I'm Brett Spencer, manager of the hotel."

The middle aged fellow Englishman introduced himself. A tall man almost equalling Sam in height, trim and fit with a California brown tan.

"Mr Spencer, I'd like to speak to you in private, perhaps your office?"

Sam took immediate control of the conversation, as his mentor had taught him.

"… Of course."

The manager replied, a brief hiatus manufactured by this stranger's confident approach which he felt was rather off putting. He led the way back to the private quarters of the building and into his office,

"Plea…"

Brett began, but stopped in his tracks as Mr Lowell had already helped himself to a seat before the man had turned back, the hefty duffle bag hit carpet with a dull thud.

Sam imparted a deep and serious stare, as if he were preparing for an important scene. Mr Spencer stood feeling increasingly awkward in his presence. Yet he was no fool, sensing the negative atmosphere surrounding this meeting. A dread of the unknown – yet suspected – truth built within him. Reluctantly trapped in this moment, Brett took his own seat.

"Mr Spencer I'm going to cut to the chase,"

Sam stabbed confidently into the tense silence,

"I am here to inform you that your employment is immediately terminated."

The blow came in the guise a cold and calculative tone that sliced like a steel blade right into Mr Spencer's core.

"You're firing me?"

Emotion fuelled perplexity shook his voice.

"We are, yes."

The equally blunt reply came back.

"Just like that. No explanation, you just walk in here, someone I've never met before and kick me out?"

The voice was raised as dismay gave way to anger.

"I'm sure Mr Keaton's decision was not made lightl…"

"Oh fuck you, asshole!"

Mr Spencer lost complete control of his composure and set his emotions free,

"You just stroll in here like you own the place and take my job, my livelihood, away from me?"

"Mr Spencer I'm not here to argue with you, the decision is final. I suggest you compose yourself and deal with the situation like a man."

Sam's advice sharply whipped across the ex-employee's desk, apparently irritated with the man for not acting in a professional manner. Sam had experienced what awaited you at the bottom end of life, and now had no pity for anyone who wasted their opportunity to stay above it.

Brett Spencer took a moment to gather his emotions before pleading one last time.

"Please! I have a family to support. Two daughters in college…"

Tears escaped, the victim now horrified at his reality; that of returning home to his dependent family, jobless.

But the shiftless response beat him down as far as he could go,

"That's not my problem Mr Spencer, it's yours."

Sam terminated the meeting as he got up, reaching for the duffle bag and heading back towards the door.

"You're a heartless bastard Lowell!"

The ex-employee's parting shot was flung across the room.

Sam stopped in his tracks and replied before walking out the door.

"I'm not heartless Mr Spencer, I'm just doing my job, as you should have been."

Sam retreated to his suite, ordering some much needed room service before falling into a blissful and seemingly conscienceless sleep.

Chapter 27

Night out in LA

Sam awoke gently, checking his new timepiece to see it was 8:35 PM. Immediately, his consciousness begged for a drink, which he didn't object to. He decided to journey down to the bar for one... or two,

'I've certainly earned it!'

This thought had become an increasingly regular source of justification for this developing habit, alongside,

'I work hard, therefore I deserve a drink.'

The clever lie clouded the underlying truth; that his new addiction kept him going. The demands of the job boiled up inside him, a pressure-cooker disaster waiting to happen.

Sam took the elevator down to the lobby and ambled into the bar. Several muffled conversations pervaded the atmosphere of the dark room; black walls, velvet curtains and track lighting creating a relaxed ambiance.

A young man in smart attire stood at the chocolate wooden bar, ready and waiting to greet Sam,

"Good evening, sir. What can I get for you?"

The question asked in a confident and upbeat manner.

Sam paused for a moment, he knew he craved a drink but that was as far as the thought had developed. Ordinarily, champagne would have been the automatic response, however, the vast array of wines and spirits lined up along the glass shelves before him fogged decisiveness.

Following an internal debate, Sam decided to hold back and start things off slowly, finally fixing on,

"A beer."

He perched upon one of the stools and waited impatiently, his fingers beginning to tap restlessly upon the cold wooden surface. The tall glass of golden refreshment was placed before him.

"That drink and you don't really add up."

A feminine voice sounded from the right. Sam turned his head and threw a glance at the glamorous woman, with olive skin and flowing hair as black as the walls, a cigarette held softly between her dark purple lips. She was a mysterious, dark looking creature, Sam's instincts told him she was trouble.

"You disapprove?"

"Greatly."

She answered with feeling, her hazel eyes refusing to deviate, hypnotically holding onto Sam's gaze.

"I didn't realise this was the smoking section."

Sam stated, the dull tone of his voice making the intent unclear. His serious and professional attitude not easily turned off, even by this dark beauty.

"Ooh, you going to get me thrown out?"

The woman joked seductively, taking another long drag of the cigarette in gleeful defiance.

Sam let a brief smile slip and proceeded to join in the game.

"I could, but I'll let it slide if you can pick out an alternative I like."

The siren leant gently upon the bar, taking a moment to look Sam up and down in judgement, her long fingers with their black tipped nails trailing through her thick hair. Flashing a wide Cheshire cat grin, she turned her attention to the barman.

"Manhattan, for the gentleman."

Their eye contact resumed and this mysterious player lifted the veil of mystery.

"Lilly Marino."

The beguiling intonation confirmed Sam's suspicions; the Italian name matched the accent. Lilly held out a hand, as a lady would to be kissed.

Sam had never encountered such elegant custom, nonetheless he dove in, lightly clutching at her fingers and kissing her hand.

"Sam Lowell."

"You work here?"

Miss Marino inquired, speculating from his playful yet seriously stated, I could get you kicked out, comment.

Sam chuckled, as if such a post were beneath him.

"No, I, well I work all over the place, London, New York. Soon will be settled in Singapore though."

Sam's mood took a nosedive for a moment as his thoughts wandered towards Seren, but the moment swiftly passed as Lilly continued.

"Mm, I love a man of culture."

Miss Marino's beautiful accent intensified the sexual electricity more than should be allowed.

"Well, I'm not that."

The response was blunt.

"What are you then?"

"A businessman."

"The image of sophistication. A weakness of mine."

Lilly's smile was this time returned, slowly but surely she worked on Sam's hardened exterior, continuing immediately, as if the questions were prearranged.

"What sort of businessman?"

"Do you always ask strangers so many questions?"

Sam's only defense was to fight fire with fire. He didn't want to talk about work right now, yet everything seemed to lead back to it.

"Only the ones who that interest me."

Lilly pushed, using her seductive sexuality to keep Sam's defensive temper at bay.

"I work with the owner of the hotel."

"Alexander."

"You know him?"

Now Sam sat up and took note.

"Only by reputation. You could say we mix in the same high flying, dark, scheming corners of society."

Lilly explained causally, the words somewhat disturbing as they were delivered.

"I wouldn't know about that."

Sam murmured, unsure whether he should invest any faith in this stranger.

"How much do you know about the man?"

Miss Marino's enthusiasm for the conversation also increased.

"Well…"

Sam began, considering his answer.

"He's the definition of the word entrepreneur; driven, ruthless, intelligent, a brilliant businessman and completely unreadable. Scares me to death sometimes but he's my mentor, I consider him a genius and a great man. I owe him everything."

Lilly took another drag. She seemed to be drawing this moment out, enjoying it.

"So, you know the PR'd identity. Only half the story of such men."

"You know something I don't?"

Sam asked, the words arranged as if in jest, however, his tone was deadly serious and forceful.

'If you know something, you'd better tell me.'

But the thought bubble was moot, Lilly Marino was a social climber and therefore an unstoppable gossip.

"I only hear rumours, whispers from dark corners. No one really knows the man, he's a ghost, exceptionally good at hiding what's under that thick skin. Seems he's Mr Perfect… However, I do recall a particularly sinister tale that circled the social tables, back in 2011, I think. The year I married my second husband…"

Lilly suddenly stopped and turned her attention to the cigarette she stubbed out. Leaving what was beginning to sound like an intriguing story open, much to Sam's irritation. Though he hid it well, having learnt from the master.

"I'd like to hear that story."

Sam insisted. Yet again his words were cleverly polite, but the serious and intimidating undertone of a ruthless man poked through.

"My husband was a contractor out here in California, he had a contact, a property developer, Vincent Morgan was his name. I only met him once at a party, a garish and loud man, my husband used to call him *the land baron*. Vincent seemed to own all the prime land in LA, including this spot right here. When Alexander came to buy the land he refused, Vincent was going to build a nightclub or some such venue. The offer went up and up but the answer was still no. The situation became very… turbulent. It was an act of spite, all the money in the world couldn't have convinced the stupid man to sell to Alexander… Then two weeks later he was found in his Malibu home, decapitated. It was in all the papers, the police believed it was the mafia."

"Jesus…"

Sam uttered under his breath, the story seeming a tad dramatic. Lilly bore a wide mirthless grin. It seemed this young lady liked to shock her audience.

"You can't really think it was Alexander? Sounds like this Vincent was the sort of man who liked to make enemies."

Sam rallied to his defense.

"True, Vincent Morgan visited many dark places. Depends I suppose if you believe in coincidences… Whatever happened it worked out perfectly for Alexander, as does everything, it seems."

The deep and disturbing conversation was interrupted by the arrival of Sam's Manhattan. A rusty colour contrasted by a bright red cherry bobbing in the liquid.

He took a good sip. The whisky awakening the back of his throat.

"Well?"

It was much stronger than Sam's body was accustomed to, but he enjoyed it.

"You clearly know your stuff."

He replied, going straight back to the glass again.

"I find everybody has their own expertise. Mine is desire. I am convinced now that yours is power, it radiated from you. A carbon copy of the man himself."

Sam didn't reply to this seemingly rhetorical comment and he didn't object to its content.

"Let me show you around."

Her enthusiasm hinting at the possibilities that LA had to offer.

"Tempting, I have an early appointment in the morning."

Sam referred vaguely back to reality but his mind chose not to analyse too much.

"Come on just a bit of sight-seeing, I swear. I'll have you back by your bedtime."

Lilly's teasing was very persuasive. Her seductive, mysterious persona promised intrigue and Sam longed to know more. What was on offer seemed too intoxicating to pass up.

"I suppose a couple of hours wouldn't hurt."

Sam conceded.

"That's the spirit."

The night was everything Lilly Marino had promised. Sam had never imagined life could be such a rush.

She handled the beautiful new Porsche skilfully as they wove in and out of the lanes of traffic, the speed limits seemed too slow for this woman who lived life in the fast lane. There was something inexplicably sexy about the way she handled the 911 with such confidence and brutality. Temptation beckoned but Sam tried not to stare at her slender legs and inviting neckline.

They stopped for food at a seafront restaurant and Sam naively wanted to believe that after the feast, they would head back to the hotel. Maybe he'd get lucky, she seemed keen although he'd never developed his 'what women are thinking' skill, figuring,

'Does any man really, truly know what's going on in a woman's mind?'

As always naivety was the fool and Sam was glad, he wanted to dive into whatever this world was. Ironically stretching his father's advice to its limits. Moulding it to satisfy his own greedy longing for more and more. Enough was no longer in Sam's vocabulary.

After dinner Lilly led Sam to a club, walking straight past the line. Of course, she knew the owner. It was a place where for one night, Sam lost his sanity. They went into the back to a private room with a dozen or so other high flying socialites.

Sam was already more drunk than he'd ever been but the sea of black desire in that room kept him alert; money, gambling, guns and drugs all about the place. Cigarette and cigar smoke filled the air with a thick fog. A large green iguana that must have belonged to one of the eccentric guests sat proudly upon the table, centre-stage at a game of cards. Drinks came in an endless stream, as did voluptuous bikinied women handing out lap dances. Sam had the pleasure of many thanks to Lilly, who bizarrely footed the bill. She encouraged it, seemingly getting off on watching as her and Sam made eye contact.

It was all very reminiscent of an Ian Flemming novel. By the time they'd left Sam had welcomed all the new experiences on offer; the drugs, the gambling and even a gun. The owner had fitted a small riffle range in the basement and at some point in the evening, the crew journeyed down to the subterranean level where Sam almost caused himself a nasty injury; hitting the ground as he tried to reload the pistol in his intoxicated and narcotised state of being.

Somehow, pumped up with enough drugs to start a small pharmacy they drove back to the hotel without causing an accident. The last and by far most pleasurable experience was the sex, which of course wasn't new to Sam. Yet it felt that way. Completely different to the soft and tender lovemaking he'd enjoyed over the years with Seren, this was rough, animalistic.

Sam had become a different man and the sex reflected it. He was commanding; it was not lovemaking but fucking, hard and fast. He threw her around the room, pulling her hair back, biting her neck, overpowering and ravishing her to his whims. Seren had never screamed out for more like Lilly did that night.

Chapter 28

Mr Bodach

"Knock, knock, knock, knock."

Sam's increasingly regular routine of being awoken at some ungodly hour by a string of early birds was particularly unwelcome on Tuesday morning. The loud and impatient sound obligated his consciousness into painful, head splitting, eye stinging, muscle aching and reluctant action. The night of excessive partying had left its mark, his body crying out for pity,

'Never again!'

The exotic temptress was gone. Sam was not surprised, that goddess was the absolute definition of *free spirit*.

"Knock, knock, knock, knock."

The door persisted as Sam approached it gingerly. He psychoanalysed the ritual; these four rapid bursts of sound were far more impatient and bold than the gentle three Carter always employed. This was clearly someone else.

The answer to who lay behind door number 1 should have been obvious – it was 7:30 on the dot. However, Sam's scrambled mind recalled little in respect of last night's events, let alone any predating arrangements.

With half awake, devil may care attitude, Sam flung the door wide to reveal a shady looking character. Tall and stocky with greying flat-top hair, a pair of blacked out sunglasses hiding his windows to the soul.

"I'm Mr Bodach."

He spoke plainly.

Sam's depleted awareness took a moment to connect the dots, but before he could reply the man's attention darted left and right, as if he feared being followed. Then proceeding to dart into the suite barging roughly past Sam in a ridiculously farcical manner which Sam may have laughed at in different circumstances.

"I told The Chair I wasn't happy about this, trusting some… kid."

Mr Bodach pointed at Sam in derogatory fashion, obviously on edge and suspicious.

"The Chair?"

Sam repeated, his exhausted mind still struggling to join the dots.

"Yes The Chair, The Boss."

The condescending explanation arrived in a slowly exaggerated pronunciation, as if the explanation was being offered to a young child.

Sam's intellectual mind had understood the code names, but didn't understand the why? What was the reasoning behind them?

"I assure you Mr Bodach, I am completely loyal to…"

He stopped himself before uttering the name, the paranoia was contagious. Sam spoke again, uneasy panic rushing in on him,

"I'm Mr Low…"

"No names!"

Mr Bodach interrupted sharply.

"Where is it?"

Sam's mind was catching up with this coded speech, pretty sure what that last question alluded to. He walked to the back of the suite, opening the closet doors wide to shed light on the ominous black safe hiding at the back. His mathematical mind thankfully recalling the numbers *667459* when it mattered.

Sam retrieved the black duffel bag and held it at arm's-length towards the spectre. As Mr Bodach reached for it Sam's eyes glimpsed at a golden badge clipped on his belt, revealed by the parting of his jacket, making out the letters

F… B… before the jacket fell back into place. Feeling confident that the last letter must have been *I*.

The intimidating character studied the contents carefully before turning his full attention back to Sam. Reading his cautious distance and wild eyes, he closed the gap and spoke with evil intent.

"If you should decide to cross me, Mr Nobody, I'll personally see to it you end up in a body bag. You got that?"

Sam nodded, he couldn't speak. Far too shocked and frightened by the threat to say anything, he just wanted to get out of there, get away from this menacing maniac whose words were filled with such genuine malice. Sam had considered himself to have become a tough and confident man, but he was not cut out for this. Whatever he'd fallen into, the stakes were far too high for him. He thought himself ready for whatever Alexander threw at him, but not this.

The spectre turned and disappeared out the door, Sam released his tension and tried to relax, gather himself and evaluate,

'What the fuck just happened?'

He didn't want to dig too deep, his respect and admiration for Keaton just wanted to look past whatever this was and get on with his job, get back to the life of his dreams. But there was no way to erase this, Sam couldn't put the lid back on and ignore the facts as he had so many other times. Alexander Keaton's action had been, odd, off… peculiar. He'd looked past the sometimes unethical and harsh methods of business his mentor employed, realising this was the big game, sometimes muscle was the only way,

'Who am I to question the billionaire?'

But whatever this was, awe for his mentor couldn't blind him from the smell of illegal dealings and,

'Whether you like it or not, prat. You are involved.'

There was no logical reason that he could think up which would explain why Alexander Keaton was paying an FBI agent a small fortune.

Sam's intelligent mind couldn't help but start connecting dots between this event and Simon Crow. He recalled the

257

man's words at that board meeting, the words which had so enraged Keaton, clearly pressing a button.

"I knew you had friends in high places Alex! I didn't realise they extended all the way to the government, at least now we know what you were doing out in LA!"

His mentor had come out to LA, conveniently enough just before Crow's downfall. Could he really have falsified the evidence? Someone in the FBI could have done, couldn't they?

Sam replied Crow's accusation,

"Alexander Keaton does not exist, Sam. He's just a phantom."

The phrase hauntingly reiterated over and over. Sam's faith was definitely shaken,

'Who exactly is *Alexander Keaton?'*

Last night, Lilly had said he only knew the PR'd version. Was Alexander Keaton a placebo, created by whoever the real man was. As he boggled, scenarios grew more and more out of hand and farfetched, his head almost splitting in the process, the theory seemed ridiculous,

'You're getting paranoid. All successful businessmen have a few skeletons. It goes with the territory!'

Sam was reluctant to consider his mentor may be guilty of criminal activities.

'He's just had to get a bit creative is all.'

Sam concluded that this was a far more palatable reality to accept, thus ending the internal debate.

Chapter 29

Lifting the veil

Sam arrived back in New York Tuesday afternoon, just as Keaton had instructed. No time wasted. His life had swiftly become an intricately structured web of time management, filled with meetings, appointments and deadlines to fulfil. A life completely orchestrated by the billionaire, something Sam had overlooked; up to this moment he had had no time to do much independent thinking, such was Alexander Keaton's genius. So completely swept up in his new life's perfection – not to mention the taxing workload – its flaws had eluded him. Unspoken promises of anything and everything his heart desired masked the truth. Sam remained blissfully oblivious.

However, after the strange events that took place involving the twitchy and intimidating Mr Bodach, the veil had slipped somewhat as had Alexander's halo. The utter surety and confidence Sam had invested in the billionaire had no doubt been shaken by seemingly suspect and frankly criminal actions.

The bastion still stood high upon a podium, how could he not? The man had picked the insignificant and insecure Sam up, dusted him off and with a few tricks turned him into a man with confidence and ability. And that was the God's honest truth, no matter how he chose to look at things, no matter the road he took, those were the facts… How could he turn his back on a man who had bestowed such a priceless gift? Not to mention, the dream trip to New York and of course the billionaire's most recent gift. The wristwatch which Sam discovered to his shock possessed an eye watering $17,795 price tag. If he'd known, he may have experienced some qualms before shackling it so casually upon his wrist.

But still, there was doubt. A whisper crept into the corner of his mind, an idea that refused to die in the shadows. Sam had believed he'd expelled it that very morning, fighting to erase doubt,

'This is ridiculous, you're being paranoid, you're tired, exhausted in fact!'

Yet the skeptic would not yield and continued to pick at the uncertainty,

'Who is Alexander Keaton?'

Sam accepted he could not possibly know the absolute truth of the complete persona. He'd lived in the real world too long, seen too much to deny the terrifying reality; we never truly know what anyone is thinking, do we? What lies beyond that thin veneer? And Alexander Keaton was a master of disguise, Sam had known that from the very beginning, the man's poker face was unmatched.

That blank face and the black suit his mentor wore, a mask he'd assumed was just part of business. You needed to protect your interests after all. But the events carried out in that hotel room had changed everything, the PR image, the inscrutable fascia no longer impressed Sam. His main interest now was in what lay behind it, thoughts forged in equal parts, curiosity and fear.

The real truth was, that underneath all the conflicting thoughts one feeling was now embedded, uncertainty. For Sam knew, if his recollections of what had happened in that LA hotel room were accurate, then unwilling or not he had dropped dead centre into criminal activity. No choice, no chance to walk away had been afforded to him. The decision had been made for him and there was nothing he could do about it,

'Apologies for bribing an FBI agent Your Honour, but honestly, I didn't know what I was doing!'

Even in Sam's head the speech sounded ridiculous. Thoughts being far more cogent than our words.

After the clusterfuck of thoughts and ideas that clashed in his mind over that long flight back to the Eastern seaboard, Sam exited that jet with a single clarity. That the only play he had was to go to Simon Crow. To do what his mentor had taught him so very well, to be a man, stand up and face reality head on.

No more hiding behind his boss, it was time for answers and Mr Crow certainly had something. Something, so juicy in fact it had got him fired, the successful and confident businessman had been railroaded into a scared old boy. What did Simon actually know? Sam reached for his phone with every intention of finding out, he knew he could get Crow's number easily enough, from Lynn.

The number was dialed and answered,

"Simon, it's Sam Lowell. We need to talk."

The Keaton had sent a car to collect Sam from the airport. Sam, whilst silently appreciating the absence of the ubiquitous Carter – luckily was otherwise engaged – provided the address as they drove away from the airport; 1 West 72nd Street, The Dakota, being the address Crow had provided. It rang a bell of familiarity, but took him a good while to connect the dots. It was the home of former Beatle John Lennon, and more poignantly, the location of his murder. Sam had never been an avid Beatles fan, the band's high being long before his era. However, his father was and Sam reflected upon the last conversation the two men had. His engorged ego would still not yield to the decision he'd made to quit medical school and disappoint his father, nor all the sharp truths he'd spoken, but for one, that snide and thoughtless comment,

"Well she isn't here is she Dad!"

Now that Sam reconsidered his words he struggled to accept they were in fact his. Snide and thoughtless didn't define such an act, it was downright cruel. What had come over him that caused him to speak in such a disrespectful manner towards those who'd raised him with nothing but

261

love and affection. Yes, he had been exhausted and frustrated, the woman he loved had just left him for dead, or at least that's how it had felt, so he had felt somewhat emotionally unstable.

Still, the excuses kept coming and Sam was beginning to realise his actions were becoming more and more extreme, more and more inexcusable. There was no excuse in the world that could account for disrespecting a caring parent and Sam finally noticed this new man he'd become had gone too far. He had lost control of his emotions and more importantly, his family. The two most important people in his life were slipping away and he'd not even noticed! How was such blindness possible?

'Could it have really been the money? Or something (more likely, someone) else?'

The car pulled up outside a German gothic style building. Thick stone walls, which appeared grey in the dull evening light led up to triangular spires and rounded turrets. An impressive structure that subtly expressed class and elegance. Sam had expected nothing less; he could tell the old gentleman was a traditionalist, a rare breed indeed.

Simon buzzed him in with the instruction to go all the way to the top. Naturally, the top floor. Numbed to the appreciation by Keaton's unequalled extravagance, Sam ignored the surroundings, lost in his own regretful fancies. However, the birdcage that creaked slowly up the levels was of some architectural interest, reminiscent of James Cameron's 'Titanic', Sam's vivid imagination throwing him a distraction from reality.

The cage stopped and Sam flung the metal mesh door across, hesitating for a moment as two imposing figures stood guarding the numbered door he was bound for.

"I'm here to see Mr Crow, he's expecting me."

Sam announced as he approached the two giants.

"I'm going to need to see some ID, sir."

The one statue moved only to speak, both assessing this potential threat. Sam rooted for his wallet and handed over the first proof he happened upon, a driver's licence. It was scrutinised thoroughly before the tension dissipated and he was allowed to pass. A grand hallway introduced the seemingly untouched 1880's style of the building. Intricately carved and varnished dark wood dominated. But Sam's eyes rejected the fine architecture, immediately alighting instead upon a man, who sat at some distance, scotch in hand. The posture was familiar, Sam had seen that depressed state before, in the board room. He recognised the man, yet still felt the need to double check.

"Simon?"

He cautiously approached, the ancient floorboard creaking and slowly, the static body unbent and Crow replied.

"Ah, the devil's apprentice, come to deliver a message. What does he want now – my soul?"

There was a sharp edge to the man's voice. He was a paranoid and shifty shadow of his former self. Naturally, the man had presumed Keaton had dispatched his apprentice for unknown yet sinister reason.

"I want the truth."

Sam replied forcefully, continuing his steady approach. Crow took a large swig of scotch.

"No you don't, you're just like all the other money whores out there, I've seen hundreds like you. Blinded by your childhood dreams, you're Alexander's speciality, kid, his latest bitch. But I tell you right now such reckless ignorance comes at a cost. You're just an innocent, running blindfolded through a minefield, and eventually you'll stumble across something you're not prepared for, as I did."

Sam conceded to this philosophical diagnosis,

"I already have."

And his heavy heart was ashamed. He was Alexander's disciple and yes, on a rudimentary level, his bitch, but a little of him still clung to his preferred version,

'Isn't that normal in the business world?'

Simon's practiced radar picked up on the seriousness of Sam's spoken words. The kid really wasn't here under his mentor's instruction. Despite the paranoia and mild intoxication, Simon Crow was still at heart a good man. Deep down he wanted to believe he could help Sam, even though it was probably too late. He was not prepared to witness yet another young soul fall victim to the deep dark pit of greed.

"What did you find?"

"An FBI agent."

"Don't say another word."

Crow blurted rapidly, his reaction hinted intrigue mixed in with a far larger helping of fear, glancing to the right. Sam drew ever closer, peering round the corner to see what captivated the old man's erratic eyes. A woman sat reading by a roaring fireplace. Sam correctly deduced this to be Simon's wife, oblivious to her husband's shenanigans. Pity jerked him back to his errand,

"I need to know the truth Simon,"

"Something is going on below the superficial facade of this company and now I'm involved, whatever it is you know I want you to share with me; this is my life."

Simon sighed regretfully, wishing desperately it was someone else's responsibility to do this, to shatter the kid's world, lifting the veil to reveal the truth.

"You'll need a drink first."

Crow struggled to his feet, a wizened shadow of his former self, the stress and excessive drinking had left him weak, slowly deteriorating. Sam followed the older man through two impressive rooms; the first a maze of antique furniture and oil paintings, the second a library with countless books lining the walls and reaching up to the high ceiling. Finally, they entered a relatively modest space, another roaring fire enclosed by two club chairs. Simon looked back through the doorway and after convincing himself they were alone, closed it.

"May I presume you handed over the package, the cash?"

Simon walked over to the globe bar in the far corner of the room.

"Yes."

"Yes it was cash, or yes you handed it over?"

A brief flash of optimism passed over Crow's countenance.

"Both."

Regret was now the dominant emotion, the conversation's dark mood gathering pace, apprehension adding to the mix about the unknown, with Sam heading for an unknown destination.

"Then, its game, set and match and the devil has won."

The glimmer of hope faded as a generous splash of Dalmore 25-year old scotch was poured into crystal.

"What do you mean – won? Won what? What are you talking about? This isn't a game."

"To him it is Sam. This world you've haplessly stumbled upon is his playground, and he's just won his latest coveted prize – you!"

Simon handed the drink over before making his way for one of the leather club chairs.

"No, no – Alexander is my friend, he took me in, gave me a life worth living. He was the only one who believed in me, he gave me everything!"

Sam fought back, still refusing to believe his mentor had anything but the best intentions for him, the two men mirrored each other, a gloomy pair.

"Alexander has made you what he needed, nothing more. You think, for one second, that he did it for you? You're deluded kid. He doesn't care about you – you just serve a purpose, that's all. He's brainwashed and manipulated you and he's such a fucking genius because you couldn't even see it happening."

"No – that's bullshit! Why me? He could have hired any money crazed business student, a banker or broker with the credentials and work ethic, why would he pick out a gutter rat with no experience, no confidence, unless he cared!"

Sam's tone became fierce and determined. He could begin to accept that there may be some dodgy, even illegal, dealings going on under the skin of the company. But, he refused to accept the man he looked up to felt nothing for him beyond cynical contempt.

Simon dropped back into the chair in frustration, he didn't have an answer to the question '*why?*' and could see this poor sap wouldn't be persuaded, Alexander's hooks were buried deep. The only play left was to show him the truth, as hard as it would be. With caution, he proceeded.

"I don't know why Alexander chose you, but I know who he is… I don't pretend to be an intelligent man Sam, I'm a simple businessman living in an age beyond me. But, if there is one thing I am it's a great judge of character, it's been the key to my success… As a boy I lived with my mother – a small run down town outside the city – we didn't have much besides each other and an annual holiday she saved for all year. When I was sixteen, 1949, heading down to Florida we came across a hitchhiker, he was pacing up and down at a junction, hoping for a sympathetic passer-by, which is where my mother came in. We stopped and he walked over, I took one look at that characterless face, those black eyes… there was no life in them, no humility no humanity, just an animal. I knew exactly what he was. Like the scared child I was, I pleaded with my mother to drive on and she did… I'll never forget that face, it haunts my nights. A couple of months later I saw it again, in the paper, that same dull stare. Turns out he'd murdered and decapitated a family of four, stole the car and casually dumped their bodies on the side of the road for some unfortunate witness to discover."

A lingering silence drew out as Sam allowed the chilling story to percolate. Still, his narrow mind failed to recognise its significance.

"Simon what are you trying to say?"

"The point is, I know people. And no matter how much you try to hide who you really are with fancy clothes, accents, mannerisms, whatever! It doesn't change who you are, beneath the skin. People don't change, they merely adapt and Alexander is not who you think he is… he's a monster, a predator, just like that hitchhiker."

"You think Alexander Keaton is a killer? You're fucking crazy!"

266

Sam wore an expression that passed for scepticism and went on to judge the old man's sanity.

"No I'm not kid, no I'm not! I'm the only one left playing this game with any clarity at all. The man is a killer, not by his own hand he's too smart for that, but I promise you, he'd eat you alive if you stood in his way and so help me God your gonna know the truth because I know you too Sam, you're a good person, you don't belong in this world and there is still a chance you could get out!"

"I'm not listening to any more of this shit. I'm leaving, I never should have come!"

Sam stood up and sprung back towards the door, regretting his decision to go behind his mentor's back like this, he saw it for the betrayal it was. He wished he'd just gone straight to Keaton, asked him about the FBI agent face to face. The broken man had one more stab,

"Why did you call me?"

Sam stopped in his tracks, the door half opened.

"If you're so convinced your boss is such an angel, why come to me?"

Sam gave no answer.

"Because I told you what deep down you already suspected about him. You know, don't you? You don't want to believe it but you know exactly what's going on behind the veil of wonder he drew you into. Extortion, corruption, take your pick, it's all there. You're just afraid to find out. Because as soon as you do, this whole world you're caught up in of elegance and luxury and fucking fairy dust, and your hero, will reveal themselves to be all they truly are – criminal!"

Sam hadn't moved an inch, a statue of conflicting views.

"Please Sam… I'm not asking you to believe me, I'm just asking you to look at the evidence."

In the end, the unknown was just too intriguing to ignore. Sam turned back and spoke.

"What evidence?"

Simon had not uttered another word, silently taking Sam through to another of the seemingly endless passageways of the wooden maze and into his office. Retrieving a large brass key from his velvet smoking jacket he turned it in the lock. The two men entered and Sam was hit by the thick scent of burned paper filling the air with a musky smoke. Behind the desk was yet another fire place, this one not yet lit but containing a pile of papers, many half burned or singed, clearly the source of the smell.

"What happened in here?"

Sam's natural curiosity found its voice.

"Over the last two years I hired a private investigator to dig up everything he could on Alexander Keaton. Keaton's genius is getting people to trust him and I fell for it. But my conscience would no longer abide my ignorance. Finally, I made the decision to trust my instincts and I became convinced he was bent. Until recently nothing surfaced. You will find Sam, that the closer to death you get, the bolder your conscience becomes."

Crow's tone was awash with regret. It was clear the pit was far deeper than he'd imagined.

"You did what? Jesus Christ! Simon, this isn't CSI you can't just go around invading people's privacy!"

Sam's ego continued to defend his mentor with the notion this was just as illegal as whatever Keaton was up to. Yet, Simon continued, shutting Sam's words out. He didn't care, his actions were irrelevant now, too late to go back.

"When I found the truth that's when Alexander had me kicked out, somehow he found out, he's got people everywhere, knows everything. I had to burn the evidence, I couldn't risk my family's safety, not now I know what he's capable of…"

Simon rambled as he darted past his desk and dropped to his knees at the fireplace, erratically searching through the charred remains. Hoping now, for Sam's sake, some piece of the evidence he so desperately tried to dispose of was still legible.

"You burned the evidence? Convenient!"

Sam was growing sick of hollow words, Crow reminding him more and more of a duplicitous politician.

"When I told you Alexander Keaton was a phantom I meant it! That's why my guy couldn't find any trace of him, that name has no past."

Flicking through the papers, most of which broke apart in his hands, he found it. Amongst the cremated scraps, by some miracle, a scanned newspaper article was just about legible. Cautiously, Simon picked it out and turned with it towards the desk, floating it gently down upon the hard surface.

Sam approached, his eyes fixated on the humble and battered article. Headed, *The Star,* and dated, *Sunday, October 11th 1998.*

"Benjamin B Barnes?"

Sam spoke with doubt filled scrutiny the name which lay amongst the articles title, *Benjamin B Barnes, the shocking story of a son's betrayal.*

"Look at the photograph."

Simon's finger gently hovered over the fragment as it targeted a school portrait of a teenage boy. Sam held the paper closer, bringing the poorly printed black and white image into focus. It looked very much like a young Alexander Keaton. The resemblance was uncanny, a mature looking young lad; those same defined cheek and jaw bones, the black hair and matching eyes, he even bore that signature poker face now so familiar to his protégé. He studied the cold and lifeless facsimile before him. It was undeniable but still, Sam harboured doubts,

"So he changed his name, so what? Lots of people do."

"Read it," Simon instructed, Sam began to scan the text.

The heartbreaking story of the Barnes family of four is enough to turn the stomach of any parent. From a middle class family living in England, Benjamin B Barnes was, according to neighbours, just your average teenage boy, or so he appeared. The father, a Mr Andrew B Barnes owned and ran a local and successful brewery alongside his wife and Benjamin's mother. The youngest member of this, as

269

described by a neighbour, "Tight nit family," was Annabella Barnes, Benjamin's fourteen-year-old sister.

Despite appearances, local police have confirmed the shocking news that has torn this family and their tranquil community apart. Earlier this week, on Monday 5th of October, the sixteen-year-old Benjamin emptied his parents' bank accounts before disappearing, without a trace. Police first suspected the boy had been abducted. However, CCTV footage obtained from a local bank has confirmed the teenager forging his father's details in order to clear out the family business and personal accounts, before vanishing into oblivion. It is speculated that Benjamin has now left the country, as no traces of his whereabouts have surfaced. Mr Andrew Barnes shared the following statement,

"We were completely devastated to find out that our own son felt such desperate need to get away from us, we can't understand it. But now, all we feel is relief and gratitude that he is alive and unharmed. We do not care about the money or what Benjamin has done, all we wish is to have our boy back. Please, come back to your family, come home."

It is simply horrific to think a child could do such a thing to the parents who so lovingly raised him.'

"…What the fuck is this?"

Sam turned back to Simon as a wild concoction of confusion and disbelief entered his consciousness.

"That is the man you work for. There is no Alexander Keaton, Sam. Never was. It's just a pseudonym, a PR stunt to present his perfect image. Benjamin B Barnes, that's our man."

Sam couldn't believe it; how could he have missed this? It wasn't just the horrific and unthinkable crime, the lie was somehow even worse in this moment, as he recalled the billionaire's slick deceit on the plane,

"When I was sixteen my parents died in a car crash. I took the insurance money and decided to make something of my life. I started my own business, another sixteen years later here I am."

270

The man he'd looked up to as a mentor, a hero even! Was nothing more than a common criminal, the likes of which Sam had never imagined meeting, let alone following with the devoted loyalty of a dog. It made him sick, and furious. The world he'd known had been turned upside down. Everything he'd absorbed; the money, the hotels, the cars, the luxury, even the advice he had so willingly taken on board was now tainted. He felt the colossal weight of the mistake he'd made as the regret of everything he'd given up hit him like a train; His principals, ethics, everything he stood for, not forgetting of course a promising career!

Sam glimpsed behind the veil and finally saw himself, and the world he had become part of, for what they truly were. A fool, strung up on the devil's strings. Yet, the worst and most disturbing of revelations was still to come. Sam Lowell felt the full momentum of this newfound clarity; it freed his better self to inspect his worse self, and he was horrified at what he saw. Firing that poor, and no doubt, innocent man out in LA who had pleaded for the sake of his family... The fact he'd turned his back on his father and Seren, the two people who had loved and stood by him unconditionally. The vicious force of this intelligence now painted him as wicked as the horned one himself.

Tortured by the memories to near implosion, right now, Sam needed to come back to the present and pressing situation he was in. Realisation settled upon him as the deep and dark hole he'd dug himself closed in on him.

"Jesus Christ, Simon... what do we do?"

"There's nothing we can do! The man's into everything, he knows people in the highest and lowest circles. The FBI, the mafia, he has connections everywhere. He's untouchable!"

Sam recalled the story Miss Lilly Marino had told him, about the land baron Vincent Morgan who had ended up without a head. It was no longer a stretch to imagine Mr Barnes orchestrating the hit! It was terrifying to think what a teenager capable of betraying his own blood, could become as a man. Simon and Sam could easily end up the same way as poor Mr Morgan, how can you fight a man with such limitless power?

"What about the police? We can go together, show them everything you have…"

"It's too late for that kid and you know it…"

Simon interrupted.

"He has you right where he wants you. If he can forge evidence of extortion onto me he could drum up any manner of changes on you! We have no idea how many cops he's got on the payroll. He could have you locked away till the end of your days at the click of his fingers, that's the sort of power we are dealing with here. You're now in his orchestra, and he will play you and play you until you wear out. The only advantage you have is that he doesn't know you found the truth, and you better hope he doesn't. Or you'll be lying awake at night with a revolver under your pillow like yours truly!"

"Shit."

Sam felt he had hit the bottom of the pit and that there may be even further to travel. Downing the scotch he still clung to, fathoming the horrific comprehension of his grim situation.

"Yeah, shit indeed!"

"So what am I supposed to do? Continue working for the fiend and just turn my back on all of this?"

"Yes… that's exactly what you have to do, you have no choice…"

Sam let himself fall into the desk chair, sinking right down, completely defeated.

"I'm sorry, truly I am. But the fact is you got yourself into this mess. You weren't forced, or coerced. The real mistake you made, was not ambition, or even greed, but being so naive as to believe you could live in such an obscene world without paying anything more than the price tag."

Sam felt completely pathetic, fraudulent; the truth hit him in the gut – he could no longer remain oblivious and cower beneath the whip,

'Even if it means death, I will stand up and be a man, a real man.'

If Sam's end was nigh, it would be on his own terms. He now spoke with conviction,

"No, there's no going back. I have to confront him, it's the only chance at dignity I have left."

"Sam don't! Do yourself a favour and keep your head down."

"I can't, this ends now!"

And Sam left, taking his newly discovered conviction with him.

Chapter 30

Dilemma

Sam headed from The Dakota straight towards the office, and his target. The taxi ride allowing his concerns and regrets further opportunity to percolate, catalysing an intense animosity towards Alexander Keaton, or Benjamin B Barnes, whoever the man was, it didn't matter anymore. All that mattered was Sam's only objective, his desperate desire to confront his nemesis face to face. Simon had given him so much, opening his eyes to the truth and for that he would be eternally grateful. Still, that was not nearly enough, Sam needed to hear it from the source's mouth. His rage needed to be expressed and directed at his enemy, the orchestrator of his downfall.

Reaching Keaton & Co Sam's focus looked beyond the front desk, even ignoring Miss Fox's objection as he burst into the office belonging to his boss. The room was empty, turning back to the secretary he spoke tersely.

"Where is he?"

Lynn stood up to address her superior formally.

"Mr Keaton's not been in all day, Sir. He left you this last night, before leaving the office, said you'd be in to collect it."

She handed over a folded piece of A4, Sam straightened it out and read.

'Sam,
432 Park Avenue, floor 83. I'll be expecting you.
Alexander'

A cold shiver of icy dread ran up Sam's spine. This couldn't have been a mere coincidence, could it? This was the first day he'd known the workaholic to take off. Perhaps he wanted a quiet and secluded spot for the next act in his production. The conversation Sam brought was not one the billionaire would want to hash out in public, before prying eyes and ears… witnesses.

No, this was planned, all of it. Somehow, Benjamin B Barnes had known yesterday that his apprentice would find out the truth today. Another harsh tutorial – never underestimate the lengths some people are willing go to. Sam was learning the hard way.

Clenching his fist around the paper Sam's poker face failed in spectacular style, giving way completely to his anger and frustration towards the brute he'd been countless steps behind since the beginning. Sam believed he had found a glimmer of consolation. However, this feeling was brief. The innocuous piece of paper confirmed that he was still under the devil's watchful eye, dangling from the puppet strings and walking into what was, no doubt, a trap. But events were already in motion and Sam's dim hope of reclaiming any measure of pride left no option. He was going to 432 Park Avenue.

Lynn's concern grew as Sam continued to stare into space, rage fuelling a maelstrom of thoughts in his turgid mind.

"Mr Lowell? Are you alright… Sir?"

She placed her hand softly upon his arm, in an attempt to bring him back, which it did with shocking consequences when Sam lost control for a split second, releasing his anguish upon his unfortunate colleague.

Lynn gave a high pitched yelp of pain as Sam grasped the forearm that had reached out to him in kindness, shouting out,

"Keep your fucking hands off me!"

The red mist vanished as swiftly as it had come and Sam was instantly mortified. Releasing his crippling grip, he tried desperately to undo what he had done.

275

"Lynn, I'm so sorry, I… I don't know what came over me."

Sam took a step back as shame for the man he'd become consumed him. The animal which had bided its time in the shadows had finally emerged. At last, Sam could see who he'd become, the twisted, stressed and crazed tyrant, blinded to its wicked intent.

Lynn slid along the wall she'd reversed up against and regaining balance she backed away. Her eyes remained fixed on Sam. The violation had completely shattered her confidence and trust in him. Both of them knew no matter what their relationship had been; professional, personal or inappropriate, it was over.

"Truly, I'm sorry."

Sam made one last attempt at redemption before walking away with his head bowed.

Sam got a taxi to Park Avenue, arriving just as night consumed the city, the bright New York lights bursting into life. But Sam didn't see them, he saw only darkness. This city, like his life was now tainted, and neither would ever be the same again.

However, his inspiration was briefly stirred, at the sight of the tallest residential building on the Western hemisphere. At 1,396 feet 432 dominated the cityscape, towering even over the Empire State building. It was an engineering marvel, the ultimate statement of power and, of course it was where the egoist lived. Sam strode towards the overbearing building, holding on to the one positive element that had emerged from his situation – his absolute confidence.

The elevator stealthily approached floor 83 and, as the numbers escalated Sam realised he had no plan whatsoever, what would he say? How would he say it? Going up against the king of manipulation without so much as a vague scenario now seemed ridiculous as this impresario would surely try to manipulate the situation. He would have to be strong, and hold on to those ethics and values he'd so readily left behind. The elevator doors parted, giving way to a white corridor with a door at the far end. Sam approached, but hesitated for moment as the crack in the doorway came into view, it had been left ajar. He didn't knock, or even speak but instead decided to play out this dramatic and orchestrated game. The door swung open with a light push and Sam closed it behind him.

It was dark, all the interior lights were off. There was just the whisper of faint light created by the distant cityscape, which was visible beyond the large square windows that gave way to a stunning 360-degree bird's eye view of the world below. The space was, of course, vast and beautiful with modern and minimalistic design, using the highest quality materials and finish. The floor and walls were polished white marble, intricate grey markings running through stone. A symphony of Bach filled the space with the gentle sound of the harpsichord, it's eyrie sound reaching out in the darkness. Sam noticed a punch bag in the corner, hung from the ceiling. Sam moved cautiously along the only inner wall, still his soft steps upon the marble echoed faintly. The wall gave way abruptly to the back of the apartment. A seating area, sofas, chairs, rugs and even a grand piano scattered about the space. As his eyes frantically scanned a mysterious silhouette came into view, lurking in the darkness, sat back in one of two identical club chairs which faced off each other beside one of the stunning views. The distinctive voice spoke.

"How's Mr Crow?"

Sam approached the chair, replying with honesty.

"Terrified, truthful... Mr Barnes."

A sadistic white smile flashed across the dark figure's face but was quickly eclipsed by the glass of scotch.

"He should be. I made you a drink, though you'll likely presume I've poisoned it."

Benjamin gestured towards a glass of scotch resting precariously upon the arm of his chair's twin. Sam sat down, staring for a moment, aiming his vitriol towards the figure in the dark which interrupted the tense silence in a disturbingly casual tone.

"You know, I've never had the pleasure of witnessing true, no holds barred, hatred before… Sorrow, anger maybe, never the pure abhorrence you brought with you. First time for everything."

"Well you've earned it, I should fucking kill you!"

Sam let his emotions rip fleetingly before reigning them back in. The shadowed figure leant forwards and into a dim white ghost beam of light which fell upon the lifeless face, back eyes glinting.

"Give it a go."

Sam's frustration yearned for a foothold that would scratch and claw until his prey was dead. However, Benjamin B Barnes was no gazelle, and Sam's logic didn't fancy his chances in a fist fight. Instead, he asked the only question that still mattered.

"What do you want?"

Barnes conveyed a look of contempt.

"You, Sam."

"Why? I don't understand – why me? Out of everyone, why choose me!"

Sam had lost control once more, bellowing in frustration.

"Because you provided a challenge. I took a worthless, insecure and pathetic shop boy, and I turned you into so much more."

"You turned me into a monster!"

Sam snapped back.

"No, I made you a man, I took you from the bottom of the world to the top, I gave you everything. You are the peak of evolution, the top of the fucking food chain because I made it so. You're my greatest creation, my most successful project."

"Project?"

Bewilderment settled in as he contemplated himself as a piece of work to be completed.

"Of course, it was planned, Sam, all of it. I told you the last test was to see if you could be ruthless and you passed. Congratulations, you're my star pupil, out of all my students over the years none turned out as well as you did."

"Simon was right; I was just a fucking dummy…"

"Don't flatter yourself! You were no different to any of the other sniffling, whining, gutter rats when I found you, complaining about how shitty and unfair your lives are instead of doing something about it and making something of yourself."

"I was making something of myself, I could have been a doctor, respected, valued!"

Sam looked back once more at the painful view of the reality he turned his back on.

"Cosmic, a GP on seventy grand a year and a pension. That's nothing, not in this day and age, just another one of the cattle."

"I could have been a good person, not this fucking monster you created!"

"A good person? Sam, don't be such a naive little bitch. I've told you before there is no good, there is no right or wrong in this world, no God measuring the scales and giving you a pat on the back if you've been a good little boy. The world doesn't work like that so why should the afterlife?"

"This is not about God or the afterlife. It's about me and my conscience, I can't be you. I could never be so heartless as to betray my own family."

"You never had my family, my father… You grew up in a home where the world was sugar coated, whereas I grew up in the real one. Ruthless, that's what the world is Sam and I learned from an early age you fight for yourself, or you fold."

"You murdered a man."

"I've never murdered anybody."

"You had Vincent Morgan killed."

"… I've had lots of people killed."

"You're pure fucking evil."

"I'm not evil, Sam, I'm a realist. I see the world for what it really is and I don't apologise for taking down anyone that stands in my way, I live the way nature intended me to."

"You're a psychopath, then."

"I'll take that."

"I won't, I refuse to become you. Nothing is worth this."

"Of course it is. Look around you, this is the pinnacle of existence, the top of the world. Wealth is the only thing worth having."

"You're wrong, there's more to life than money, and I let it go because I lost sight of what truly matters. I thought you stood for something great, that you were a man of principals. Now I see you're just a criminal, a fraud."

"What, you want to go back to that shit box excuse for an apartment, selling groceries?"

"How do you know where I live? Where I worked? How do you know what I was studying? Who the fuck are you?"

"The omega, Sam. I hear, see and know everything. My fingers are in all the pies; Police, FBI the mafia, I can't lose. I am the closest thing this world has to a God, and I want you to be my right hand. That's what all this has been for, I want you to run the company with me. Together we will live like kings."

"I won't follow you."

"You know I can't let you leave, not now. If you walk back out that door you will never be free. I will bring you a cage with no light and no air, for the rest of your life. You can have everything, or you can have nothing. Decide."

Sam was locked in this dilemma of unfathomable proportions. How did you decide between your dignity and your freedom? His humanity screamed out for its survival, yet the dreaded notion that if he continued along this path of recklessness, he would spend the rest of his life filled with a deep and painful regret that no amount of money, drinking, drugs or women could ever stem. Sam would like to think he had devotion to his dignity, the likes of which all those martyrs had shown before him. Though if that were true, would he have gotten himself into this situation in the first place?

'How did I get here?'

Sam was stuck between two different hells with no real power to call his own.